Teacher Preparation Classroom

TEACHER PREP

MERRILL
PRENTICE HALL

www.prenh...

D1450340

Your Class. Their Careers. Our Future. Will your students be prepared?

We invite you to explore our new, innovative and engaging website and all that it has to offer you, your course, and tomorrow's educators! Preview this site today at www.prenhall.com/ teacherprep/demo. Just click on "go" on the login page to begin your exploration.

Organized around the major courses pre-service teachers take, the Teacher Preparation site provides media, student/teacher artifacts, strategies, research articles, and other resources to equip your students with the quality tools needed to excel in their courses and prepare them for their first classroom.

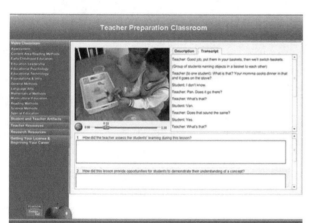

This ultimate online education resource will provide you and your students access to:

Online Video Library. More than 250 video clips—each tied to a course topic and framed by learning goals and Praxis-type questions— capture real teachers and students working in real classrooms.

Student and Teacher Artifacts. More than 200 student and teacher classroom artifacts—each tied to a course topic and framed by learning goals and application questions—provide a wealth of materials and experiences to help your students observe children's developmental learning.

Lesson Plan Builder. Step-by-step guidelines and lesson plan examples support students as they learn to build high-quality lesson plans.

Articles and Readings. Over 500 articles from ASCD's renowned journal Educational Leadership are available. The site also includes Research Navigator, a searchable database of additional educational journals.

Strategies and Lessons. Over 500 research-supported instructional strategies appropriate for a wide range of grade levels and content areas.

Licensure and Career Tools. Resources devoted to helping your students pass their licensure exam; learn standards, law, and public policies; plan a teaching portfolio; and succeed in their first year of teaching.

Word Identification Strategies

Building Phonics into a Classroom Reading Program

Fourth Edition

Barbara J. Fox
North Carolina State University

PEARSON

Merrill
Prentice Hall

Upper Saddle River, New Jersey
Columbus, Ohio

Library of Congress Cataloging-in-Publication Data

Fox, Barbara J.
  Word identification strategies: building phonics into a classroom reading program / Barbara J. Fox. — 4th ed.
    p. cm.
  Includes bibliographical references.
  ISBN 0-13-156130-8 (a. k. paper)
  1. Word recognition. 2. Reading—Phonetic method. 3. Reading (Elementary) I. Title.
  LB1050.34.F69 2008
  372.4' 65—dc22

                                                                    2007000051

Vice President and Executive Publisher: Jeffery W. Johnston
Senior Editor: Linda Ashe Bishop
Senior Production Editor: Mary M. Irvin
Senior Editorial Assistant: Laura Weaver
Design Coordinator: Diane C. Lorenzo
Project Coordination: Carlisle Publishing Services
Cover Design: Candace Rowley
Cover Image: Artville
Production Manager: Pamela D. Bennett
Director of Marketing: David Gesell
Marketing Manager: Darcy Betts Prybella
Marketing Coordinator: Brian Mounts

This book was set in Palatino by Carlisle Publishing Services. It was printed and bound by R. R. Donnelley & Sons Company. The cover was printed by R. R. Donnelley & Sons Company.

Pearson Education Ltd.   Pearson Education Australia Pty. Limited
Pearson Education Singapore Pte. Ltd.   Pearson Education North Asia Ltd.
Pearson Education Canada, Ltd.   Pearson Educación de Mexico, S. A. de C.V.
Pearson Education—Japan   Pearson Education Malaysia Pte. Ltd.

                                        10 9 8 7 6 5 4 3
                                   ISBN 13: 978-0-13-156130-4
                                   ISBN 10: 0-13-156130-8

Preface

This fourth edition of *Word Identification Strategies: Building Phonics into a Classroom Reading Program* invites you, the teacher, to support children as they develop the word identification strategies that make it possible to read and learn new words. It has been over half a decade since the report of the National Reading Panel was published and the No Child Left Behind Act was enacted. One might arguably conclude that these two connected events resulted in pressure on educators to teach phonics directly, systematically, and early.

Often lost in the continuing debate about the teaching of phonics is the idea that we need to keep phonics in perspective. Whereas phonics is necessary to learn to read a language like ours that uses an alphabet, it is not the most prominent component of classroom reading programs. We could create a long list of important strategies and attitudes. For example, children need comprehension strategies, a large reading vocabulary, the ability to activate their prior knowledge, strategies to fix miscues, and, of course, to develop a love of reading that lasts a lifetime, to name a few.

With so many components crowding the classroom reading program, what is the role and proper place of phonics? The perspective I take in this book is that we must teach phonics, but we cannot afford to overdo it. Phonics is the knowledge of relationships among letters and sounds, and a group of strategies that children develop as they learn to read, not a single letter-sound by letter-sound pathway to pronunciation. Children learn phonics so they can read and learn new words and, in so doing, build a large fluent reading vocabulary. Therefore, my perspective is that phonics, while important, is a means to an end, not an end in and of itself.

Core Beliefs about What Makes a Good Phonics Teacher

I believe a good phonics teacher knows how the letter patterns of phonics match the sounds in words. A good teacher understands and knows how to teach the prefixes, suffixes, syllables, and other multiletter groups in the structure of long words. Also important for good teaching is understanding how children develop competence in reading new words and the strategies children use at different stages in their development as word learners. A good teacher understands that a well-balanced, effective classroom program provides phonics instruction in proportion to children's needs.

This book is for kindergarten through fifth-grade teachers getting ready to enter the classroom for the first time, for practicing teachers who already have classroom experiences, for teachers whose primary responsibility is the teaching of reading, and for teachers who coach others in ways to provide the best reading instruction for each individual learner. This book offers a comprehensive, easy-to-understand explanation of what children do when they first begin to pay attention to print; how children learn and use the letter-sound patterns of phonics; and the contribution that knowledge of prefixes, suffixes, and syllables makes to learning new words. This book offers a theory-based, developmental perspective on teaching word identification and describes teaching activities that are consistent with this theoretical perspective. The strategies in this text can be used to support students' individual needs in conjunction with a basal reading program.

Principles Guiding Phonics Teachers The first guiding principle for phonics teachers is that learning to read new words unfolds in a predictable developmental sequence that begins long before children ever pay attention to the specific words in books and ends when children rapidly, accurately, and effortlessly recognize all the words in everyday reading. The second guiding principle is that we teach children how our writing system works so that they can develop a large reading vocabulary and, ultimately, become independent readers. Children may begin kindergarten with only a foggy understanding of our alphabetic writing system, but they leave fifth grade with a wide and rich body of words that they recognize quickly, accurately, and effortlessly. A third and final principle is that ultimately successful teaching is measured by children's ability to learn new words on their own, to read independently, to easily recognize many different words, and to focus their full attention on connecting with meaning.

New in This Edition

Each bulleted item describes a new feature of this fourth edition:

- English language learners are an increasing presence in our classroom and, therefore, the focus on these children has been expanded to include research-based guidance for effective teaching.
- Also new to this edition are Spare-Minute teaching activities that call for little, if any, advance preparation and are suitable for brief periods of time.
- The importance of phonemic awareness for phonics, spelling, and reading fluency is explained in greater detail to help readers of this book develop insight into how phonemic awareness affects learning to read.
- Because developing reading fluency is now a more visible component of classroom reading programs, Chapter 1 includes an explanation of how phonics contributes to fluent reading.
- Also new to this edition is a section in Chapter 5 describing the overall elementary school program for teaching letter-sounds and a similar section in Chapter 6 explaining the program for teaching multiletter chunks.

What the Reader of This Book Will Learn about Teaching Word Identification

Readers of this book will learn about the different word identification strategies children use to read and learn new words and also how to effectively teach these strategies. Chapter 1 considers the proper place of phonics in today's classroom reading programs, the cues children use to read new words, and the stages of learning to read and spell new words. Chapter 2 explains the sequence in which phonemic awareness develops, best teaching practices, tests for assessing phonemic awareness, and activities for developing rhyme and phonemic awareness.

Chapter 3 explains the first strategies children use to read words. Chapter 4 explores how children use the letter patterns in known words to read unknown words; how to help children cross-check, self-monitor, and self-correct; best teaching practices; and activities for teaching the rimes and onsets in word family words. Chapter 5 describes the letter-sound strategy, the letter-sound patterns of phonics, a sequence for teaching letter-sound patterns, the proper way to use decodable books, best teaching practices, and activities for developing knowledge of letter and sound relationships. Chapter 6 explains the multiletter groups in words; how readers use the large multiletter chunks to identify long words; how long words consist of prefixes, suffixes, or Greek and Latin roots that give readers insight into word meaning; how long words are constructed of syllables; and activities to develop knowledge of word structure. The last chapter, Chapter 7, focuses on English language learners and children who need extra help because they are not yet successful at reading new words on their own.

This book is a ready reference for teachers in every elementary grade. In taking a developmental approach to word identification, it gives teachers the information they need to match what is taught to what children need to learn. I hope that this cross-grade developmental approach combined with the new additions to this revision will support effective teaching in every grade. The ultimate objectives are, after all, developing children's ability to read new words and enabling their steady progress toward becoming accomplished readers who instantly recognize all the words they read in everyday text.

ACKNOWLEDGMENTS

I am indebted to the many teachers who welcomed me into their classrooms, to the children who were willing readers and eager participants in the activities their teachers shared, and to the principals who encouraged and supported their teachers. Without them this book could not have been written. I would also like to thank the reviewers of this text for their insightful comments and welcomed recommendations: Marsha Riddle-Buly, Western Washington University; I. LaVerne Raine, Texas A&M University-Commerce; Peter Quinn, St. John's University; and Timothy Rasinski, Kent State University.

Contents

CHAPTER 2

Phonemic Awareness: Becoming Aware of the Sounds of Language   23

CHAPTER 3

Early Word Identification: Using Logos, Pictures, Word Shape, and Partial Letter-Sound Associations to Read New Words   67

CHAPTER 4

Analogy-Based Phonics: Using the Predictable Patterns in Known Words to Read New Words 83

CHAPTER 5

Letter-Sound Phonics: The Strategy of Using
Letter-Sounds to Read and Learn New Words   121

CHAPTER 6

Structural Analysis: Using the Chunking Strategy
to Read and Learn Long Words   173

CHAPTER 7

Teaching English Language Learners and Children at Risk   221

APPENDIX A

Rimes for Word Reading and Spelling

APPENDIX B

Letter-Sound Patterns

APPENDIX C

Generalizations for Adding Suffixes

APPENDIX D

Greek and Latin Roots

Key Vocabulary

Index

CHAPTER 1

Word Identification in Your Classroom Reading Program

This chapter explains the proper place of word identification in your classroom reading program. You will learn about methods to teach word identification, how children read new words, and how to determine the most appropriate balance between word identification and other components of the reading program. You will also learn how children use a combination of language and letter and sound cues to read unfamiliar words; the stages of word learning; and why understanding these stages is important for teaching children to read and learn new words.

KEY IDEAS

- Emphasis on word identification should be in proportion to children's individual needs.
- Phonics helps children develop rich reading vocabularies, contributes to reading fluency, and supports reading independence.
- Readers may use a combination of (letter and sound) sentence structure (syntactic), and meaning (semantic) cues to read new words.
- With an understanding of how word learning develops, you will teach exactly what children need to know to add new words to their reading vocabularies.

KEY VOCABULARY

Alphabetic principle

Analogy-based phonics

Analytic phonics

Consonants

Embedded phonics (letter and sound) cues

Letter-sound phonics

Meaning (semantic) cues

Metacognitive awareness

Sentence structure (syntactic) cues

Structural analysis

Synthetic phonics

Vowels

You instantly recognize all the words you commonly encounter when reading. Instead of figuring out words, you focus on comprehension. This is exactly as it should be. However, consider what it is like for young readers who come across many unfamiliar words. Meeting a large number of new words is a major impediment to comprehension, and so it is not surprising that these children concentrate on developing their reading vocabularies.

Consider the note in Figure 1-1 written by Maria. If you speak and read Spanish, Maria's message is crystal clear. The words are easy to recognize, the sentences are well formed, and you know why the picture and the message are a perfect match. Suppose instead that you speak Spanish but cannot read it. Now the format of the note and Maria's drawing are the only reliable clues to meaning. You might make an educated guess based on information gleaned from the picture and your own background knowledge. From the heart-shaped drawing, you might logically infer that this is either a Valentine or a love letter. But unless you recognize the words Maria wrote, your grasp of meaning is limited, and your comprehension is at best an approximation of Maria's message.

To go beyond supposition, you must learn the same things beginning readers learn—how to use phonics and the multiletter groups, or chunks, in word structure (the -er in *sharper*) to read new words. Just recognizing words is not enough; you must also know the meaning of the words Maria wrote, understand the sentence structure, and appreciate the social context in which notes such as this are written and read. (See the translation of Maria's note at the end of this chapter.)

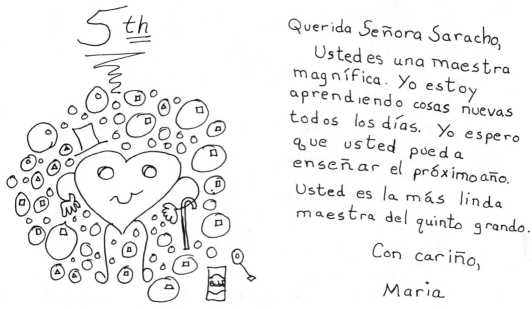

Figure 1-1   Maria's note: Can you get the message?

WHY DO WE TEACH PHONICS?

Our written language is based on the *alphabetic principle*. This is the principle of using letters to represent sounds. An alphabetic writing system makes it possible for any reader who knows the code—the relationship between letters and sounds—to pronounce words the reader has never seen in print before. For the purpose of illustration, let us suppose *bat* is a word readers do not recognize. In order to read this word, readers use their knowledge of letter and sound relationships—the alphabetic principle in action—to associate sounds with letters (b = /b/[1], a =/a/, t = /t/), and then blend the sounds together to pronounce a familiar spoken word (/b/ + /a/ + /t/ = /bat/).

   In a perfect alphabet, only one letter represents only one sound, and so readers can pronounce any written word by simply associating sounds with letters. *Phonics* consists of the relationship between the letters and sounds, and approaches for teaching these

---

[1] In this book, for simplicity, instead of using a standard system of phonetic symbols, letters that typically stand for sounds are used and placed between slashes (/ /). Single vowels represent short vowel sounds, while long vowel sounds are either described as such, identified by spelling pattern (ou, ee) or indicated by the use of a macron (¯).

relationships. Letter-sound relationships are a set of visual directions—a map, if you will—telling readers how to pronounce words they have never seen before. You teach phonics when you demonstrate that the letter *b* represents the sound heard at the beginning of /banana/, /boat/, and /bubble/. In helping children compare and contrast the sounds represented by the letters in *hid* and *hide*, you are teaching phonics. When you challenge readers to think about a word that begins with *c*, ends with *t*, and makes sense in the sentence *Mark's _____ eats tuna fish*, you are a teacher of phonics. And when you encourage writers to spell a word "the way it sounds," you help children think about and analyze our alphabetic writing system, which is what you do when you teach phonics.

Teachers include word identification in their classroom reading programs for three reasons:

1. Phonics makes it easier to read and learn new words. With a relatively small amount of information, readers can identify a large number of words. For instance, the children in your class who know the sounds that *t* and *ur* represent can figure out the pronunciation of words that share these letters, such as *turn, hurt,* and *turtle.*

2. Phonics helps children develop a large reading vocabulary. Phonics is a bridge between the spoken words children already know and the written words they do not recognize. Readers identify unfamiliar words by associating sounds with letters to read new words. Remembering how the letters in written words represent sounds in spoken words helps children learn words, even when words are visually similar (Adams, 1990; Ehri, 2005). The more children read and write the same words, the stronger their memory becomes and the faster they recognize the words (Ehri, 2006). Eventually the sounds, spellings, and meanings of words are joined together in memory. Children then recognize words instantly, at a glance. Instant word recognition includes information on the word's spelling, sound, and meaning.

3. Phonics contributes to fluent reading. Fluent oral reading is smooth and sounds like talk. It is expressive, accurate, and appropriately paced. Accurate, expressive reading is possible only when readers instantly and accurately recognize the words in text (Eldredge, 2005). Phonics plays an important role in fluent reading as a bridge between unfamiliar written words and familiar spoken words. Fluent reading is not possible without instant word recognition. Instant word recognition develops as children use phonics to read and learn new words. Let us consider why instant word recognition is so important for fluent reading.

Effortless word recognition is a hallmark of fluent reading. Effortlessly reading words frees readers' minds to think about reading with expression. Readers who do not immediately recognize words have several choices, none of them conducive to fluent reading. Readers might skip words, stop to decode them, or guess. In so doing, readers change the focus from reading in meaningful phrases and with expression to decoding or guessing. This, of course, disrupts expressive, fluent reading, and, additionally, interferes with comprehension.

Instant, accurate word recognition develops as children use phonics to read and learn new words (Ehri, 2005). Good decoders in the first, second, and third grades are more fluent readers than their classmates who struggle with phonics (Neuhaus, Roldan, Boulware-Gooden, & Swank, 2006; Schwanenflugel, Hamilton, Kuhn, Wisenbaker, & Stahl, 2004; Speece & Ritchey, 2005). Good decoders have larger reading vocabularies (Eldredge, 2005), and read faster than poor decoders (Neuhaus, et al., 2006). By the end of first grade, the good decoders in your classroom will read twice as fast as their classmates with poor phonics skills (Speece & Ritchey, 2005). This means that fluent readers read twice as much as poor readers in the same amount of time. This affords twice as many opportunities for fluent readers to read known and new words, and develop larger reading vocabularies.

Phonics affects fluency as early as the first grade. Developing expressive, accurate, fluent reading in first grade is important. Once the trajectory toward fluency is established, children seem to stay on the same course unless the classroom reading program is adjusted to provide more reading instruction. High-fluency readers at the end of first grade are high-fluency readers at the end of the second grade; low-fluency readers at the end of first grade are likely to be low-fluency readers at the end of second grade (Speece & Ritchey, 2005).

Phonics is important for developing fluency, but it does not make children fluent readers, as we see in Figure 1-2. Fluent reading is a complex skill. Like all complex skills, fluent reading is based on several more basic skills. The basic skills must be in place or developing appropriately in order for readers to carry out complex skills. Phonics is one of the basic skills that supports oral reading fluency. Phonemic awareness is another basic skill. You will learn more about phonemic awareness and its contribution to fluency in Chapter 2. Phonics does not guarantee fluency. You may teach a few good decoders who cannot read fluently. But you will never teach a fluent reader who does not instantly recognize almost all the words in text. Although knowing phonics does not automatically result in fluent reading, it is a critical basic skill. Phonics is a tool for learning words. Knowing words, in turn, makes it possible to read fluently.

4.   Phonics helps children become independent readers. You will find that the good readers in your classroom are also good at phonics (National Reading Panel, 2000). Knowing and using phonics, in turn, makes it possible for these children to read many new words in text. Because children with good phonics are able to read on their own the new words in books suitable for their grade, they can read any of these books at any time in any place. These children have better attitudes toward reading and better self-concepts of their ability to succeed in school than children who do not use word identification strategies (Tunmer & Chapman, 2002).

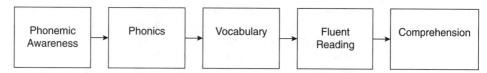

Figure 1-2   The relationship of phonics to vocabulary and fluency.
Figure constructed from the findings of Eldredge (2005) and Schwanenflugel, Hamilton, Kuhn, Wisenbaker, & Stahl (2004).

Your classroom reading program will be successful when you teach phonics early, systematically, directly, and meaningfully, and when children have many opportunities to use their letter-sound knowledge in reading and writing. The first step in well-planned, direct instruction is for you, the teacher, to explain, model, and demonstrate how to use phonics when reading and writing. Second, children practice under your guidance. Should children encounter difficulty, you are there ready to help them use phonics and correctly apply information. If children need more instruction, this is the time to provide further explanation and additional demonstration of how to use phonics. Last, as children become more skilled, you gradually withdraw your support, until finally children are successful on their own, without your aid.

By early, we mean beginning in kindergarten or first grade, well before children are independent readers (National Reading Panel, 2000). As for systematically, there is no research-based sequence in which letter-sound associations should be taught, as explained in Chapter 5. This said, it is important to have an overall plan for teaching letter-sounds, to teach them in a logical sequence, to make sure the plan is implemented, and to assure that all children have an equal opportunity to learn useful letter-sound relationships.

Phonics instruction also needs to be meaningful; that is, we want to teach phonics within the context of words that not only illustrate certain phonics letter-sound relationships, but also are important for everyday reading and writing. You must also consider what children need to know to be better readers and then provide instruction in proportion to children's needs, which brings us to the topic of balance in your classroom program.

WORD IDENTIFICATION IN A BALANCED CLASSROOM READING PROGRAM

When something is balanced, it is in proportion. Phonics is in balance with the other components in your classroom reading program when you select just the right approach, just the right materials, and just the right emphasis to develop the reading potential of every child. A balanced program includes many teaching methods, all in proportion to children's individual needs.

The things children need to know to improve their reading achievement change as their reading ability develops. As a consequence, the role of word identification in first grade is quite different from its proper place in a fourth-grade classroom. Yet the goal—to give children the tools they need to develop a large reading vocabulary—remains the same across grades. We want children to become independent readers who use the word identification strategies we teach them to learn new words on their own and develop the ability to instantly read all the words they see in everyday text.

In a balanced program, kindergarten, first-, and second-grade children learn to identify words by letter-sound patterns, which is the traditional grist of letter-sound phonics (Chapter 5). However, in this book we will also include in a balanced reading program the teaching of analogy-based phonics (Chapter 4), which teaches children to identify new words by noticing shared letter groups, such as the *at* in *hat* and *fat*, and teaches large multiletter groups, or chunks, in the structure of words (Chapter 6), such as prefixes (the *re-* in *rerun*) and suffixes (the *-ed* in *jumped*). And, of course, balanced programs ensure that children have many and varied opportunities to use their knowledge of phonics, analogous letter groups, and multiletter chunks in word structure when they read and spell.

The International Reading Association's (1997) position is that teachers should ask *when, how, how much,* and *under what circumstances* to teach phonics. We can see from this statement that phonics is not an all-or-nothing curriculum component. Rather, it is a portion of the curriculum that complements other reading and writing activities, and enables children to read and spell independently.

When Do We Teach Phonics?

The answer to *when* depends on the level of children's development as readers. For children to develop a large vocabulary of instantly recognized words, classroom reading programs must dedicate a significant amount of time to phonics in the early grades. Because children in third grade and above already know how to use phonics, a balanced program for these children focuses on the multiletter chunks in word structure (prefixes, suffixes, base words, contractions, syllables, and root words, including Greek and Latin roots), as well as advanced comprehension strategies and study skills. Thus, the answer to the question of *when* to teach phonics is that letter-sound phonics should be taught in the first few grades (National Reading Panel, 2000), and word structure in grades three through five. This brings us to the next point—*how* to teach phonics.

How Do We Teach Phonics?

Although there are a plethora of phonics teaching materials available, phonics instruction can be distilled into five teaching methods: (1) synthetic, (2) analytic, (3) embedded, (4) analogy-based, and (5) structural analysis. If you teach reading or language arts in an elementary school, you will use one or more of these methods.

1. *Synthetic* (explicit) phonics is part-to-whole letter-sound instruction. Synthetic phonics starts with letter-sounds. Children "sound out" new words by first associating letters with sounds and then blending the sounds together. For example, children would first learn that the letter *s* represents /s/, *i* represents /i/, and *t* represents /t/. Then children blend these three sounds together to pronounce /sit/ and, in hearing a familiar word, read the word *sit*.

2. *Analytic* (implicit) phonics is whole-to-part-to-whole letter-sound instruction. Children learn whole words first, and later are taught, or encouraged to discover, which sounds go with which letters. This avoids asking children to pronounce sounds in isolation. For example, children would learn to read many different words with a short /a/ letter-sound, as we hear in *bat*. Then the teacher writes a known word, *bat,* on a chart, and asks children to pay special attention to the short /a/ sound. The teacher now writes other short *a* words the children already know how to read, such as *fan, mad, Sam, bad, ham,* and *map.* Everyone studies the word list and draws the conclusion that a single *a* in a short word stands for /a/. Children do not pronounce isolated sounds in the analytic approach; sounds are pronounced only within the context of whole words.

   3.   *Embedded* phonics does not follow a prescribed teaching sequence. Phonics is taught "as needed"—that is, teachers teach only those letter-sound associations that children need to decode words in the books they are reading. Because each book has a different set of words, and since many of these words are likely to contain different letter-sound patterns, embedded phonics does not teach letter-sound relationships in a prescribed order (Armbruster, Lehr, & Osborn, 2001). Consequently, as children move from kindergarten to the first and second grades, they may bring to text a highly personal, and therefore highly individualistic, storehouse of phonics knowledge. Bear in mind that the National Reading Panel (2000) concluded that teaching phonics in a prescribed sequence is more effective than teaching phonics on an as-needed basis.

   4.   In *analogy-based* instruction children learn the predictable letter patterns in words, and how to use the parts of words they know to identify new words that share the same patterns. Analogy-based phonics groups words with the same patterns into word families (the *it* family, for example, consists of *sit, fit,* and *lit*), teaches children how to pronounce and spell families, and emphasizes wide-range reading and writing. Here the teacher helps children learn the basis for a word family, such as *it,* saying something like, "*It* says /it/. Words with *it* belong to the *it* family." The teacher and children then participate in activities that call attention to *it* family words. You will learn more about this approach in Chapter 4.

   5.   In *structural analysis* children learn to analyze long words into multiletter chunks. Children learn to recognize prefixes (the *pre-* in *precooked*), suffixes (the *-ed* in *precooked*), and Greek and Latin roots (the Greek roots *astro-* and *-naut*), and how these multiletter chunks affect word meaning. Children also learn the basic syllable patterns, and how syllables represent sounds in multisyllable words (*dem-on-strate*).

How Much Time Should We Spend Teaching Phonics?

How much time and energy you spend on phonics depends on children's knowledge of the alphabetic principle, and their ability to use this knowledge when reading and writing. Unfortunately, there are no hard and fast rules for how much time to spend teaching phonics. Generally speaking, we spend proportionally more time teaching phonics in kindergarten through second grade when children do not know letter-sound relationships. In grades three through five, teachers teach children how to use word structure to read long words. (Chapter 6 has more information on teaching word structure.)

   The precise amount of the school day to spend on phonics varies, depending on the teaching materials and methods available to you in your classroom, and on children's development as readers. Research shows that it is effective to spend up to 20 minutes a day teaching phonics in kindergarten (Johnston & Watson, 2004). Struggling readers benefit from more phonics instruction, up to 50 minutes a day (Blachman et al., 2004; McCandliss, Beck, Sandak, & Perfetti, 2003). This said, it may be difficult to translate research findings into your own classroom reading program because (a) you may teach children who are different from those in the research study or (b) you may use teaching materials that set out a different amount of time for teaching phonics.

To strike the right balance in your classroom reading program, consider children's needs and then select the intensity (how much) that is the best match for the individuals and groups you teach. Greg and Sharon illustrate how beginning readers from the same first-grade class have different levels of phonics knowledge. As illustrated in Figure 1-3, Greg fluently recognizes only a few words, relies almost entirely on pictures to guess at meaning, inconsistently uses beginning and ending letter-sounds to identify words, and forgets words from one day to the next. He does not always separate words with white spaces when he writes and does not consistently use letters to represent sounds.

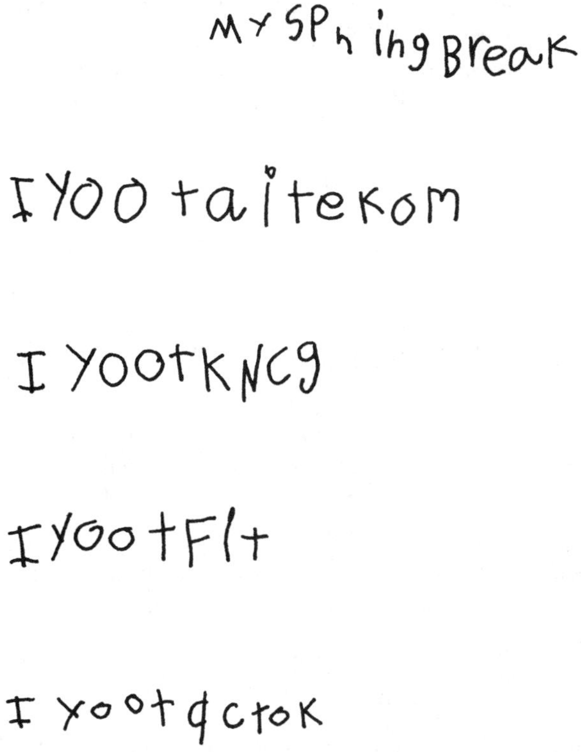

MY SPh ing Break

I YOO ta i te Kom

I YOOtK NC9

IYOOtFlt

I Yo ot q c to K

Figure 1-3   At the end of the first grade, Greg knows only a handful of words. He will benefit from explicit instruction in all aspects of reading, including phonics, and from opportunities to use letter and sound relationships when reading and spelling.

Sharon, whose work can be seen in Figure 1-4, understands what she reads, uses phonics and context clues to read new words, and uses letter-sound relationships when spelling. Her reading vocabulary is growing rapidly, and she is developing reading independence. We can see from her writing that Sharon correctly spells many words in her reading vocabulary, understands the sounds most *consonants* represent, and is learning how *vowels* represent sounds. While both Greg and Sharon will benefit from more phonics knowledge, Greg has far more to learn than Sharon. For this reason, an appropriate classroom balance would include more phonics instruction in consonant and vowel patterns (*fin* versus *fine*, for example) for Greg than it would for Sharon. So, we see that the answer to *how much* phonics to teach in the early grades depends on children's understanding of letter-sound relationships and on their ability to use these relationships in everyday reading and writing.

Under What Circumstances Should We Teach Phonics?

The answer to *under what circumstances* depends on how teachers differentiate instruction. Children may learn (a) all together in a large group, (b) in small groups, (c) in flexible skill groups, or (d) individually. Large groups typically include everyone, or nearly everyone, in the class, while small groups include a handful of children who are reading on or near the same level. Another kind of group, a flexible skill group, consists of children reading at vastly different levels who need to know

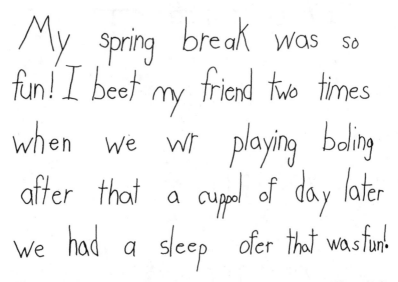

Figure 1-4   While Sharon, Greg's first-grade classmate, will benefit from learning more about how letters represent sounds, she knows and uses many more letter-sound associations when she reads and writes than Greg. An appropriate classroom balance would include less concentration on phonics for Sharon than it would for Greg.

more about specific letter-sound associations, specific reading strategies, or specific reading skills. These groups are disbanded once children know and apply the information and strategies when reading. And last, children may be taught individually. According to the National Reading Panel (2000), all types—large groups, small groups, and whole classes of children—are effective, provided that instruction is systematic.

You will find that different teachers in your school conceptualize balance differently. Naturally, when children's needs differ so too does the emphasis teachers place on teaching phonics. Many factors go into finding the right balance among phonics and other components of your classroom reading program—the grade you teach, children's ability to use letter-sound relationships when reading and writing, and the size and growth of children's reading vocabulary, to name a few. A classroom phonics program for a child like Greg, who brings less phonics knowledge to reading and writing, looks quite different from a program for a child like Sharon, who has more phonics knowledge. Even though the individual teachers in your school may not agree on the answers to when, how, how much, and under what circumstances to teach phonics in a balanced program, they all teach children how to use a combination of meaning, sentence structure, and letter-sound cues to read new words in text, which is the topic of the next section.

MEANING, SENTENCE STRUCTURE, AND LETTER AND SOUND CUES

Good readers bring to print a deep understanding of the meaning, word order, and sounds of the spoken language. Letter-sound relationships of phonics, word order of the text, and the meaning of language are three types of information—or cues—that support readers as they make sense of authors' messages.

Meaning (Semantic) Cues

Meaning (semantic) cues are the sensible relationships among words in phrases, sentences, and paragraphs. This is the basis on which readers decide whether an author's message is logical and represents real-world events, relationships, and phenomena. Readers use these meaning cues to narrow down word choices and to verify that an identified word makes sense within the larger scope of the sentence or passage. For example, meaning cues make it possible for readers to determine that the relationship among words in *The little dog chewed on the bone* makes sense and that the relationship among the words in *The little bone chewed on the dog* is not. Readers also use meaning cues to limit their choices for the words that belong in sentences. For example, we know that the missing word in *The mother _____ had five brown and white puppies* is almost certainly going to be *dog*. When readers use meaning-based cues, they ask themselves, "Does this make sense?"

Sentence Structure (Syntactic) Cues

Sentence structure (syntactic) cues are the basis on which readers decide whether an author's word order is consistent with English grammar. These cues help readers predict words in phrases and sentences. For example, in *The little _____ chewed on a bone*, readers know that the word following *little* is a person or an animal (a noun). Sentence structure cues also give readers insight into meaning. Readers who use these cues know that the meaning of phrases, sentences, and paragraphs may change when words are sequenced in different ways, for example, *The little dog chewed on a bone* versus *The dog chewed on a little bone*. Though the first sentence refers to a small dog and the other to a small bone, both conform to the structure of English. But the sentence *The chewed on a dog bone little* makes no sense at all. Hence, when readers use word order cues, they ask themselves, "Does this seem like language?"

Meaning and sentence structure cues, together with the overall conditions under which materials are read, create a rich base on which word identification and reading comprehension rest. When readers use the reading context, they draw on the cues available to them, selecting and combining information to construct authors' messages. Brian's note, seen in Figure 1-5, illustrates how meaning and sentence structure cues work together. You, the reader, instantly recognize all the words as belonging to your reading vocabulary except one: *spreencler*. If you were to try to decode

Figure 1-5 Brian's note: How do you figure out the meaning?

this word without thinking about context, it would be difficult to figure out what Brian meant to say. However, *spreencler* is surrounded by other words that contribute valuable clues to its identity.

From word order cues, you infer that *spreencler* is a noun, not a verb, adverb, or adjective. From meaning cues, you surmise that this unknown object is something children play with, which rules out such things as spoons or spades. If you know the types of activities Brian and Mike enjoy, and if you also know the types of things Mike has to play with, you can use this prior knowledge to narrow your choices even further. For many readers, this information is enough to deduce the identity of *spreencler.*

Letter and Sound Cues

Though the meaning and sentence structure cues are rich, if you want to be absolutely certain about the word, you will turn your attention to cues that are a combination of how words look and sound. *Letter and sound cues* consist of the visual cues to pronunciation. The letter and sound cues in *spreencler* help you further narrow the field of possible words. When readers use letter and sound cues, they ask themselves, "Does this word sound and look right?"

When using all three cues to identify words, readers think about words that make sense in passages, and hence keep the focus on meaning. Given the unconventional way Brian spelled *spreencler,* simple letter and sound cues might help you approximate pronunciation. The easiest way to combine letter and sound, meaning, and sentence structure cues is to ask, "What word begins with *spr,* ends with *er,* and makes sense in Brian's message?" With this combination of cues, your chance of making an educated guess increases substantially because the letter and sound cues help you narrow the field of possible words. If the guess you make is sensible, you discontinue decoding, confident that you understand Brian's message.

If the beginning and ending letter and sound cues in *spreencler,* as well as the meaning and sentence structure cues, are not enough to figure out this word's identity, then you consider all the letters in spelling. Should you choose to do this, you would probably sound out *spreencler* letter-sound by letter-sound. But, having sounded out *spreencler,* you still have not pronounced a recognizable word. Brian's spelling is unconventional, and so the outcome of sounding out is a nonsense word. Yet this nonsense word is quite similar in sound to a meaningful word in your speaking vocabulary that fits nicely into the overall reading context.

There is a curious and very interesting phenomenon at work here: In using letter and sound cues, readers do not always have to perfectly pronounce the words they are figuring out. Pronunciation need only sound enough like a real word to trigger recognition. By combining information from different cues, you know without a shadow of a doubt that Brian intended to write that he is playing in Mike's *sprinkler.*

While all types of cues contribute to understanding messages like Brian's, this does not imply that every cue is equally helpful in every reading situation.

Children's reasons for reading affect the importance they assign to accurate word identification. For example, a fifth grader who reads her science textbook for information needs to pay close attention to the words the author wrote. A third grader who is reading an article in a children's magazine is more likely to be concerned with the overall ideas in the article, not with detailed information. Correct identification of nearly all words is far more important for understanding the information in science textbooks than it is for enjoying magazine articles.

Insofar as Brian's note is concerned, if your reason for reading is to find out who Brian is playing with, you might make an educated guess for *spreencler,* having found out that Brian is in Mike's company. Conversely, if you are concerned with knowing precisely what Brian is doing, you will analyze *spreencler* to determine exactly what type of play Brian is engaged in. All in all, the amount of mental attention you allot to word identification depends on how concerned you are about absolute understanding. Your concern for understanding is, in turn, determined in part by the reason you are reading Brian's note in the first place.

Over-relying on any one cue is inefficient, time-consuming, and likely to result in poor comprehension. Good readers know this and hence balance their use of cues with the type of text they are reading, the reading environment, their own reasons for reading, and their own background knowledge. Although it is not necessary to distribute attention equally to all cues, it is necessary to be able to take maximum advantage of the information cues provide, should reading situations call for it.

HOW CHILDREN READ FAMILIAR AND UNFAMILIAR WORDS

Familiar Sight Words

Children read *known* words from memory. Children recognize these words quickly, accurately, and effortlessly. This type of instant word recognition is the bedrock of fluent reading (Wolf & Katzir-Cohen, 2001). These words are on the "tip of the tongue," always ready and immediately available any time children see them.

Reading Unfamiliar Words

In reading *new* words, children may take advantage of all the cues in text, including meaning and sentence structure cues. They may also look at pictures for cues to meaning, and bring their own real-world experiences to bear on deciding which words authors are likely to use to express ideas. All these sources of information—meaning cues, sentence structure cues, picture cues, prior knowledge cues—help readers narrow word choices. However, even with these rich sources of information, readers still must look inside *new* words to identify them; that is, readers must pay attention to the letters in words and to the sounds those letters represent.

Readers use different strategies when they pay attention to the letters and letter groups in new words. A strategy for identifying new words is a deliberate plan of action—a set of steps, if you will, that when completed result in reading and understanding an unfamiliar word. Unlike the mythical Greek goddess Athena who sprang fully grown from Zeus's head, word identification strategies do not emerge fully formed from a few incidental experiences with print. Strategies are systematic, organized procedures for identifying words and as such require careful nurturing and a supportive environment in which to develop. This does not mean a drill-and-kill approach to learning in which readers memorize isolated letter-sound combinations. Rather, it means giving readers many opportunities to understand how our alphabetic writing system works, and many chances to strategically use this information as they read and write every day. There are three strategies from which to choose: (1) analogy, (2) letter-sound, and (3) structural analysis.

Analogy: In using the analogy strategy readers look for familiar letter groups in new words, and then match those letter groups to letters in known words. For instance, on seeing a new word, *hat*, readers realize that *at* is also in a known word, *sat*. Readers then use this information (*at*) to read *hat*. When spelling, children realize that the /at/ in /hat/ also is in /sat/, a word they already know how to spell. On remembering that /at/ in /sat/ is spelled *at*, spellers then use this analogous information in combination with the beginning letter-sound (/h/ = *h*) to spell *hat*.

Letter-Sound: Readers associate sounds with letters, say the sounds, and blend all the sounds together to pronounce a familiar spoken word. For example, on seeing *hat* for the first time readers associate the /h/ with the letter *h*, the /a/ with *a*, and the /t/ with *t*. Having pronounced each sound individually, readers then blend these sounds together to pronounce the whole word, /hat/. On hearing /hat/, children recognize it as a word in their speaking vocabulary and, therefore, associate both meaning and sound with *hat*. In spelling, writers associate letters with the sounds they hear in a word, and then write those letters. In our example, spellers listen for the sounds in /hat/, associate a letter with each individual sound (/h/ = *h*, /a/ = *a*, /t/ = *t*), and then write the letters to spell (*hat*).

Structural Analysis: Children who analyze word structure bring to reading a thorough knowledge of how to pronounce large letter groups, or chunks, and, when appropriate, what the large multiletter chunks mean. For example, on seeing the new word *precooked*, readers look for familiar multiletter chunks in word structure. In this example, readers would notice the *pre-*, meaning before, and the *-ed*, indicating past tense. This leaves the word *cook*, which the readers recognize as a word in their reading vocabularies. By associating sound and meaning with the large multiletter chunks in word structure, readers understand how the new word sounds and have insight into its meaning. (Refer to Chapter 6 for more information.)

The strategy readers choose to use for reading new words—analogy, letter-sound, or the multiletter chunks in word structure—depends on the reading context; whether the word is long or short; and what readers know about letters, sounds, and word structure. Your role as the teacher is to demonstrate and explain how letters represent sound, to model and demonstrate strategies, and to discuss with children the strategies they use.

METACOGNITIVE AWARENESS

Metacognitive awareness is the self-conscious understanding of our own knowledge, skills, and strategies. From a word identification perspective, metacognitive awareness is knowing how, when, and why to use different word identification strategies. It is the self-awareness, or personal insight, into what an individual reader knows about letters and sounds, why this knowledge is important, and how and when to use certain strategies. To develop and apply word identification strategies, readers need to become aware of their own strategy use and how letters represent sound. Children who possess metacognitive awareness monitor their own word identification while reading, cross-check to make sure that the words they read make sense, and correct their own miscues. (This is explained further in Chapter 4.)

Thinking analytically and critically helps children become conscious—metacognitively aware—of their own strategy use and, in so doing, gain greater control over word identification strategies. When children explain in their own words what they know about how our alphabetic writing system works and give reasons for using the strategies they do, they develop a self-conscious awareness of their own knowledge, as well as an appreciation of why and when to use different strategies. To help children become aware of what they know about letters and sounds, and how and when to use word identification strategies, ask questions such as these:

1. When would you use this same way to figure out another word?
2. What other kinds of words can be figured out just the way you figured out this one?
3. What do you do when you come to a word you do not know?
4. How did you know that _____ (pointing to a letter or letter group) makes the _____ (indicating the sound or describing the sounds, such as the long vowel sound) in _____ (the word the child correctly read)?
5. When you see a _____ (describing a particular phonics pattern, such as a *vowel-consonant-e*, as in *home*), what sound should you try first?
6. If the first try doesn't make a real word, what sound(s) could you try next? (This question helps children develop flexibility in decoding.)
7. How would you write _____ (a word with a letter-sound association children are learning in your classroom)? Then follow up with the question: "Why did you write it this way?"
8. What did you learn today that will help you be a better reader?

As children answer questions like these, they organize observations, form generalizations, change or alter information and ideas, and, perhaps most important, become sensitive to how the use of word identification strategies supports comprehension. Children move through different word learning stages as they become more and more skilled at reading new words. Each stage is associated with the ability to use different word identification strategies, as you will learn in the next section.

THE FIVE STAGES OF WORD LEARNING

Children move through four word learning stages—prealphabetic, partial alphabetic, alphabetic, and consolidated—on their way to the fifth stage, the instant recognition of all the words in text, as shown in Table 1–1 (Ehri, 2000). As children enter each new stage, they use new strategies. Strategies develop in a reasonably predictable sequence that begins long before children read storybooks and long before they go to school. Though the exact order in which strategies develop is not completely understood, we do know that readers use some strategies before others. The earliest strategies are used when children are in the prealphabetic stage.

1. Prealphabetic

Prealphabetic word learning begins in preschool and usually ends some time during kindergarten. Children in this stage may not understand that words are separated by white spaces, and that one written word matches one spoken word. Children know few, if any, letter names, and do not yet know how letters represent sounds. The earliest strategies do not call for paying attention to the letters and sounds in words. Children associate meaning with pictures in familiar books, recognize words by their familiar everyday surroundings, or recognize words because of their unique shapes, as explained in Chapter 3. We cannot read what these children write because there is no association among letters and sounds. In writing, children may scribble, draw pictures, make mock letters, or randomly string letters together.

2. Partial Alphabetic

Children enter the second stage, the partial alphabetic stage, sometime in kindergarten or at the beginning of first grade, as described in Chapter 3. Partial alphabetic word learners know most, if not all, letter names. Children also know the sounds of most consonants, and some children are learning some vowel sounds, usually short vowel sounds as heard in *bad, bet, bit, hot,* and *hut.* Children read a few words from memory, and recognize new words by associating one, maybe two, letter-sounds with them. Children may also use letter names to recognize words, provided that the letter names contain a portion of the letter-sounds. For example, children might use the name of the letter *s* to read *stop* because the letter name—/sss/—contains part of the letter sound, /s/. In spelling, children use one

TABLE 1–1   *Stages of Word Learning*

Stages of Word Learning	What Children Know and How They Use Their Knowledge
Prealphabetic	Children do not yet understand the alphabetic principle. *Children* (a) memorize text, (b) associate meaning with pictures, (c) associate meaning with environmental print, and (d) identify words by their unique configuration. *Children are learning* (a) how print is oriented on the page, (b) how to match written words with spoken words, (c) that white spaces separate words, (d) letter names or letter-sounds, and (e) how to identify beginning sounds and rhymes in words. *When writing, children* (a) make scribbles, (b) make up their own mock letters, (c) write letter strings, and (d) draw pictures. Children do not use letters to represent sounds in words.
Partial Alphabetic	Children are beginning to understand the alphabetic principle. Children's reading vocabulary slowly increases. *Children* (a) give the names and sounds of most letters, (b) match spoken and written words, (c) find words in sentences, (d) find letters in words, (e) automatically recognize a few words, (f) use one or two letter-sounds or letter names to read new words, and (g) associate meaning with picture cues. *Children are learning to* (a) combine picture cues with beginning letter-sound cues to read new words, (b) find letters that represent rhyming sounds (the rime), such as the *at* in *hat* and *sat,* and (c) use parts of known words to read unknown words. *When writing, children use* one or more consonants to spell words (*dg = dog*).
Alphabetic	Children understand the alphabet principle, and their reading vocabulary rapidly increases. *Children* (a) use the analogy strategy to read new words, (b) sound out new words with the letter-sound strategy, (c) separate spoken words into sounds and blend sounds into words, (d) use meaning, sentence structure, and letter and sound cues in words, (e) cross-check, self-monitor, and self-correct during reading, (f) read some text independently, (g) read some text fluently, and (h) teach themselves new words through reading and writing. *When writing, children* (a) conventionally spell known words, (b) invent the spelling of unfamiliar words, and (c) write at least one letter for every sound in a word.
Consolidated	Children's reading vocabulary rapidly increases. *Children* (a) use the multiletter chunks in word structure to read new words, (b) read long words, (c) teach themselves new words through reading and writing, and (d) focus most all of their attention on comprehension. *When writing, children* (a) correctly spell most words and (b) use alternative spellings to represent some sounds (*naim* for *name*).
Automatic	Children's reading vocabulary is large and continues to grow. *Children* (a) automatically recognize all the words they see in print, (b) teach themselves new words through reading and writing, (c) recognize more words in print than they use in conversation, (d) read independently, and (e) focus entirely on comprehension while reading.

or more letters, usually consonants, to write whole words (*k* for *cat; dg* for *dog*). Children's reading vocabulary is growing, but only slowly and with a great deal of repetition in reading and writing.

3. Alphabetic

The third stage, the alphabetic stage, begins when children pay attention to and learn about vowel letter-sounds. Children usually enter this stage in late kinder- garten or early first grade. Children in the alphabetic stage pay attention to vowel letters when reading and spelling new words. Alphabetic word learners also pay attention to the beginning, middle, and ending letters in the new words they read. Children in the alphabetic stage sound out new words, discussed in Chapter 5, or read new words by analogy, discussed in Chapter 4. When children spell, they in- clude a letter for every sound heard, although not always in a conventional way (*truk* for *truck*). Children's reading vocabulary grows rapidly, and they learn words on their own through reading and writing. They are becoming independent read- ers and spellers.

4. Consolidated

Toward the end of second grade, and most certainly by fourth grade, children enter the consolidated stage. Children have had enough experience reading and writing to recognize large multiletter chunks in word structure, including prefixes, suffixes, syllables, base words, and root words. The strategy of analyzing word structure (de- scribed in Chapter 6) is a streamlined approach to reading and spelling new words. And, not surprisingly, children's reading vocabulary grows rapidly, and children learn the majority of new words on their own through reading and writing. Chil- dren now read books independently, without the help of their teachers.

5. Automatic

Children reach the automatic stage when they instantly recognize all, or nearly all, the words they see in text. Words are read rapidly, accurately, and effortlessly. Readers pay full attention to comprehension because they do not need to spend energy on word identification. At this point in their development as readers, chil- dren recognize more words in print than they use in conversation. Now, at last, the size of the reading vocabulary surpasses the size of the speaking vocabulary. And because text consists of words in readers' sight vocabulary, reading is pleasurable, rapid, and fluent.

Movement toward instantly recognizing a large number of words is gradual. Children seem to move from one stage to another, slowly learning and using more complex information and strategies. When children begin using a new strategy, their ability to apply the strategy and their understanding of print and speech re- lationships is immature. With instruction, and ample reading and writing experi- ences, children's knowledge gradually matures and their ability to use the new word identification strategy improves. When children are relatively comfortable using a certain strategy and have a good understanding of the print and speech relationships that support it, they gradually move into the next higher stage, which calls for utilizing a more efficient strategy based on a more elaborate understanding of print and speech relationships.

As is to be expected with any complex learning process, sometimes children will use strategies to read and spell words that are characteristic of more than one stage. For instance, in reading a short storybook, a child may use letter-sound relationships to sound out the new word *made* (a strategy consistent with the alphabetic stage), and then on the next page use only the beginning and ending letters to read the new word *duck* (a strategy consistent with the partial alphabetic stage). Gradually, however, the strategies from earlier stages fade away so that, whenever possible, readers use their most streamlined strategy to read and spell words.

When you, the teacher, are familiar with the stages and understand the knowledge and abilities that underpin the use of strategies in the different stages, you can make decisions that will help children move from one stage to the next. A good word identification program is balanced with other components of the literacy curriculum, to be sure, but it is also related to children's stages of word learning. When you understand the stages of word learning and the strategies that children in various stages use to read and spell new words, you have the information you need to relate what you teach to what children need to know to move to the next word learning stage. You can use this knowledge to select just the right material to match the skills and abilities of children, and challenge children to develop new and more effective strategies. You become a more effective teacher because you are teaching exactly what children need to know to become better at reading and spelling the new words that may stand in the way of understanding text.

Our goals are to develop readers who have such large fluent reading vocabularies that they seldom see words they do not already know how to read and to produce writers who correctly spell nearly all of the words in their fluent reading vocabularies. Instant word recognition takes readers' attention away from word identification and completely shifts it to comprehension, which is exactly what we expect of accomplished readers. When all is said and done, word identification is not *the* goal of reading instruction. Rather, it is a means to an end, a way to help children learn new words on their own so as to support fluent reading, and, in the process, become confident readers who focus their attention on understanding text, on learning from text, and on enjoying reading as a leisure activity throughout their lives.

Translation of Figure 1-1, Maria's Valentine
Dear Mrs. Saracho,

You are a great teacher. I am learning new things every day. I hope that you will be able to teach here next year. You are the nicest teacher in fifth grade.

Love,
Maria

REFERENCES

Adams, M. J. (1990). *Beginning to read: Thinking and learning about print.* Cambridge, MA: MIT Press.

Armbruster, B. B., Lehr, F., & Osborn, J. (2001). *Put reading first: The research building blocks for teaching children to read kindergarten through grade 3.* Washington, DC: National Institute for Literacy.

Blachman, B. A., Schatschneider, C., Fletcher, J. M., Francis, D. J., Clonan, S. M., Shaywitz, B. A., & Shaywitz, S. E. (2004). Effects of intensive reading remediation for second and third graders and a 1-year follow-up study. *Journal of Educational Psychology, 96,* 444–461.

Christensen, C. A., & Bowey, J. A. (2005). The efficacy of orthographic rime, grapheme-phoneme correspondences, and implicit phonics approaches to teaching decoding skills. *Scientific Studies of Reading, 9,* 327–340.

Ehri, L. C. (2000). Learning to read and learning to spell: Two sides of a coin. *Topics in Language Disorders, 20,* 19–36.

Ehri, L. C. (2005). Learning to read words: Theory, findings, and issues. *Scientific Studies of Reading, 9,* 167–188.

Ehri, L. C. (2006). More about phonics: Findings and reflections. In K. A. D. Stahl & M. C. McKenna (Eds.), *Reading research at work: Foundations of effective practice* (pp. 155–165). New York: Guilford Press.

Eldredge, J. L. (2005). Foundations of fluency: An exploration. *Reading Psychology, 26,* 161–181.

Goodman, K. (1996). *On reading: A common-sense look at the nature of language and the science of reading.* Portsmouth, NH: Heineman.

International Reading Association. (1997). *The role of phonics in reading instruction: A position statement of the International Reading Association* [Brochure]. Newark, DE: Author.

Johnston, R. S., & Watson, J. (2004). Accelerating the development of reading, spelling, and phoneme awareness skills in initial readers. *Reading and Writing: An Interdisciplinary Journal, 17,* 327–357.

McCandliss, B., Beck, I. L., Sandak, R., & Perfetti, C. (2003). Focusing attention on decoding for children with poor reading skills: Design and preliminary tests of the word building intervention. *Scientific Studies of Reading, 7,* 75–104.

National Reading Panel. (2000). *Teaching children to read: An evidence-based assessment of the scientific research literature on reading and its implications for reading instruction: Reports of the subgroups* (NIH Publication No. 00-4754). Washington, DC: U.S. Government Printing Office.

Neuhaus, G. F., Roldan, L. W., Boulware-Gooden, R., & Swank, P. R. (2006). Parsimonious reading models: Identifying teachable subskills. *Reading Psychology, 27,* 37–58.

Schwanenflugel, P. J., Hamilton, A. M., Kuhn, M. R., Wisenbaker, J. M., & Stahl, S. A. (2004). Becoming a fluent reader: Reading skill and prosodic features in the oral reading of young readers. *Journal of Educational Psychology, 96,* 119–129.

Speece, D. L., & Ritchey, K. D. (2005). A longitudinal study of the development of oral reading fluency in young children at risk of reading failure. *Journal of Learning Disabilities, 38,* 387–399.

Tunmer, W. E., & Chapman, J. E. (2002). The relation of beginning readers' reported word identification strategies to reading achievement, reading-related skills, and academic self-perceptions. *Reading and Writing: An Interdisciplinary Journal, 15,* 341–358.

Wolf, M., & Katzir-Cohen, T. (2001). Reading fluency and its intervention. *Scientific Studies in Reading, 5,* 211–239.

CHAPTER 2

Phonemic Awareness

Becoming Aware
of the Sounds of Language

This chapter describes how children develop insight into the sounds of language. You will learn about the importance of language awareness for learning to read, different types of language awareness children bring to your classroom, and tests to determine children's insight into the sounds in words. In this chapter you will find best practices for teaching phonemic awareness and many engaging activities to use in your classroom to develop children's ability to recognize rhyme, separate words into sounds, and blend sounds into words.

KEY IDEAS

- Phonemic awareness is the ability to think analytically about the sounds in words and then act on the basis of this analysis to separate words into sounds and blend sounds into words.

- Phonological awareness refers to awareness of the words, syllables, rhymes, and sounds in language. Phonemic awareness is a subset of phonological awareness that is important for using phonics to read and learn new words.

- Awareness of the words, rhymes, and sounds of language develops in a relatively predictable sequence that begins with awareness of the words in language and ends with awareness of the sounds in words.

- The ability to separate words into sounds and the ability to blend sounds together are the key components of phonemic awareness.

- Children with good phonemic awareness are better word learners, better readers, and better spellers than children with low phonemic awareness.

KEY VOCABULARY

Adding sounds

Blending

Deleting sounds

Isolating sounds

Manipulating sounds

Phoneme

Phonemic awareness

Phonological awareness

Rhyme awareness

Segmenting sounds

Substituting sounds

The language children bring to school serves many purposes. Language gives children a way to interact with others, express their feelings, and learn about their environment. When children carry on everyday conversations, they concentrate on communication, and not on the individual sounds from which the words are created. All this changes when children begin to learn to read. As they move toward literacy, children begin to think about spoken language in a totally different way: They stand back from the meaning of language in order to analyze speech. As they do this, children discover that the words they use in everyday conversation consist of individual sounds.

Nadia is discovering the individual sounds in spoken words and learning how letters go with sounds. When Nadia writes, as in the note in Figure 2-1, she thinks about the sounds in the words she wishes to spell and then associates letters with them. When Nadia reads, she looks for familiar letter patterns in unfamiliar words, considers the reading context, and then reads a word that fits both the reading context and the sounds that the letters represent.

Unlike Nadia, Marty is not aware of the sounds in words, and he does not know how letters represent sounds. Yet Marty does know that writing is important and that writing goes from left-to-right (see his writing in Figure 2-2). Marty experiments as he writes a few recognizable letters, uses some mock letters, and simulates cursive writing with scribble writing (the long wavy line traversing

Figure 2-1   Nadia uses her emerging awareness of the sounds in words and her developing knowledge of letter-sound patterns to write: I went to Sue's and ate pizza.

the page). As Marty becomes aware of the sounds in words and as he learns how letters go with sounds, he will begin to use letters to represent the sounds in the words he wishes to spell and, consequently, we will be able to read his writing.

WHAT IS PHONEMIC AWARENESS?

The word *phonemic* comes to us from the French who borrowed it from the Greek language. A *phoneme* is the smallest sound that differentiates one word from another. For example, the phonemes /s/ and /r/ differentiate /sat/ from /rat/. While a few English words have only one phoneme, most consist of two or more phonemes. For example, /bē/ consists of two phonemes (/b/, /ē/), *fish* has three phonemes (/f/, /i/, /sh/), *frog* has four (/f/, /r/, /o/, /g/), and *zebra* has five (/z/, /ē/, /b/, /r/, /a/). The -*ic* is Greek for pertaining to; hence, *phonemic* means pertaining to phonemes.

Figure 2-2 Marty, a kindergartner, is not yet aware of the individual sounds in words and how letters represent sounds. He uses a few real letters, mock letters, and scribbles as he experiments with writing.

Phonemic awareness is the ability to analyze language, and the ability to act on this analysis to separate words into sounds and to blend sounds into words. Children with well-developed phonemic awareness can arrange, rearrange, add, and delete sounds in words, and can blend individual phonemes into words. For example, these children will tell you, their teacher, that /man/ consists of /m/-/a/-/n/; that /a/ is the middle sound in /man/; that taking the /m/ away leaves /an/; and that the sounds /m/ + /a/ + /n/ blend together to make /man/. In the absence of phonemic awareness, children perceive speech as a continuous, undivided stream and therefore do not understand the principle of alphabetic writing—that print represents speech at the sound level. Phonemic awareness refers *only* to awareness of the sounds in words. Phonological awareness is a broader term that includes awareness of the sounds in words and awareness of larger language units.

WHAT IS PHONOLOGICAL AWARENESS?

The *phon-* in *phonological* is of Greek origin, meaning *sound* or *voice*, as in *telephone*. *Logy* also comes to us from the Greek language, and means the *study of*. Phonological, then,

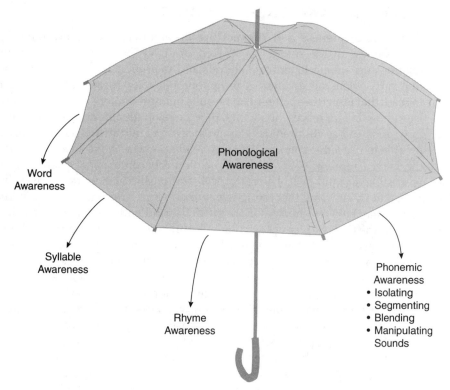

Figure 2-3 Phonological awareness and phonemic awareness.

pertains to the study of sound. When applied to the teaching of reading, *phonological awareness* refers to awareness of the words, syllables, rhymes, and sounds in language, and to the ability to blend individual sounds into words. We might think of phonological awareness as a large umbrella, as illustrated in Figure 2-3, that covers awareness of all the different units in speech. Children with good phonological awareness know that (a) sentences consist of individual words, (b) words consist of syllables, (c) some words rhyme while others do not, (d) words consist of individual sounds, and (e) blending individual sounds together produces meaningful spoken words.

The child who can tell you that *My dog* consists of *my* and *dog* has word-level awareness, a phonological awareness skill. Likewise, the child who announces that /mad/ and /dad/ rhyme is aware of rhyming words, another phonological awareness skill. Later in this chapter we will explore rhyme awareness, a phonological awareness skill taught in many preschool and kindergarten classrooms.

PHONEMIC AWARENESS AND PHONICS

Phonemic awareness and phonics are different. Phonemic awareness pertains to awareness of the sounds in spoken language, while phonics pertains to the relationship among letters and sounds and to approaches for teaching these relationships. Phonemic awareness and phonics develop reciprocally as children learn to read; that is, getting better in one results in improvement in the other. As children learn how letters represent sounds, they develop greater awareness of the sounds in words. And as children develop greater phonemic awareness, they become better able to use letter-sound patterns to read new words. For instance, learning that the letter *t* represents /t/ may help children become aware of the /t/ sound in words like *top* and *tiger*. The reciprocal relationship also works in the other direction; that is, knowing that the spoken words /top/ and /tiger/ begin with the /t/ sound may help children associate the /t/ sound with the letter *t* in *top* and *tiger*.

In the first chapter we discussed the linkage between phonics and fluency. As it turns out, phonemic awareness also plays a role in developing fluent reading (as we see in Figure 1-2 in the preceding chapter). Kindergartners and early first graders who are just learning to read have few words in their sight vocabularies. However, as early as kindergarten the foundations for fluency are being established through developing phonemic awareness. Children need some level of phonemic awareness in order to make sense of the principle of alphabetic writing and effectively use phonics. Children need phonics to identify new words, develop a large reading vocabulary, and spell new words when writing. A vocabulary of instantly recognized words makes it possible to read fluently. As we can see, in developing phonemic awareness children are taking an important early step toward fluency. It is not surprising, then, that phonemic awareness is a good predictor of later reading success (Schatschneider, Fletcher, Francis, Carlson, & Foorman, 2004). If you teach kindergarten, first, or second grade, look for the children with good phonemic awareness to be better at using phonics, have a larger reading vocabulary, and have better fluency than children who are less phonemically aware.

PHONEMIC AWARENESS DEVELOPS SEQUENTIALLY

Phonemic awareness develops in a relatively predictable sequence in which children first become aware of large language segments and then become aware of increasingly smaller ones (Lonigan, 2006). Awareness of the words in everyday conversations develops first. While some children may discover words as early as age 3, many become aware of words at about age 4. Most children begin kindergarten with word awareness. These children can separate sentences and phrases into individual words. For example, a word-aware child can tell you that /John ate dinner/ consists of /John/, /ate/, and /dinner/.

Rhyme and syllable awareness are generally thought to develop after word awareness (Bradley & Bryant, 1978), although there is not universal agreement on this sequence (Macmillan, 2002). Rhyme awareness develops before awareness of sounds (Blaiklock, 2004). Generally speaking, most 4-year-olds can divide long words into syllables, and by ages 4 and 5, preschool children are learning to identify rhyming words and beginning sounds (Justice, Invernizzi, Geller, Sullivan, & Welsch, 2005).

Children who are aware of rhyme can identify words that do and do not rhyme (/wag/ and /tag/ rhyme, but /wag/ and /sit/ do not), and can think of their own rhyming words (/mad/, /sad/, /bad/). As children develop awareness of rhyming words, they also become aware of beginning sounds. Some children find rhymes easier to identify than beginning sounds (Cardoso-Martins, Michalick, & Pollo, 2002), while others become aware of beginning sounds before they are aware of rhyme (Walton & Walton, 2002). Awareness of beginning sounds (/mop/ begins with /m/) and rhyme awareness (/mop/ and /hop/ rhyme) are thought to be one single level of language awareness (Armbruster, Lehr, & Osborn, 2001). Therefore, you can expect children to become aware of beginning sounds and rhyming sounds at approximately the same time or at least within a relatively short period of time (Anthony & Lonigan, 2004).

Identifying individual sounds in words is more difficult than identifying rhyme (Cardoso-Martins, et al., 2002). To identify the individual phonemes in words, children must (a) recognize that sounds are nonmeaningful portions of words, (b) understand that words consist of sounds, (c) be able to say each of the sounds in words, and (d) be able to blend disconnected sounds into complete, meaningful words. Phonemic awareness is, therefore, far more demanding than rhyme awareness. The sounds in words are much smaller than rhymes and, not coincidentally, the sounds themselves last only a very short time. Typically developing children become aware of sounds sometime in kindergarten or early first grade as they learn to read and write. Generally speaking, children develop awareness of beginning sounds first, followed by ending sounds and then middle sounds (Cassady & Smith, 2004). Children increase their phonemic awareness through direct instruction in phonemic awareness, instruction in the letter-sounds of phonics, and with opportunities to use letter-sound knowledge when reading and spelling.

RHYME AWARENESS

Some children as young as 3 may be sensitive to rhyme (MacLean, Bryant, & Bradley, 1987). Kindergartners who have experience with poetry and rhyming language games are generally quite good at identifying rhyming words (Treiman & Zukowski, 1991). Kindergartners with good *rhyme awareness* tend to be better readers later in school than kindergartners who are not sensitive to rhyme (Bradley & Bryant, 1978). Justin, who was aware of rhyming language as a kindergartner, demonstrates rhyme awareness in a poem he wrote after his first-grade class had shared the book *Ten Apples Up on Top!* (LeSieg, 1961). This book, which tells the rhyming story of animals balancing apples and being chased by an angry bear with a mop, clearly influenced Justin's thinking as he composed. Notice in Figure 2-4 how Justin uses two of the rhyming words from the storybook—*top* and *mop*—to create his own special poetic mood, message, and expression.

Apples

APPLES ON THE BOTTOM

APPLES ON TOP

APPLES ON THE CEILING

AND AN APPLE MOP!

Figure 2-4   Justin's rhyming poem, "Apples," shows that he has developed an awareness of rhyming sounds in language.

Rhyme awareness, coupled with awareness of beginning sounds, may make it possible for beginning readers to learn short words (Stahl & Murray, 2006). There are two ways rhyme awareness may help Justin as he learns to read: First, rhyme awareness may act as a scaffold to help Justin identify the sounds in words (Goswami, 2001). And second, rhyme awareness may prime Justin to look for the letters in written words (*mop* and *top*) that represent the rhyme /op/ in spoken words (Goswami, 2001). Children like Justin who are aware of rhyme (/mop/ and /top/) may think of the rhyme (/op/) as one category of sound, and the beginning sounds (/m/ and /t/, in this example) as another category. In so doing, children separate the beginning sound (/m/ or /t/) from the rhyming sound (/op/). These children may then be able to learn to substitute one beginning sound for another (Norris & Hoffman, 2002). For instance, Justin might begin by saying the word /mop/ and then substitute an /h/ for an /m/ to pronounce /hop/. *Substituting*, or swapping, one sound for another is important for reading new words by analogy, as explained in Chapter 4.

HOW CHILDREN DEMONSTRATE RHYME AWARENESS

Children show us they understand the rhyme in language when they identify rhyme, think of rhyming words, and separate words into beginning sounds and rhyming sounds (Armbruster et al., 2001). Let us take a closer look at each of these skills:

1.   **Identifying rhyme.** In identifying rhyme, children say which words rhyme and which do not. This is the easiest of the three rhyming skills. Children

who can identify rhyme will say that /pig/ and /big/ rhyme, but that /big/ and /cat/ do not. To help children learn to identify rhyme, ask questions like: "Does /man/ rhyme with /can/?" "Does /man/ rhyme with /rat/?" "Which words rhyme—/box/-/car/-/fox/?" "Do these belong together? /mad/ - /sad/ - /bad/?" "Which one doesn't belong? /mad/ - /dad/ - /boy/?"

2. **Thinking of rhyming words.** Children think of rhyming words on their own. For example, if you say /hot/, children might say /cot/ or /dot/. Help children learn to think of rhyme by asking them to "Say a word that rhymes with /cat/. With /man/. With /dog/." You might also ask children to "Say *a word that sounds like* bat." Another alternative is to ask, "If I say mouse, you would say. . . ." Children then answer with /house/ or another rhyming word.

3. **Separating words into beginning sounds and rhyming sounds.** This is the most difficult of the three rhyme skills. Children split words into two parts: the beginning sound and the rhyming sound. You may see the word *alliteration* in teachers' manuals and instructional guides. Alliteration is another term for words that begin with the same sound. Tongue twisters are a good example of alliteration: Peter Piper picked a peck of pickled peppers. Help children pay attention to beginning sounds by asking, "Say the first sound in /mop/." Help them pay attention to the rhyme by asking, "Say the rhyming sound in /mop/ and /top/." And help them split a word into its beginning sound and rhyme by asking them to "Say /mop/. Say the first sound in mop." /m/ "Now say the rhyming sound in mop." /op/. (Chapter 4 has ideas for teaching activities to encourage and support children as they apply this skill to reading and writing words.)

ACTIVITIES FOR DEVELOPING RHYME AWARENESS

Although children are naturally drawn to rhyming language, they may not develop rhyme awareness by simply participating in normal classroom activities (Layton, Deeny, Tall, & Upton, 1996). It is important, therefore, to support those children in your classroom who are not yet aware of rhyming language. Activities that ask children to produce their own rhyming words have been shown to improve children's rhyme awareness, even when those activities are brief, lasting only 4 minutes or so (Majsterek, Shorr, & Erion, 2000). Therefore, even relatively short activities, when consistently and repeatedly used with children like Nadia (see Figure 2-1) and Marty (see Figure 2-2), help children develop rhyme awareness. While the focus of these activities is on rhyming language, many can be easily adapted to develop awareness of beginning sounds. Along with these activities, read rhyming books and poems, recite nursery rhymes, and call children's attention to the jump rope rhymes they hear older children recite on the playground.

 **Activities**

2.1 *Predict Rhyming Words*

Skill: Think of rhyming words.

Children in small groups predict familiar rhyming words in often-read poems.

Things You'll Need: Poems on large charts; sticky notes.

Directions:

1. Write a familiar poem on a large chart.
2. Cover up one or more rhyming words with sticky notes.
3. Read the poem together with the children in chorus. Ask children to supply the hidden rhyming words.
4. Then remove the sticky notes to reveal the rhyming words.
5. Reread the poem in chorus; point to each word as it is read. Ask children to think of other rhyming words.

2.2 *Match Rhyming Words*

Skill: Identify rhyming words.

Children in small groups read familiar poems aloud and then match rhyming words on cards with the rhyming words in poems.

Things You'll Need: Rhyming poems on laminated charts; laminated rhyming word cards with masking tape loops on the back.

Directions:

1. Have the children read familiar poems and jingles together with you in chorus. As children read together, track words by moving your hand under the words as they are read to (a) focus children's attention on the print, (b) demonstrate left-to-right orientation, and (c) demonstrate the connection between spoken words and written words.
2. Give children rhyming word cards. Have them put the rhyming word cards on, next to, or under the rhyming words in the poem.

2.3 *Rhyming (or Beginning Sound) Picture Bookmark*

Skill: Identify rhyming words or beginning sounds.

Children make a handy bookmark with this small group or center activity.

Figure 2-5 Making rhyming picture bookmarks is fun, gives children extra practice recognizing rhyming words, and results in a handy place marker for the books children enjoy at school or at home.

Things You'll Need: A bookmark pattern on sturdy paper with room for a picture in the top square, as shown in Figure 2-5 pictures that do and do not rhyme with the top picture (or pictures that do and do not begin like the top picture); scissors; glue.

Directions:

1. Have the children cut out pictures that rhyme with the picture at the top of the bookmark pattern and glue the rhyming pictures in the bookmark squares.

2. Extend this activity to written language by having children watch as you write the words under the pictures on their bookmarks. Or, you might ask children to join you in interactively spelling one or two words.
3. Laminate finished bookmarks.
4. Say the picture names on the bookmarks with children in chorus.

To develop sensitivity to beginning sounds, ask children to cut out and glue pictures with the same beginning sound, thereby making beginning sound bookmarks.

2.4 *Rhyming and Beginning Sound Picture Sorts*

Skill: Identify rhyming words or beginning sounds.

Children work with partners, individually, or in learning centers to sort rhyming pictures (or pictures that begin with the same sound).

Things You'll Need: Pictures taped to two or three lunch sacks for each child or set of learning partners; rhyming pictures (or pictures that begin alike) on 3-inch-by-5-inch cards.

Directions:

1. Discuss rhyming words or words that begin alike.
2. Show children the picture-cards.
3. Have children name each picture. It is important to have children name the pictures because sometimes children use a picture name we do not anticipate. When this happens, the sort does not work.
4. Ask children to sort the picture-cards by putting them into sacks that have a rhyming picture on them, as shown in Figure 2-6, or by putting pictures that begin alike into sacks. Or, if children do not put cards into sacks, have children tell you or another adult the names of the pictures they sort.

If you place this sorting activity in a learning center, ask children to fold over the top of the sack when they finish sorting and to write their names on the back. This way you have a record of the learning center activity, and you know who sorted correctly and who did not.

2.5 *Rhyming Picture-word Mobiles*

Skill: Identify rhyming words or beginning sounds; match written words with pictures.

Children in small groups make mobiles that feature pictures and words that either rhyme or begin with the same sound.

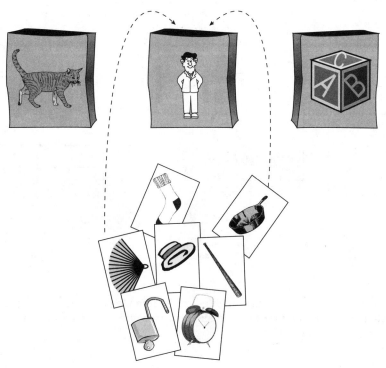

Figure 2-6   Sorting rhyming pictures into paper lunch sacks gives children an opportunity to analyze the rhyme in words and to differentiate one set of rhyming sounds from another.

Things You'll Need: Old magazines and catalogs; scissors; colorful construction paper cut into geometric shapes; glue; colorful yarn cut into different lengths; coat hangers to hang the mobiles; hole punch.

Directions:

1. Have the children cut out pictures with names that either rhyme or begin alike, and then paste the pictures onto one side of the colored pieces of construction paper.
2. Write the word for the picture on the opposite side.
3. Punch a hole in the top of each geometric shape, thread a colorful strand of yarn through the hole, and then tie the yarn to a coat hanger (see Figure 2-7).

   Integrate with math: Integrate this activity with mathematics by discussing the circles, triangles, squares, and rectangles that adorn the mobiles.

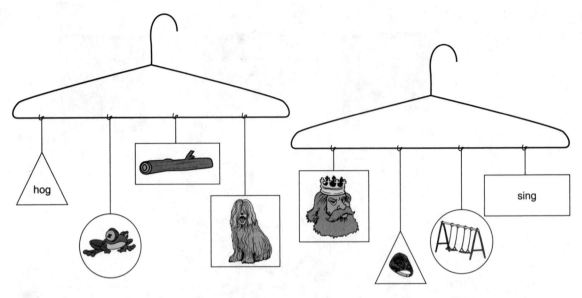

Figure 2-7 In making rhyming mobiles, children think about and read rhyming words and, if construction paper is cut into circles, triangles, squares, and rectangles, you have an opportunity to integrate language arts and mathematics.

2.6 *Rhyming Picture Collage*

Skill: Identify rhyming words or beginning sounds.

Small groups make collages of rhyming pictures or pictures that begin with the same sound.

Things You'll Need: Lots of pictures; oak tag; tape or glue.

Directions:

1. Give children a few pictures, some that rhyme and some that do not—or, if focusing on beginning sounds, some that begin alike and some that do not.
2. Have children select rhyming pictures or pictures with the same beginning sound, and then glue or tape pictures onto a large sheet of paper.
3. When the collage is finished, have the children say the picture names in chorus.
4. Extend this activity to written language by writing words on cards and asking children to match the words with the pictures on the collage.

Figure 2-8 After Gerald drew this pair of rhyming pictures, his kindergarten teacher shared them with the class. The rhyming pictures are: bat-cat; goose-moose; mouse-house.

2.7 *Draw Rhyming Pictures*

Skill: Think of rhyming words.

In this small group, individual, or learning center activity, children draw pictures that rhyme and then share the pictures with their classmates.

Things You'll Need: Paper folded in half; crayons.

Directions:

1. Have children draw two rhyming pictures, one picture on one side of the folded paper and a different picture on the other side, as shown in Figure 2-8.
2. Write the words under the pictures. Ask children to share the rhyming pictures with their classmates.

2.8 *Picture-Rhyme Memory Game*

Skill: Identify rhyming words or beginning sounds.

This is a rhyming or beginning sound picture version of the ever-popular Concentration®, and is a good game for children to play with a partner or while pairs of children visit the centers in your classroom.

Things You'll Need: A deck of cards with pairs of rhyming picture-word cards, as shown in Figure 2-9, or pictures of words that begin alike.

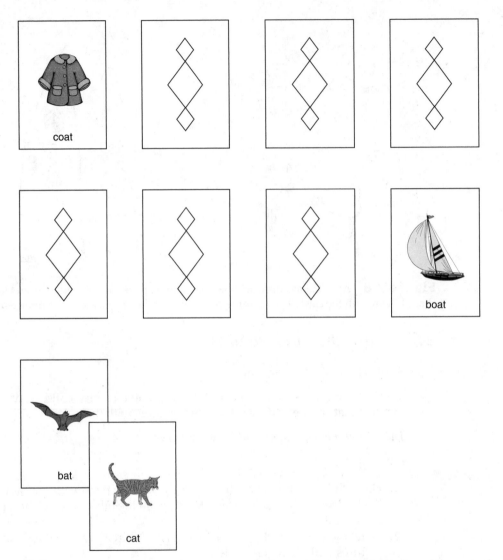

Figure 2-9   A rhyming picture-word memory game. Recognizing pairs of rhyming picture-word cards reinforces sensitivity to, and awareness of, rhyme in spoken and written language.

Directions:

1. Children put the rhyming (or beginning sound) pictures face down on a table and take turns flipping up two picture-word cards.
2. Players keep pairs of picture-word rhyming or begin-alike cards. Cards that do not rhyme or begin alike are turned face down again. The player with the most cards wins.

2.9 *Shoe Box Rhyme*

Skill: Think of rhyming words or words that begin with the same sound.

Small groups or individuals say words that rhyme with (or begin with the same sound) as pictures or objects hidden in a shoe box.

Things You'll Need: A shoe box; an assortment of small objects or pictures.

Directions:

1. Place objects or pictures in a shoe box; do not let the children watch as you do this.
2. Put your hand in the shoe box and grab an object or picture. Show it to the children. Ask the children to think of a word that rhymes with the name of the object or picture, or to think of a word that begins with the same sound.
3. Set that object aside and take another from the shoe box. You might also want to write the words that children suggest, thereby connecting spoken words with written words.

2.10 *Shower Curtain Rhyme Toss*

Skill: Think of rhyming words or words that begin with the same sounds.

In this large muscle activity, small groups toss a beanbag onto a shower curtain with pictures taped on it and then say a word that rhymes with or begins with the same sound as the picture-name.

Things You'll Need: Plastic shower curtain; beanbag; pictures; tape.

Directions:

1. Tape pictures to a shower curtain and put the shower curtain on the floor.
2. Children stand around the curtain and take turns tossing a beanbag onto (or near) a picture.
3. Children say the picture-name and then say a word that rhymes with it or that begins with the same sound.

SPARE MINUTE ACTIVITIES FOR DEVELOPING RHYME AWARENESS

2.11 *Rhyming Word Lists*

Skills: Identify rhyming words; read rhyming words.

Make lists of words that rhyme with the words in a familiar poem. For example, if *swing* is a rhyming word in a poem or book written in verse, ask children to suggest other words for the list, such as *king, ring, sing*. Leave the charts up in your room; refer to the charts when talking about rhyme; use them as resources for interactive writing. Interactive writing is writing in which the teacher scaffolds by supplying information the children do not yet have and helping them apply the information they do have. Look in Chapter 5 for a more detailed explanation.

2.12 *Create Rhyming Chalkboard (or Whiteboard) Chains*

Skill: Think of rhyming words or words that begin with the same sound.

Write on the board the rhyming words children suggest, draw circles around the words, and then connect the circles with lines, thereby creating a chain of rhyming words. Make several chains; count the words in each chain. Read the chains in chorus. Point out the letters in rhyming words that represent rhyming sounds. (Be sure to use words that sound alike and are spelled alike—jam-ham, not jam-lamb.)

2.13 *Frame Rhyming Words*

Skill: Identify rhyming words.

Read rhyming poems. Call attention to rhyming words by framing them (cupping your hands around words). Also use a word window—a piece of oak tag with a "window" or hole in the middle—to frame words. Have children use their hands or the word window to frame rhyming words.

2.14 *Use a Puppet to Pique Interest in Rhyme*

Objective: Think of rhyming words or words that begin with the same sounds.

We find that a colorful puppet is a good way to keep children interested in rhyme activities and to encourage children to participate in rhyme activities. The puppet says two (or more) words, and children decide if the words rhyme or begin alike. Children put their thumbs up for rhyming or begin-alike words, down for nonrhyming words or words that begin differently. When the puppet's words do not rhyme or begin alike, the puppet asks the children to suggest rhyming words or words that do begin alike.

PHONEMIC AWARENESS

At 6 years old, Melanie already knows how letters represent sounds. Look at Figure 2-10 and the clever way she writes sn-snow balls, ch-chillier, ch-ch-ch-chilly, and ah ah ah ahchoooooo! She literally separates language into sounds before her readers' eyes. Melanie can separate words into sounds, and she can blend

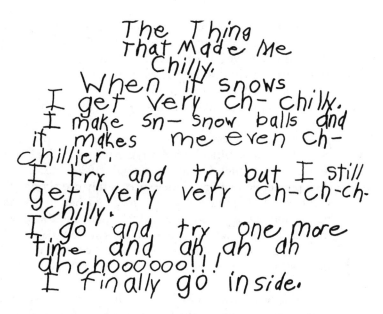

The Thing
That Made Me
Chilly.
When it snows
I get very ch-chilly.
I make sn-snow balls and
it makes me even ch-
chillier.
I try and try but I still
get very very ch-ch-ch.
chilly.
I go and try one more
time and ah, ah ah
ah chooooooo!!!
I finally go inside.

Figure 2-10   Melanie demonstrates sound awareness when she separates the beginning sounds from words in her story to help her readers experience the sensation of being cold.

individual sounds into meaningful words. Children like Melanie who begin school with high phonemic awareness make faster reading progress than children with low phonemic awareness (National Reading Panel, 2000; Muter, Hulme, Snowling, & Stevenson, 2004; Schatschneider et al., 2004; Strattman & Hodson, 2005). The positive relationship between phonemic awareness and reading achievement is evident whether children grow up in economically advantaged families (Nicholson, 1997; Spira, Bracken & Fischel, 2005), are at-risk of reading difficulty (Carroll & Snowling, 2004), or speak English as their second language (Manis, Lindsey, & Bailey, 2004). What's more, children with more phonemic awareness typically have larger reading vocabularies than the children with less awareness (Lonigan, 2006).

Phonemic awareness is important for reading and spelling. Phonemic awareness is more important for reading and spelling than rhyme awareness (Yeh, 2003). Whereas rhyme awareness calls for insight into rather large bundles of sound, phonemic awareness requires children to identify single sounds. The phoneme, as we have learned, is the level at which our alphabet represents sound. Not surprisingly, kindergartners with good phonemic awareness become better readers than their classmates who have good rhyme awareness but less well developed phonemic awareness (Savage & Carless, 2005). In fact, increasing rhyme awareness in kindergarten may not result in better reading if this instruction reduces the opportunity to develop phonemic awareness (Nancollis, Lawrie, & Dodd, 2005).

Phonemic awareness makes it possible for children to use phonics to read and spell new words. Phonics, in turn, is necessary for learning to read new words (Eldredge, 2005; Strattman & Hodson, 2005). Consequently, children with good phonemic awareness have larger reading vocabularies than their classmates with low awareness (Strattman & Hodson, 2005). All things considered, if some of the children whom you teach have not discovered the sounds in language, they will benefit from activities that increase phonemic awareness, becoming better readers and better spellers as a consequence.

Phonemic awareness helps children realize that the sounds they hear in spoken words are represented by the letters in written words. Children with low phonemic awareness do poorly when they must use letter-sound associations because they have difficulty identifying the individual phonemes in words that letters represent (Juel, Griffith, & Gough, 1986). However, when children improve their phonemic awareness, they successfully use phonics to read new words (Elbo & Petersen, 2004; Hindson et al., 2005). Generally speaking, learning the letter names and the letter-sounds fosters phonemic awareness. While some children may develop insight into the sounds in language before learning the letters (Hulme, Caravolas, Maliková, & Brigstocke, 2005), most develop phonemic awareness as they learn letter names and letter-sounds in kindergarten and early first grade.

Phonemic awareness also is important for spelling. Children with good phonemic awareness are better spellers than children with poor awareness (Caravolas, Hulme, & Snowling, 2001; Frost, 2001; Kroese, Hynd, Knight, Hiemenz, & Hall, 2000). When beginning spellers do not know how to spell a word, they match letters with sounds by (1) saying the word to themselves, (2) listening for individual phonemes, and (3) then writing the letters that represent the sounds they hear. Matching letters to sounds calls for carefully analyzing the phonemes in words. This might explain why phonemic awareness increases when kindergartners are prompted to "spell words like they sound" (Martins & Silva, 2006). We would expect the effect of phonemic awareness to be most evident in the early grades before children have memorized the spellings of many different words. It makes sense, then, that the words that first and second graders correctly separate into sounds are spelled with greater accuracy than the words children incorrectly separate into sounds (Foorman, Jenkins, & Francis, 1993).

How Children Demonstrate Phonemic Awareness

Children with good phonemic awareness step aside from the meaning of language to consider the smallest units of sound—the phonemes—in our language. In so doing, children analyze and think about the individual sounds in words and blend these sounds to pronounce words. While there are many ways for children to show us they are aware of sounds, the most common are isolating sounds, segmenting sounds, manipulating sounds, and blending sounds into words.

1.   **Isolating sounds.** Children isolate sounds when they pronounce the beginning, ending, or middle sound in a word. For example, children may tell you that /man/ begins with /m/ or that /sun/ ends with /n/. Help children isolate sounds by asking them questions like "What's the first sound in /soap/?" "What's

the first sound in /moon/ /milk/ /made/?" "What's the last sound in /cat/?" "What sound do you hear in the middle of /boat/?"

2. Segmenting sounds. In segmenting, children pronounce each phoneme in the same order in which it occurs in a word. For example, when asked to say the sounds in /coat/, children would say, "/c/ - /oa/ (long o) - /t/." Encourage children to segment by asking "What sounds do you hear in /rain/?" or "Say all the sounds in /soap/."

3. Manipulating sounds. When children manipulate sounds, they deliberately change the sounds in one word so as to pronounce a different word. Children do this by *adding* a new sound to a word, removing (*deleting*) a sound, or substituting a sound. For instance, children might add /r/ to the beginning of /at/ to pronounce /rat/, or /t/ to the end of /bee/ to say /beet/. An example of sound deletion is taking the /s/ away from /sat/ to pronounce /at/. Children substitute a sound when they exchange the /t/ in /sat/ for a /d/ to pronounce /sad/.

Prompt children to add sounds by asking "What word do we get when we add /r/ to /at/?" Or you might say "Start with /an/. Add a /t/ to the end. What's the word?" Prompt children to delete sounds by encouraging children to "Say /meat/ without the /m/." You also might ask children to "Say /meat/. Now say it again without the /t/." Another way to phrase sound-deletion questions is to ask, "What is left when we take /m/ away from /meat/?" "Can you say /ham/ without the /h/?" Encourage children to substitute beginning sounds by asking them to "Say /cat/. Now say /r/ instead of /c/." Prompt children to substitute ending sounds; ask children to "Say /cat/. Say it again, but now say /n/ instead of /t/." Encourage children to substitute middle sounds by asking them to "Say /pan/. Change the /a/ to /i/."

4. Blending sounds. Children show us they know how to blend when they combine phonemes to pronounce a whole word. Children might, for example, blend /sh/ + /ip/ to pronounce /ship/, or they might blend /sh/ + /i/ + /p/ to say /ship/. In both cases, children must fold sounds together. In so doing, the sounds themselves are somewhat altered. Children cannot simply "say it fast" because this essentially results in saying one isolated sound after another in close succession. In successful blending, sounds overlap somewhat, something like the shingles on a roof. Help children blend sounds by saying "What word do these sounds make? /l/ /a/ /p/." "What word is this? /b/ /e/?" "What word do we get when we blend together /s/ /o/ (long o) /p/?" "If I say /m/ /a/ /n/, you say _____."

BEST PRACTICES FOR DEVELOPING PHONEMIC AWARENESS

You can expect the children whom you teach to develop greater sensitivity to the sounds in words when you include phonemic awareness in your balanced classroom reading program. In following these best practices, you ensure that phonemic awareness instruction is effective and in proportion to children's needs:

1.   **Teach awareness of beginning sounds, followed by awareness of ending sounds, and then awareness of middle sounds** (Cassady & Smith, 2004). This is the sequence in which phonemic awareness typically develops in most children.

2.   **Teach phonemic awareness, letter names, and letter-sounds together** (Christensen & Bowey, 2005). Teaching phonemic awareness along with letter names and letter-sounds is more effective than teaching phonemic awareness alone. If your classroom program weaves an emphasis on phonemic awareness into the fabric of phonics instruction, you may not need to provide the average reader with additional phonemic awareness instruction beyond that included in your well-planned, sequenced, and explicit program (Johnston & Watson, 2004). For the child who needs more phonemic awareness instruction, combine some of the activities in Chapters 3 and 5 with activities in this chapter.

3.   **Teach one or two skills at a time.** Teaching one or two phonemic awareness skills is twice as effective as teaching many skills at once, perhaps because children do not really master skills when many different skills are taught at the same time (Ehri et al., 2001; National Reading Panel, 2000).

4.   **Teach phonemic awareness early, in kindergarten and first grade.** Becoming aware of the sounds in language is important for understanding the alphabetic principle in the kindergarten (Ehri et al., 2001), and necessary for using phonics to read and spell new words in first grade.

5.   **Teach in small groups.** Teaching small groups of children is more effective than teaching large groups (National Reading Panel, 2000). Children in small groups may have more opportunities to personally respond to you, their teacher. And you may have more opportunities to observe the effects of instruction when you teach small groups of children.

6.   **Pace instruction to the needs of the child** (Ehri et al., 2001). Children differ in the level of phonemic awareness they bring to your classroom. Consistent with a balanced view of instruction, spend more time teaching phonemic awareness to children with low awareness and move high-awareness children on to other reading and writing activities.

7.   **Show children how to use phonemic awareness when reading and writing new words** (Juel & Minden-Cupp, 2000). We cannot assume that children will automatically infer how to use their developing phonemic awareness skills when they read and spell. Therefore, you will be a more effective teacher when you model how to use phonemic awareness to read and spell new words and when you give children opportunities to practice, under your guidance, the phonemic awareness skills they are learning.

8.   **Begin with short, two-sound words** (Uhry & Ehri, 1999). It is easier to separate short, two-sound words into phonemes (/at/ = /a/ - /t/) than to segment three- and four-sound words. What's more, two-sound words that begin with a vowel, such as /ape/, /it/, and /eat/, are easier to segment into individual sounds than words that begin with a consonant, such as /be/, /tie/, and /two/. Introduce three- and four-sound words when children can segment and blend two-sound words.

ACTIVITIES FOR DEVELOPING PHONEMIC AWARENESS

The activities in this section develop awareness of the sounds in words and the ability to blend. Consistent with best practice, we find these activities to be most effective when we teach in small groups. By and large, you will want to use these activities with younger children, say kindergartners or first graders, or older children who lack phonemic awareness and, therefore, have difficulty using phonics to read new words. In addition to these activities, you may wish to modify some of the rhyme awareness activities to use them to develop phonemic awareness. Modify these activities to suit your own teaching style and use them along with the letter and sound activities in Chapters 4 and 5.

Activities

2.15 *Rubber Band Sound Stretching*

Skill: Segmenting.

The teacher says a word slowly while children listen for sounds. Rubber band stretching helps children hear sounds in words.

Things You'll Need: Nothing special.

Directions:

1. Call attention to sounds by saying a word slowly, keeping the sounds connected while at the same time stretching them out, much as you pull a rubber band. For instance, in stretching /man/, you would stretch the word to pronounce something like "/mmmaaannn/."
2. Children listen to a rubber band sound stretched word and tell you the beginning, middle, and ending sound.
3. Next, bring your hand up to your mouth and "pull" the sounds as you stretch them.
4. Repeat, only this time ask the children to bring their hands to their mouths and sound stretch along with you.

2.16 *Colored Squares for Segmenting*

Skills: Segmenting and associating sounds with letters.

Children in a small group line up a colored square for each sound in a word.

Things You'll Need: One-inch colored construction paper squares.

Directions:

1. Give each child three or four colored squares. Say a word slowly, stretching it to clearly pronounce all the sounds.
2. Children move one colored square for each sound heard.
3. Then have children point to individual squares that represent specific sounds in the word. For the purposes of illustration, let's assume that children pushed three squares for /fan/. You might have children, "Point to the square for the first sound in /fan/." Or, you might ask, "What's the first sound in /fan/? Point to that square." Another option is to ask children to "Point to the /f/." Similar questions might be asked for middle and ending sounds.
4. Extend this activity to written language by writing letters on the squares after children have moved them into a line. This increases awareness of the connections between the sounds in spoken words and the letters in written words and helps introduce letter-sound relationships.

2.17 *Colored Squares for Manipulating Sounds*

Skills: Manipulating sounds and associating sounds with letters.

Things You'll Need: One-inch colored construction paper squares.

Directions:

1. Children line up squares for the sounds in a word, as described in the previous activity. Now, if *adding sounds,* children add an extra square to represent a new sound; if *deleting sounds,* children remove a square to take a sound away; if substituting sounds, children swap one color square for another. For example, suppose children line up a red square for /p/, a green square for /a/, and a blue for /n/ to represent /pan/. Children might substitute the red square (/p/) for a black square (/m/) to represent /man/. Now the squares consist of black, green, and blue to represent /man/. Children then might substitute a yellow square (/t/) for the blue to represent /mat/. Substituting middle sounds is the most difficult task, so ask children to do this after they are able to substitute beginning and ending sounds.
2. Have children pronounce the new word.
3. Write the letters on the squares and then refer to the word wall to find examples of other words that begin or end with the letters on the squares.

2.18 *Sound Boxes*

Skills: Isolating, segmenting, and blending.

Sound boxes are connected boxes where each box represents a sound in a word. Variations of this activity have been used since the 1970s when a

Soviet researcher, Elkonin, developed a method in which children move tokens for the sounds in words. Today, a similar technique is used in Reading Recovery lessons (Clay, 1985). This activity may be used with small groups or when working with individual children.

Things You'll Need: Sound boxes, as shown in Figure 2-11a; tokens; pictures with two-, three-, or four-sound names (optional).

Directions:

1. Give each child a piece of paper with several groups of sound boxes. You may also wish to give children pictures to help them remember the words they are segmenting.
2. Rubber band sound stretch a word. Children push a token into a box for each sound heard. When children do not have much experience with sound boxes, pronounce words with beginning and ending sounds that you can say without interrupting airflow, such as the /mmm/ and /nnn/ in /man/. It is easier to demonstrate sounds when we can stretch them—/sss/ and /aaa/ (short *a* as in *fan*). Later, introduce sounds in which the airflow is interrupted, as the /t/ and /b/ in /tub/. Sounds in which the airflow is interrupted (/t/, /p/, /g/, for instance) cannot be effectively stretched and, therefore, are somewhat more difficult for you to demonstrate in the sound boxes activity.

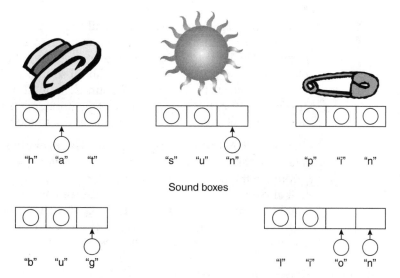

Figure 2-11a   Phonemic awareness increases when children move tokens into boxes for the sounds they hear in words and point to the tokens that represent beginning, middle, and ending sounds.

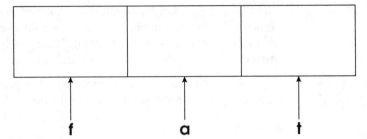

Figure 2-11b   Connecting sounds with letters helps children gain insight into the principle that letters represent the sounds children hear in words.

3. Once children have moved a token for each sound heard, ask them to point to the box that represents a single sound and to tell the sound's position—beginning, middle, end—in the word. For example, you might say, "Point to the box that stands for the /m/ in /man/." Then ask, "Does /m/ come at the beginning, middle, or end of /man/?"
4. Ask children to say together in chorus the individual sounds in the word by pointing to each box as they say the sound.
5. Last, have children blend sounds to pronounce the whole word, tracking (sweeping) their fingers under boxes as they say the sounds.

2.19 *Sound Boxes with Letters*

Skills: Isolating, segmenting, and blending; associating sounds with letters.

This sound box activity introduces children to the letters that represent the sounds. In so doing, we combine phonemic awareness with rudimentary phonics. The letters help children remember the sounds and, additionally, provide a good platform for talking about sounds and calling attention to word wall words that contain the sounds. Sound boxes with letters are appropriate for children who have some phonemic awareness and are developing the concept that letters represent sounds.

Things You'll Need: Sound boxes, plastic letters or other letters, perhaps letters on cards, as shown in Figure 2-11b. If you use boxes with the letters printed in them, bear in mind that when children move tokens into boxes that already have letters in them, the tokens cover up the letters. Therefore, you will want to take extra care to make sure that children peek under the tokens (or move the tokens above or below the boxes) to look at the letters when you ask children to tell you the names of letters that represent sounds.

Directions:

1. Begin by rubber band sound stretching the word and then pronounce the word normally.

2. Children move a letter into a sound box for each sound in a word. (If letters are written in the boxes, move a token into each box for each sound heard.)
3. Ask children to say the name of each letter as they (or you) identify the letters that go with the sounds (see Figure 2-11b.).

2.20 *Graph Sounds*

Skill: Segmenting.

Children working in small groups under your guidance make a graph showing words with two, three, or four sounds.

Things You'll Need: Pictures; tape; a large piece of newsprint. Beforehand, draw two, three, and four connected boxes at the top of the newsprint, distributing groups of connected boxes fairly far apart. Fasten the newsprint to a bulletin board.

Directions:

1. Children count the sounds in picture names.
2. Children then tape the pictures below the connected boxes that match the number of sounds in the names. When finished, children have made a graph similar to the graph in Figure 2-12.
3. *Integrate this activity with mathematics* by adding up the words under each group of connected boxes, as well as the total number of words found.

2.21 *Sort Pictures for Sounds*

Skill: Isolating sounds.

Children working individually, with a partner, or in a learning center sort pictures according to beginning, middle, or ending sounds.

Things You'll Need: Two or more sacks for each individual or set of partners; pictures on cards. Tape a picture to each sack. The pictures on cards should have a beginning, middle, or ending sound in common with one of the pictures on each sack.

Directions:

1. Place two or three sacks with a picture and a letter that corresponds to the target sound on a table in a learning center.
2. Children sort pictures by putting them into the sack that has a picture and letter with a shared sound. For example, to sort for the same

Figure 2-12 Graphing sounds gives children practice identifying the number of sounds in words, and the finished graph is a wonderful resource for integrating language arts with mathematics.

beginning sound, children would put pictures of a *bus, bee, bear, banana, bat,* and *balloon* in a sack with a picture of a *ball* and the letter *b*, and pictures of a *doll, doughnut, duck,* and *drum* go in a sack with a *dog* and the letter *d* on the front. Have children follow the same procedure when sorting for ending or middle sounds.

2.22 *Picture-Sound-Letter Sort*

Skills: Isolating sounds and associating sounds with letters.

In this activity children sort pictures according to shared sounds and then identify the letters that represent the shared sounds.

Things You'll Need: A large piece of chart paper divided into two or three columns with a letter and a picture at the top of each column.

Directions:

1. Prop up pictures on the chalk tray. Hold up one picture. Ask children to say the beginning sound. Talk about the letter that represents that sound. Find the letter in the alphabet display in your classroom. Look for the letter in the words on the word wall.
2. Have a volunteer glue the picture in a column under the letter that represents the beginning sound. Figure 2-13 shows a paper for sorting pictures into groups that share the same beginning letter-sound.
3. Write the letter beside each picture on the chart.

2.23 *Interactive Spelling*

Skills: Segmenting, blending, and associating sounds with letters.

Interactive spelling is a technique in which you, the teacher, ask children to join you in spelling words by listening for sounds and then associating letters with them.

Things You'll Need: Nothing special.

Directions:

1. Begin by pronouncing a word slowly, rubber band sound stretching it so that all the sounds are clearly heard, yet connected together. Ask the children what sound they hear at the beginning and what letter goes with that sound. Write the letter on the board.
2. Again pronounce the word, only this time emphasize the second sound as you rubber band the pronunciation. Have children tell you the letter that goes with that sound, and write that letter on the board.
3. Continue rubber band sound stretching and emphasizing the sounds children are to match with letters until the entire word is spelled.

Figure 2-13   Associating letters with sounds (picture-sound-letter sort) and sorting by beginning, ending, or middle letter-sounds gives children practice listening for sounds and associating letters with sounds.

4. To give children practice blending sounds, read the word with them, sliding your finger under the letters as the sounds are pronounced. This helps children develop greater phonemic awareness, reinforces letter-sound knowledge, and supports conventional spelling. Interactive spelling is most successful when used with *phonetically regular words*—that is, words that sound like they are spelled, such as *man*, *lime*, and *see*.

Activities for Developing Blending

2.24 *Finger Puppet Talk*

Skill: Blending.

Children listen to a finger puppet say words sound by sound and then blend sounds together to pronounce the word.

Things You'll Need: A finger puppet.

Directions:

1. Using a special finger puppet, explain that this special puppet talks only in sounds. For example, the puppet might say, /m/ - /a/ - /n/. Ask the children to identify the word the puppet said, /man/.
2. Continue pronouncing words sound by sound and asking the children to say the whole words.

2.25 *Arm Blending*

Skill: Blending.

Arm blending is a tactile, kinesthetic approach to blending that children can use on their own when reading all sorts of materials in all sorts of places.

Things You'll Need: Nothing special.

Directions:

1. Have children imagine that they place sounds on their arms. For example, to blend /f/, /a/, /n/, children put their right hand on their left shoulder (reverse for left-handed children) and say /f/, their hand in the crook of their arm and say /a/, and their hand on their wrist and say /n/.
2. Children blend by saying sounds as they slide their hands from shoulder to wrist.
3. When finished, the children again pronounce the whole blended word. Mentally "placing" sounds on their arms helps children remember the right sounds in the right order. The motion of the sweeping hand sliding down the arm is a kind of tactile analog for what the voice does when sliding sounds together during blending.

2.26 *Finger Blending*

Skill: Blending.

Children use their fingers to anchor sounds in memory and to guide blending. Finger blending requires more dexterity than arm blending and is appropriate for children who easily can touch together the fingers on one hand.

Things You'll Need: Nothing special.

Directions:

1. For the purposes of illustration, let's suppose that children are blending /b/, /e/, /l/, /t/ into /belt/. Children touch their forefinger to their thumb while saying /b/, their middle finger to the thumb saying /e/, their ring finger to the thumb while saying /l/, and their little finger to thumb saying /t/.
2. To blend, children place each finger on their thumb as they pronounce sounds, thereby blending sounds into /belt/.

2.27 *Knuckle Blending*

Skill: Blending.

Knuckle blending is an alternative to finger blending.

Things You'll Need: Nothing special.

Directions:

1. Children use their right forefinger to place sounds on the knuckles of their left forefinger (reverse for left-handed children).
2. To blend /ham/, children touch the innermost knuckle with their right forefinger while saying /h/, middle knuckle while saying /a/, outer most knuckle while saying /m/. In blending, children sweep their right finger over the left finger as they say sounds.

2.28 *Moving Sounds*

Skills: Blending and associating sounds with letters.

This is a kinesthetic, whole-body approach to blending. Standing at arm's length, children wearing letters take turns rubber band sound stretching their own sound while moving closer to the partner until the whole word is pronounced.

Things You'll Need: Letters written on cards for each sound in a word.

Directions:

1. Select words in which each letter represents a sound. Ask as many children as there are letters and sounds to come to the front, such as /sun/. Give each child a letter and ask the children to line up so that the word is spelled from left to right. Have children stand about an arm's length from one another.
2. The child holding the first letter (the letter *s*) slowly moves toward the child holding the second letter (the letter *u*) as *you* rubber band sound stretch /sss/.
3. When the child holding the *s* is shoulder to shoulder with the child holding the letter *u*, you rubber band sound stretch /uuu/, and the child with the *u* stands next to the child with the letter *n*.
4. When the child with the *u* is shoulder to shoulder with the child holding the letter *n*, you rubber band sound stretch /nnn/ as the child with the *n* moves to stand next to the child with the *u*.
5. Have the whole group pronounce /sun/. Repeat a couple of times to give children practice.
6. To get everyone in the small group involved, ask onlookers to arm blend /sun/ while others are demonstrating sounds on the move.

2.29 *Picture Blending*

Skill: Blending.

This activity uses pictures to develop the concept of blending (Catts & Vartiainen, 1993).

Things You'll Need: Large pictures of familiar objects; scissors.

Directions:

1. Show children a picture and say the picture name. Cut the picture into as many parts as you wish to use for blending. For example, you might cut a picture of a *boat* into three equal parts, one for /b/, one for /oa/ (long o), and one for /t/. Make blending easier by cutting the picture into two parts, one for /b/ and one for /oat/, so as to reduce the number of sounds (or sound groups) children blend.
2. Point to each picture piece and say the sound it represents. For example, point to the first part of the *boat* picture while saying /b/, to the second part saying /oa/ (long o), and to the third when saying /t/. Explain that sounds go together to make a word just like pieces of a puzzle go together to make a picture. Demonstrate by moving the picture pieces together while you blend the sounds to pronounce /boat/.
3. Then ask the children to push the picture pieces together while you blend.

4. Give the children practice by asking them to blend the sounds along with you and by blending sounds on their own. Figure 2-14 is an example of picture blending for the word /boat/.
5. Extend this activity to written language by writing the letters under each picture piece. After children blend, talk about the sounds in words and the letters the sounds represent.

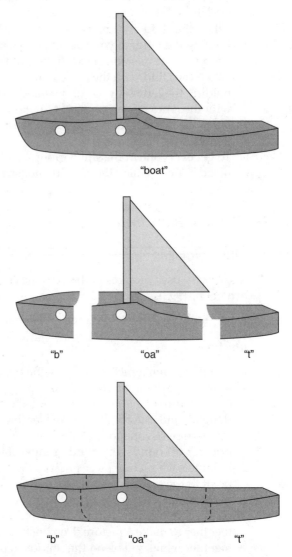

Figure 2-14 Picture blending gives children a concrete visual reference to illustrate the idea of blending sounds into words.

2.30 *Slide Sounds Together*

Skills: Blending and associating sounds with letters.

A picture of a slide depicts the blending process.

Things You'll Need: A picture of a slide sketched on the board, as illustrated in Figure 2-15.

Directions:

1. Draw a large slide on the board. Write a word on the slide, distributing letters from the top to near the bottom.
2. Demonstrate blending by pronouncing each sound as you slide your hand under each letter, adding sounds one after the other until you reach the bottom.
3. Ask children to say the whole word and then write it at the bottom of the slide.
4. Give children more responsibility by inviting a child to be the slider—the person who moves his or her hand down the slide. Ask the whole group to blend the sounds as the "slider" slides toward the bottom. The slider pronounces the whole word when the slider's hand reaches the bottom.

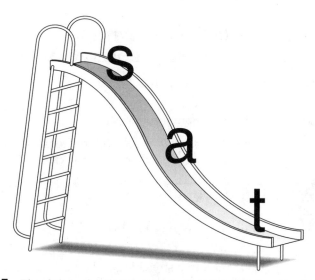

Figure 2-15   The slide in the Sliding Sounds Together activity gives learners a visual cue for blending. After sounds are blended, the whole word is written at the bottom of the slide.

2.31 *Magic Sounds*

Skills: Blending and associating sounds with letters.

The individual sounds in words give children clues to the identity of hidden objects. This is similar to the Shoe Box Rhyme activity, only here children guess magic words from individual sounds rather than beginning and rhyming sounds.

Things You'll Need: One medium-size container; many small items or pictures to put in the container.

Directions:

1. Explain that you will say magic sounds that make a word when children blend the sound together. Grab something from the container but do not let the children see what you hold.
2. Keeping the object (or picture) hidden from view, say, "Here are the magic sounds: /p/ - /i/ - /g/. What is it?" Show the *pig* when children say /pig/. Put the *pig* beside the container and grab another object, perhaps a small, plastic *cat*.
3. Generalize this activity to written language by writing the words children guess. Talk about the letters, saying the sound that each letter or group of letters represents. This helps make the sounds visible in that the letters represent sounds. End by pointing to each letter or letter group, saying its sound, and blending the sounds into the word. This reinforces the idea that the letters in written words represent the sounds in spoken words.

SPARE MINUTE ACTIVITIES FOR DEVELOPING PHONEMIC AWARENESS

2.32 *Count Sounds*

Skill: Segmenting sounds.

Say a word, such as /me/. Children count the number of sounds they hear. Children may say the number or hold up cards with the number of sounds they hear.

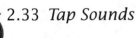

2.33 *Tap Sounds*

Skill: Segmenting sounds.

Say a word and have children tap a pencil once for each sound heard. Rubber band sound stretching and repeating words help children focus on the individual phonemes. Begin with two-sound words (/ape/). After children can tap the phonemes in two-sound words, introduce three- (/cap/) and then four-sound (/soda/) words.

2.34 *I Spy*

Skill: Isolating sounds.

I Spy is excellent for those times when the class is getting ready to go to lunch; specials like P.E., art, or the library; or home for the day. Think of something in your room and say, "I spy something that begins with /_/ (a beginning sound)." Children then think of things in the room that begin with the same beginning sound.

Focus attention on ending or beginning sounds by placing a few items or pictures on a table. Say "I spy something that ends with /_/. What is it?" Children point to or pick up the picture or object.

2.35 *Roll Call*

Skills: Isolating sounds and associating sounds with letters.

Use this activity, or your own personal adaptation of it, in lining up children for lunch, for recess, or to go home at the end of the school day. Say something like, "Line up if your name begins (or ends) with /m/." Ask children what letter their name begins (or ends) with.

2.36 *Secret Names*

Skill: Manipulating sounds.

The teacher changes a sound in children's names and children guess the name. For instance, Dave might become Mave. You might say, "Whose name am I saying in a secret way? Mave." Dave or others in the class say the name.

2.37 *Secret Code*

Skill: Manipulating sounds.

Tell children everyone is going to play a sound game where they make new words by changing the beginning sound. For example, desk might become besk; crayon, brayon.

2.38 *What Is It?*

Skill: Blending.

Show children three or four pictures. You might want to put pictures on the chalk tray or spread them out on a table. Say a picture name sound by sound. Children find the picture you named.

2.39 *Pass the Sound Around*

Skill: Isolating sounds.

Show children who are sitting around a table a selection of picture-word cards. Point to a card and say the picture name followed by a child's name and the position of the sound the child is to identify (beginning, middle, end) in the picture name. For example, in pointing to a picture of a pig, you might say, "Pig: Annaleise. Beginning sound." Annaleise then says the beginning sound, /p/. Annaleise now "passes" her turn to another child by pointing to a different picture-word card, saying a child's name and asking for a beginning (middle or ending) sound. The activity continues until everyone has had a turn or until all of the beginning (middle or ending) sounds are identified.

PHONEMIC AWARENESS TESTS

You now have many rhyme and phonemic awareness activities from which to choose. But before using these activities, you need to know which children in your class would benefit from increasing their phonemic awareness. One way to find out about children's phonemic awareness is to observe children as they read and write every day in your classroom. If you wish to go beyond classroom observation, you will want to use an assessment tool designed specifically to determine phonemic awareness. There are a number of assessment tools from which to choose. With a single exception, all require that you assess children individually.

The Lindamood Auditory Conceptualization Test (LAC-3) (Lindamood & Lindamood, 2004) has been used for nearly 30 years. The LAC-3, now in its third edition, is appropriate for kindergartners through adults, and requires that participants arrange colored blocks to show the sequence of sounds in nonsense words. The results are reported in minimum levels of performance for success reading and spelling at or above grade level.

The Test of Auditory Analysis Skills (TAAS) (Rosner, 1979) has 13 items that ask children to delete sounds from words. This test is suitable for children from kindergarten through third grade, and expected levels of performance are listed for each grade. Children whose performance is below expectation are candidates for more phonemic awareness instruction, according to this tool.

If you prefer a group paper-and-pencil test, consider the Test of Phonological Awareness-Second Edition: Plus (TOPA-2+) (Torgesen & Bryant, 2004). The kindergarten version assesses awareness of beginning sounds, while the first- and second-grade version assesses awareness of ending sounds. Percentile ranks and standard scores are reported. The authors suggest that the TOPA-2+ is most sensitive to kindergarten children's ability during the second half of the year.

The Test of Phonological Awareness in Spanish (TPAS) (Ricco, Imhoff, Hasbrouck, & Davis, 2004) assesses awareness of beginning and ending sounds, rhyme, and sound manipulation. In manipulating sounds, the child is asked to repeat a word, leaving out a syllable or sound.

The Dynamic Indicators of Basic Early Literacy Skills (DIBELS®) (Good & Kaminski, 2002) is a series of short, individually administered tests to assess and monitor a variety of skills important for reading success. Segmentation is measured in the middle and at the end of kindergarten and throughout the year in first grade. The Phoneme Segmentation Fluency (PSF) tests, in combination with other assessments given at each grade, are used to identify children who are performing as expected for their grade and children at risk of reading difficulty. DIBELS® is free and downloadable after you register on the website in the reference list. DIBELS® is easy to administer, score, and interpret.

The Comprehensive Test of Phonological Processes (CTOPP) (Wagner, Torgesen, & Rashotte, 1999) is a norm-referenced assessment of phoneme awareness, blending, memory, and rapid naming. Scores include percentile ranks; age and grade equivalents; and quotients for phoneme awareness, memory, and rapid naming. With its dual focus on phonemic awareness and rapid naming, this instrument is appropriate for assessing learning disabled and struggling readers.

The Yopp-Singer Test of Phoneme Segmentation (Yopp, 1995), intended for kindergartners and beginning first graders, has 22 items that measure children's ability to segment two- and three-sound words into phonemes.

The Roswell-Chall Auditory Blending Test (Roswell & Chall, 1997) assesses children's ability to blend from two to three sounds. First published in 1963, this test consists of 30 items and classifies blending as adequate or inadequate.

The Phonological Awareness Test (PAT) (Robertson & Salter, 1997) is intended for 5- through 9-year-olds, and includes rhyme awareness, sound segmentation, sound deletion, sound isolation, sound substitution, blending, phonics, decoding nonsense words, and invented spelling. The Phonological Awareness Profile (Robertson & Salter, 1995), a criterion-referenced test for children ages 5 through 8, assesses essentially the same areas as the PAT. The profile can be used as pre- and post-teaching measures.

Phonological Awareness Handbook for Kindergarten and Primary Teachers (Ericson & Juliebo, 1998) includes pre- and post-teaching measures for rhyme awareness, blending, sound segmenting, and invented spelling. (Spell words the way they sound.) You will also find tests for classroom use in Phonemic Awareness for Young Children: A Classroom Curriculum (Adams, Foorman, Lundberg, & Beeler, 1998).

Of the many tests from which to choose, we use the PAT most often. The PAT is easy to administer, quick, and you, the teacher, can pick and choose which portions of the test you wish to administer. We also like the PAT because it yields good information on the phonics letter-sound patterns children know and the patterns they do not know. We find that a combination of information on the child's phonemic awareness and phonics knowledge is a powerful tool for planning effective instruction. Some tests, such as the CTOPP, are helpful in identifying children at risk of reading difficulty or for learning more about struggling readers. We have found the LAC-3 yields a good idea of children's ability to segment and manipulate sounds, though it does not include blending.

TEACHING PHONEMIC AWARENESS IN YOUR CLASSROOM READING PROGRAM

We teach phonemic awareness in kindergarten and first grade. By and large, phonemic awareness receives the most emphasis in kindergarten, somewhat less emphasis in first grade, and in every grade thereafter it is not directly taught to children making average progress. Although phonemic awareness is not directly taught after first grade, teachers in second grade and above do remind children to listen for sounds while spelling and blend sounds while decoding.

Kindergarten

Kindergarten classroom reading programs usually set aside about 30 minutes or so for teaching word work (also called word study), although some programs may devote more or less time to word work. Word work in kindergarten may include instruction in phonemic awareness, letter names, phonics, and high-frequency words. Kindergarten teachers integrate phonemic awareness and phonics throughout the day and across subjects and experiences, so kindergartners may well receive much more than 30 minutes of formal instruction.

The kindergarten classroom reading program develops phonological and phonemic awareness. In developing phonological awareness, teachers may focus on syllable and rhyme awareness. Teachers call children's attention to syllables by asking them to clap for the syllables in words, provided that children are not already aware of syllables. If children are not aware of rhyming sounds, teachers develop the children's ability to identify rhyming and nonrhyming words, identify the rhyming sounds in words, and think of rhyming words. Although kindergarten teachers develop phonological awareness, phonemic awareness is the heart of the program.

If you are a kindergarten teacher, you will teach phonemic awareness every day. You will teach phonemic awareness directly and explicitly, and in combination with phonics. You will teach kindergartners to count sounds, separate words into sounds (/man/ = /m/, /a/, /n/), delete sounds (/man/ minus /m/ = /an/), substitute sounds (exchanging /c/ for /m/ = /can/), and blend (/m/ + /a/ + /n/ = /man/). You may pair phonemic awareness with instruction in letter names or letter-sounds. In either case, you will purposefully link a sound, such as /s/, with letters—a letter name (/ess/) or a letter sound (/sss/). After kindergartners know a few letter-sounds, you will show children how to blend the sounds associated with them into words. For instance, you might model how to associate /m/ with *m*, /a/ with *a*, and /n/ with *n*, and then blend the sounds into /man/. Connecting phonemic awareness instruction with phonics helps to develop the ability to separate words into sounds and blend sounds into words, and additionally, gives the kindergartners whom you teach valuable practice using phonemic awareness while using letter-sound phonics.

First Grade

First-grade classroom reading programs typically set aside a little over 30 minutes for teaching word work, which consists of phonemic awareness, phonics, spelling, and high-frequency words. Generally speaking, first-grade teachers begin the year by teaching phonemic awareness every day in connection with phonics. After a few weeks, teachers might teach phonemic awareness three or four times a week, depending on children's development as readers. Toward the middle or slightly after mid-year, phonemic awareness is taught only twice a week to average readers, usually at the beginning of the week when letter-sound associations are introduced or reviewed. Phonemic awareness is always paired with phonics and frequently paired with spelling as well. However, you may decide to give certain children more intense, supplementary phonemic awareness instruction separate from, as well as along with, phonics and spelling. By the end of the first grade, the average readers in your classroom will be skilled at manipulating sounds and blending, and children will use these skills to read and spell new words. Direct, explicit phonemic awareness instruction is not necessary for average readers in the second grade.

Second Grade

Phonemic awareness is not directly taught to second graders making average or better progress. Of course, some struggling readers who have difficulty using phonics may benefit from phonemic awareness instruction, but this is not part of the normal second grade classroom reading program. And so we see that phonemic awareness takes center stage in kindergarten and, perhaps, beginning in first grade, depending on the classroom reading program and children's development as readers. Emphasis on developing phonemic awareness begins to diminish by the middle of first grade. By the end of first grade, phonemic awareness is taught within phonics and spelling lessons only a couple of days a week, if that much. Children whose teachers follow a well-planned, sequential classroom reading program are skilled at segmenting, blending, and manipulating sounds before the end of the first grade year. For average progress or better readers, direct, explicit phonemic awareness has disappeared from the classroom reading program no later than the beginning of second grade, not to resurface for the rest of the elementary school years.

REFERENCES

Adams, M. J., Foorman, B. R., Lundberg, I., & Beeler, T. (1998). *Phonemic awareness in young children: A classroom curriculum.* Baltimore: Brooks Publishing.

Anthony, J. L., & Lonigan, C. J. (2004). The nature of phonological awareness: Converging evidence from four studies of preschool and early grade school children. *Journal of Educational Psychology, 96,* 43–55.

Armbruster, B. B., Lehr, F., & Osborn, J. (2001). *Put reading first: The research building blocks for teaching children to read kindergarten through grade 3.* Washington, DC: National Institute for Literacy.

Blaiklock, K. E. (2004). The importance of letter knowledge in the relationship between phonological awareness and reading. *Journal of Research in Reading, 27,* 36–57.

Bradley, L., & Bryant, P. E. (1978). Difficulties in auditory organization as a possible cause of reading backwardness. *Nature, 271,* 746–747.

Caravolas, M., Hulme, C., & Snowling, M. J. (2001). The foundations of spelling ability: Evidence from a 3-year longitudinal study. *Journal of Memory and Language, 45,* 751–774.

Cardoso-Martins, C., Michalick, M. F., & Pollo, T. C. (2002). Is sensitivity to rhyme a developmental precursor to sensitivity to phoneme?: Evidence from individuals with Down syndrome. *Reading and Writing: An Interdisciplinary Journal, 15,* 439–454.

Carroll, J. M., & Snowling, M. J. (2004). Language and phonological skills in children at risk of reading difficulties. *Journal of Child Psychology and Psychiatry, 45,* 331–640.

Cassady, J. C., & Smith, L. L. (2004). Acquisition of blending skills: Comparisons among body-coda, onset-rime, and phoneme blending tasks. *Reading Psychology, 25,* 261–272.

Catts, H. W., & Vartiainen, T. (1993). *Sounds abound: Listening, rhyming and reading.* East Moline, IL: LinguiSystems.

Christen, C. A., & Bowey, J. A. (2005). The efficacy of orthographic rime, grapheme-phoneme correspondence, and implicit phonics approaches to teaching decoding skills. *Scientific Studies of Reading, 9,* 327–340.

Clay, M. M. (1985). *The early detection of reading difficulties* (3rd ed.). Portsmouth, NH: Heinemann.

Ehri, L. C., Nunes, S. R., Willows, D. M., Schuster, B. V., Yaghoub-Zadeh, Z., & Shanahan, T. (2001). Phonemic awareness instruction helps children learn to read: Evidence from the National Reading Panel's meta-analysis. *Reading Research Quarterly, 36,* 250–287.

Elbo, C., & Petersen, D. K. (2004). Long-term effects of phoneme awareness and letter sound training: An intervention study with children at risk for dyslexia. *Journal of Educational Psychology, 94,* 660–670.

Eldredge, J. L. (2005). Foundations of fluency: An exploration. *Reading Psychology, 26,* 161–181.

Ericson, L., & Juliebo, M. F. (1998). *The phonological awareness handbook for kindergarten and primary teachers.* Newark, DE: International Reading Association.

Foorman, B. R., Jenkins, L., & Francis, D. J. (1993). Links among segmenting, spelling, and reading words in first and second grades. *Reading and Writing: An Interdisciplinary Journal, 5,* 1–15.

Frost, J. (2001). Phonemic awareness, spontaneous writing, and reading and spelling development from a preventive perspective. *Reading and Writing, 14,* 487–513.

Good, R. H., & Kaminiski, R. A., (2002). *Dynamic indicators of early reading skills* (6th ed.) Retrieved May 31, 2006, from http://dibels.uoregon.edu

Goswami, U. (2001). Early phonological development and the acquisition of literacy. In S. B. Neuman & D. K. Dickinson (Eds.), *Handbook of early literacy research* (pp. 111–125). New York: Guilford Press.

Hindson, B., Bryne, B., Fielding-Barnsley R., Newman, C., Hine, D. W., & Shankweiler, D. (2005). Assessment and early instruction of preschool children at risk for reading disability. *Journal of Educational Psychology, 97,* 687–704.

Hulme, C., Caravolas, M., Maliková, G., & Brigstocke, S. (2005). Phoneme isolation is not simply a consequence of letter-sound knowledge. *Cognition, 97,* B1–B11.

Johnston, R. S., & Watson, J. (2004). Accelerating the development of reading, spelling, and phoneme awareness skills in initial readers. *Reading and Writing: An Interdisciplinary Journal, 17,* 327–357.

Juel, C., Griffith, P. L., & Gough, P. B. (1986). Acquisition of literacy: A longitudinal study of children in first and second grade. *Journal of Educational Psychology, 78,* 243–255.

Juel, C., & Minden-Cupp, C. (2000). Learning to read words: Linguistic units and instructional strategies. *Reading Research Quarterly, 35,* 458–492.

Justice, L. M., Invernizzi, M., Geller, K., Sullivan, A. K., & Welsch, J. (2005). Descriptive-developmental performance of at-risk preschoolers on early literacy tasks. *Reading Psychology, 26,* 1–25.

Kroese, J. M., Hynd, G. W., Knight, D. F., Hiemenz, J. R., & Hall, J. (2000). Clinical appraisal of spelling ability and its relationship to phonemic awareness (blending, segmenting, elision, and reversal), phonological memory, and reading in reading disabled, ADHD, and normal children. *Reading and Writing: An Interdisciplinary Journal, 13,* (1–2), 105–131.

Layton, L., Deeny, K., Tall, G., & Upton, G. (1996). Researching and promoting phonological awareness in the nursery class. *Journal of Research in Reading, 19,* 1–13.

LeSieg, T. (1961). *Ten apples up on top.* New York: Random House.

Lindamood, C. H., & Lindamood, P. C. (2004). *Lindamood auditory conceptualization test* (Rev. ed.). Austin, TX: Pro-Ed.

Lonigan, C. J. (2006). Conceptualizing phonological processing skills in prereaders. In D. K. Dickinson & S. B. Neuman (Eds.), *Handbook of early literacy research, volume 2* (pp. 77–89). New York: Guilford Press.

MacLean, M., Bryant, P., & Bradley, L. (1987). Rhymes, nursery rhymes, and reading in early childhood. *Merrill-Palmer Quarterly, 33,* 255–282.

Macmillan, B. M. (2002). Rhyme and reading: A critical review of the research methodology. *Journal of Research in Reading, 25,* 4–42.

Majsterek, D. J., Shorr, D. N., & Erion, V. L. (2000). Promoting early literacy through rhyme-detection activities during Head Start circle-time. *Child Study Journal, 30,* 143–151.

Manis, F. R., Lindsey, K. A., & Bailey, C. E. (2004). Development of reading in grades K–2 Spanish-speaking English-language learners. *Learning Disabilities Research & Practice, 19,* 214–224.

Martins, M. A., & Silva, C. (2006). The impact of invented spelling on phonemic awareness. *Learning and Instruction, 16,* 41–56.

Muter, V., Hulme, C., Snowling, M. J., & Stevenson, J. (2004). Phonemes, rimes, vocabulary, and grammatical skills as foundations of early reading development: Evidence from a longitudinal study. *Developmental Psychology, 40,* 665–681.

Nancollis, A., Lawrie, B. A., & Dodd, B. (2005). Phonological awareness intervention and the acquisition of literacy skills in children from deprived social backgrounds. *Language, Speech, and Hearing Services in Schools, 36,* 325–335.

National Reading Panel. (2000). *Teaching children to read: An evidence-based assessment of the scientific research literature on reading and its implications for reading instruction: Reports of the subgroups* (NIH Publication No. 00-4754). Washington, DC: U.S. Government Printing Office.

Nicholson, T. (1997). Closing the gap on reading failure: Social background, phonemic awareness, and learning to read. In B. Blachman (Ed.), *Foundations of reading acquisition and dyslexia: Implications for early intervention* (pp. 381–407). Mahwah, NJ: Erlbaum.

Norris, A. N., & Hoffman, P. R. (2002). Phoneme awareness: A complex developmental process. *Topics in Language Disorders, 22,* 1–34. Austin, TX: Pro-Ed.

Ricco, C. A., Imhoff, B., Hasbrouck, J. E., & Davis, G. N. (2004). *Test of phonological awareness in Spanish (TRAS).* Austin, TX: Pro-Ed.

Robertson, C., & Salter, W. (1995). *The phonological awareness profile.* East Moline, IL: LinguiSystems.

Robertson, C., & Salter, W. (1997). *The phonological awareness test.* East Moline, IL: LinguiSystems.

Rosner, J. (1979). *Test of auditory analysis skills.* Novato, CA: Academic Therapy Publications.

Roswell, F. G., & Chall, J. S. (1997). *Roswell-Chall auditory blending test.* Cambridge, MA: Educators Publishing Service.

Savage, R., & Carless, S. (2005). Phoneme manipulation not onset-rime manipulation ability is a unique predictor of early reading. *Journal of Child Psychology and Psychiatry, 46,* 1297–1308.

Schatschneider, C., Fletcher, J. M., Francis, D. J., Carlson, C. D., & Foorman, B. R. (2004). Kindergarten prediction of reading skills: A longitudinal comparative analysis. *Journal of Educational Psychology, 96* (2), 265–282.

Spira, G. E., Bracken, S. S., & Fischel, J. E. (2005). Predicting improvement after first-grade reading difficulties: The effects of oral language, emergent literacy, and behavior skills. *Developmental Psychology, 41,* 225–234.

Stahl, S. A., & Murray, B. A. (2006). Defining phonological awareness and its relationship to early reading. In K. A. D. Stahl & M. C. McKenna (Eds.), *Reading Research at Work* (pp. 92–113). New York: Guilford Press.

Strattman, K., & Hodson, B. W. (2005). Variables that influence decoding and spelling in beginning readers. *Child Language Teaching and Therapy, 21,* 165–190.

Torgesen, J. K., & Bryant, B. R. (2004). *Test of phonological awareness-second edition: PLUS (TOPA-2+)* Austin, TX: Pro-Ed.

Treiman, R., & Zukowski, A. (1991). Levels of phonological awareness. In S. A. Brady & D. P. Shankweiler (Eds.), *Phonological processes in literacy* (pp. 85–96). Hillsdale, NJ: Erlbaum.

Uhry, J. K., & Ehri, L. C. (1999). Ease of segmenting two- or three-phoneme words in kindergarten: Rime cohesion or vowel salience? *Journal of Educational Psychology, 91,* 594–603.

Wagner, R., Torgesen, J. K., & Rashotte, C. (1999). *Comprehensive test of phonological processes.* Austin, TX: Pro-Ed.

Walton, P. D., & Walton, L. M. (2002). Beginning reading by teaching in rime analogy: Effects on phonological skills, letters-sound knowledge, working memory, and word-reading strategies. *Scientific Studies of Reading, 6,* 79–115.

Yeh, S. S. (2003). An evaluation of two approaches for teaching phonemic awareness to children in Head Start. *Early Childhood Research Quarterly, 18,* 513–529.

Yopp, H. K. (1995). A test for assessing phonemic awareness in young children. *The Reading Teacher, 49,* 20–29.

CHAPTER 3

Early Word Identification

Using Logos, Pictures, Word Shape, and Partial Letter-Sound Associations to Read New Words

This chapter describes four strategies that begin the development of a rich, fluent reading vocabulary. You will learn how emergent readers use cues in their environment and in pictures or recognize words by their unique configuration. You will find out how children use one- or two-letter names or sounds to read new words. You will also learn how these strategies correspond to the development of a rich reading vocabulary and conventional spelling, and about best practices for teaching children who use one- or two-letter-sounds to support word identification.

KEY IDEAS

- The earliest word identification strategies develop long before children go to school and long before they actually learn to read.

- Before children read words, they may associate meaning with cues in the environment, such as logos and product packages.

- Early in their journey toward literacy, children may infer meaning from illustrations, often "reading" by saying words that describe the pictures.

- As children begin to notice words, they may look for cues in a word's unique configuration, which consists of the word's shape and length, or an eye-catching letter.

- When children first pay attention to letters and sounds, they associate a letter-sound (or a letter name) with a whole written word.

KEY VOCABULARY

Configuration cues

Environmental cues

Partial alphabetic cues

Partial alphabetic word learners

Picture cues

Prealphabetic word learners

Precommunicative spellers

Semiphonetic spellers

The word identification strategies explained in this chapter develop before children go to school, when children are in kindergarten or, at the very latest, in early first grade. Identifying words with environmental, picture, and word configuration cues does not call for knowing anything whatsoever about the alphabetic principle or letter-sound relationships. When children do begin to consider letter- and sound-based cues, they focus on only one or two of these cues in an unfamiliar word, and hence take only minimal advantage of the alphabetic principle. Although these early strategies are not reliable ways to figure out the identity of unfamiliar words, preschool and kindergartners use them, and so it is important for you to understand how they work. With insight into these early strategies, you are in a position to guide children as they move toward using more efficient and effective strategies for reading new words.

ENVIRONMENTAL CUES: THE STRATEGY OF ASSOCIATING MEANING WITH THE PRINT IN OUR EVERYDAY SURROUNDINGS

Children in prekindergarten and kindergarten often associate meaning with the signs, package labels, and logos in their everyday surroundings. This strategy is one of the first steps toward literacy. It is one of several strategies that 5-year-old John uses to make sense of print. When reading, John associates meaning with familiar signs and logos and, when writing, copies the words *California, October, no,*

Figure 3-1   John enjoys copying the words he sees displayed in his kindergarten classroom.

stop, and *soap* from the wall chart in his kindergarten classroom, as shown in Figure 3-1.

Associating meaning with familiar objects and signs in the environment gives preschoolers a measure of control over their lives. The preschooler who recognizes the box of Raisin Yum Yum cereal on the grocery shelf might be able to talk her mother into buying that particular breakfast food. Though she quickly recognizes the cereal box, this same child cannot read the word *raisin* on the package of raisins her mother buys for midday snacks. While this preschooler might not be able to tell what the writing *Raisin Yum Yum* actually "says," in all likelihood she can give an approximation that is both meaningful and contextually acceptable.

Children give feasible approximations because they connect meaning with the everyday settings in which the print appears, not with the specific words in print. Although children do not read words when they are taken out of their familiar environmental contexts, the words from known logos and labels are easier for children to learn than words from unfamiliar environmental print (Cronin, Farrell, & Delaney, 1999). Additionally, children take an important step toward developing the concept that writing makes sense by using the strategy of associating meaning with the environmental context in which print appears.

Picture Cues: The Strategy of Inferring Meaning from Illustrations

Like the print in children's everyday surroundings, the pictures in storybooks are an avenue to meaning that does not call for phonemic awareness, understanding the alphabetic principle, recognizing specific words, remembering letters, or knowing letter-sound associations. Long before children read storybooks on their own and well before they go to school, they read their favorite books by inferring and predicting meaning from pictures. For instance, 4-year-old Thomas used the strategy of inferring meaning from *picture cues* when he proudly held up a poster of a race car his father brought home from a business trip to Detroit and announced that the poster said: "Gentlemen, start your engines." The fact that the words on the poster bore not the slightest resemblance to the message Thomas read was of little consequence to him; he focused entirely on the rich picture context.

Children who have been read to at home or in child care expect pictures to signal meaning. Turning the pages and cueing on pictures, these children say words that could have been written by the author but are not necessarily on the page. Children who use picture cues to "read" their favorite books may also use pictures when writing their own stories. Kesha, a beginning kindergartner, drew the picture story seen in Figure 3-2 after hearing her teacher read and reread

Figure 3-2 As children like Kesha begin to pay attention to written language, they may draw pictures to represent the events in familiar storybooks, and they may include pictures, letters, and words copied from their classroom.

Arthur's Halloween (Brown, 1982). Notice how Kesha faithfully renders the big scary house that is so prominent in *Arthur's Halloween,* including a smiley face on the door to show the house is not frightening. Kesha clearly understands the picture–meaning connection.

Kesha also knows that writing is an important feature of books, and therefore, in her picture story, she includes letters and a word copied from the print in her classroom. In some ways, the *O*s are part of Kesha's picture story. When Kesha read her picture story to her teacher, she described the house that she drew, and she described the events that she remembered from *Arthur's Halloween.* From Kesha's writing, we can infer that she is searching for a medium through which she might effectively communicate with her audience, as yet unaware of the way that our alphabetic writing system represents speech.

CONFIGURATION CUES: THE STRATEGY OF USING WORD LENGTH, WORD SHAPE, OR EYE-CATCHING LETTERS TO READ NEW WORDS

In their search for ways to bring meaning to print, children look beyond cues in the environment and in pictures. In so doing, they move closer to print, discovering and using the *configuration cues* in words. Configuration consists of a word's shape, its length, or an eye-catching letter. These cues are incidental to alphabetic writing inasmuch as they do not call for connecting letters and sounds. This said, these cues do require that children actively think about written words. Even though these cues essentially bypass the alphabetic principle, children who use them must be able to identify some letters and find words in print. To find words in print, children must understand the purpose of the white spaces between words and, if words are written in sentences, the left-to-right and top-to-bottom orientation of print on the page. You can expect children to use word configuration cues before they use letter-sound cues. This is true regardless of how easy or difficult words are to identify.

Jesse puts one letter after another across the page, as seen in Figure 3-3. He writes his name and copies the words *yellow* and *me,* as well as the letters of the alphabet, from the print in his kindergarten classroom. He also includes numbers and a picture. What Jesse does not do is link the letters in written words to the sounds in spoken words. Jesse does not yet understand the basic premise on which alphabetic writing rests, and therefore he writes strings of random letters when he is not copying. Jesse is interested in print, however, for his careful copying suggests that he attends to some of the words he sees in school and is aware of the importance of the words in his classroom. As Jesse carefully notices the words that surround him in his kindergarten classroom, he looks at word configuration and uses these cues to help him identify important words.

Figure 3-3 Jesse knows that words and letters are important, and he explores written language by copying the many different types of print that he sees in his classroom.

Word Shape

A word's shape is formed by letters that may be on, above, or below the line. The word *hat*, for example, has two ascending letters separated by a letter that stays on the line, so its shape looks like:

cat looks like:

pat looks like:

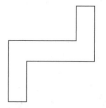

While shape does not give readers cues to sound, it does provide some information for narrowing word choices. However, this information is frequently unreliable. Because so many words have virtually identical patterns of upward and downward sloping letters (*pat, got, jet*), identifying words by their shape alone makes reading more difficult than it should be. Children who use shape to recognize the word *hat* are bound to be confused when they try to read other words that have the same shape, such as *bat, fit,* and *had.*

Word Length

Though *hand* and *homework* are the same shape ⊔⊔ a quick glance at word length tells us that *hand* and *homework* are different. It is not surprising, then, that sometimes children cue on word length alone. Length seems to be an important cue only when words differ considerably, such as the difference in length between *hand* and *homework,* or *elf* and *elephant* (Bastien-Toniazzo, & Jullien, 2001). Even without paying attention to letter and sound cues, children are far less likely to confuse *eat* with *elephant* than they are to confuse *eat* with *elf.*

Letter Shape

In using letter shape, children pay attention to the circles, arcs, humps, and lines of the letters in words. Children might, for instance, remember the word *nail* because the letter *n* has one "hump"; *took* because the two circles look like eyes; *banana* because it begins with a stick and ball (the lowercase *b*). Only paying attention to circles, arcs, humps, and lines has the potential to create all sorts of confusion. Take *g* and *j* as an example. Both *g* and *j* have "tails," so children may not think of *g* and *j* as different letters. Children who recognize *game* because it has a "tail" may misread *juice* because the letter *j* has a "tail," too.

All things considered, the configuration cues that are so helpful in one reading condition are frequently not at all helpful in another condition. As long as there is an unusual characteristic like a distinctive shape, length, or letter, children may easily identify words. However, because configuration cues have no predictable, logical association with the sounds that letters represent, these cues are very fragile and often lead to misidentifications, as well as confusion and frustration.

PREALPHABETIC WORD LEARNERS AND PRECOMMUNICATIVE SPELLERS

The children in your classroom who use environmental, picture, and configuration cues to identify new words are in the *prealphabetic stage* of word learning (Ehri, 2005). Prealphabetic word learning begins in preschool and usually ends during kindergarten. Children in this stage cannot name the letters of the alphabet or, at best, can name only a few letters. They do not know the letter-sounds of phonics and lack phonemic awareness. Not surprisingly, these children seldom read words when they are outside familiar environmental contexts, when there are no picture cues, or when words do not have a distinct configuration. Also, not surprisingly, these children cannot read their own stories a day or so after writing them because children's writing does not systematically represent speech.

Children who are prealphabetic word learners are also *precommunicative spellers*. The words they write have no relationship between sounds and letters (Gentry, 2006). Warren, a precommunicative speller, strings letters together, as shown in Figure 3-4, unaware of speech and print connections. You can easily recognize the precommunicative spellers in your classroom.

Figure 3-4   A prealphabetic reader and precommunicative speller, Warren combines mock letters with real letters, stringing them across the page, unaware of speech and print connections.

Just look for writing with these five features:

1. No white spaces or inconsistent use of white spaces (Jesse, Figure 3-3).
2. Mock letters sprinkled among real letters (Warren, Figure 3-4).
3. Pictures at least as prominent as writing (Kesha, Figure 3-2; Warren, Figure 3-4).
4. The same letter written over and over again (Kesha, Figure 3-2).
5. Writing that wanders randomly around the page (Jesse, Figure 3-3).

You will also observe that, although precommunicative spellers use uppercase and lowercase letters, they have a decided preference for writing in uppercase.

From a word identification perspective, it is important for prealphabetic word learners and precommunicative spellers to learn how to combine context cues with beginning and ending letter-sound cues when reading and writing new words. It also is important for children to learn letter names and letter sounds. Knowing letter names in kindergarten is a good predictor of success learning to read (Schatschneider, Fletcher, Francis, Carlson, & Foorman, 2004). In learning the letter-names, beginning readers discover how one letter differs from another. Learning letter names also can help children learn letter-sounds, provided that the name of the letter (*S*) contains part of the letter-sound (sss) (Share, 2004). Children are likely to have the most difficulty sorting out letters that look rather similar (*b-d*) or whose names sound somewhat similar (/p/-/t/) (Treiman, Kessler, & Pollo, 2006).

Children tend to learn the names of common letters more easily than the less common letters. Additionally, children may mistakenly call a letter they are learning by the name of a common letter they know. Therefore, you will be a more effective teacher when you give children plenty of experiences with letters and letter names, especially letters that look similar or have names that sound somewhat similar.

In the course of learning letter names, it is natural for children to recognize a letter before they can tell you the name (Lafferty, Gray, & Wilcox, 2005). A child may be able to point to the *B* when you say /bee/ (the letter name), but that same child may not be able to tell you the letter name on her own without prompting. Begin by teaching the names of easy-to-identify uppercase letters and then proceed to the more difficult-to-identify lowercase letters (Adams, 1990). When you teach letter-names, start out by teaching the names of the letters at the beginning of children's own names, followed by all the letters in children's names.

As children develop phonemic awareness, learn letter names and letter-sounds, and have a variety of reading and writing experiences in your classroom, they will begin to identify words by connecting one or two letters with sounds. When children do this, they pay close attention to a portion of the alphabetic cues in words, which is the next stage in movement toward developing a rich reading vocabulary.

Partial Alphabetic Cues: The Strategy of Using Letter Names or One- or Two-Letter-Sounds to Read New Words

When children begin to use letter-sound cues, they typically take a rather simplistic route to word learning (Ehri, 2005). Children connect a single letter-sound cue (maybe two) or a letter-name with the pronunciation of a whole word. For example, if a child sees the word *sandwich* in a storybook and if that child knows the sound associated with the letter *s*, the child may then identify *sandwich* by associating the letter *s* with the /s/ sound heard in /sandwich/. A letter name may be used as a cue if the name includes a portion of the sound heard in the word. For example, the name of the letter *s*, /s/, includes a portion of the sound the letter represents and, therefore, children may associate the name (/ess/) with the word *sandwich*.

Once emergent readers associate a letter-sound or a letter name with a written word, they may assume that the same cue always represents the same word. As a consequence, children who recognize *sandwich* because they notice the letter *s* are likely to read every word with an *s* as *sandwich*. Hence, *same* and *see* are read as /sandwich/ because each shares the same cue—the letter *s* that represents /s/.

At a *minimum*, children are aware of at least one sound in the spoken words they hear in everyday conversations, though their phonemic awareness may well be greater than this (Share, 2004). You can expect these children to be aware of the beginning sounds in words and to separate the beginning sound from the rhyming sounds (the vowel and remaining consonants). For instance, children can separate the /s/ from the /at/ in /sat/, and the /m/ from /mat/, as explained in Chapter 2. Children also know the features that distinguish one letter from another and therefore identify individual letters consistently and reliably. They know that written words consist of letters, and they also know the sounds or names of some of the letters.

Perhaps the greatest advantage of using partial cues is that children have opportunities to develop, test, and revise hypotheses about how the alphabet works. As children experiment with even a single letter-sound cue, they refine their phonemic awareness and extend their knowledge of how letters represent sounds. Though the use of partial cues is relatively short-lived, it eases children into strategically using alphabetic writing, and as such is the precursor to the development of more advanced word identification strategies.

Partial Alphabetic Word Learners and Semiphonetic Spellers

Generally speaking, the use of partial cues emerges in kindergarten and, for some children, in early first grade (Ehri, 2005). Lexi, like other partial alphabetic word learners, writes from left to right, uses white spaces to separate words, fluently recognizes a few often-used words, and can read and write her own name, as we can see in Figure 3-5. She approaches word identification systematically.

In reading new words, Lexi uses letter names when the names give sound clues, or she uses one, possibly two, letter-sound cues. Lexi might identify *father* because she hears the /eff/ in the name of the letter *f*; she might identify *monkey* because she knows the sound associated with the letter *m*. However, because Lexi does not pay attention to all the letters in words, she is likely to confuse words that begin and/or end alike. You will notice that partial alphabetic word learners like Lexi misidentify and confuse words like *father, family,* and *funny* because these words all begin alike and, additionally, *family* and *funny* end alike.

Lexi knows more about letter-sounds and has more phonemic awareness than children like James, Jesse, and Warren who are in the prealphabetic stage. Lexi has enough phonemic awareness and knows enough about letter names and letter-sounds to use one or two alphabetic cues when she reads. Although

Figure 3-5   Lexi conventionally spells words in her fluent reading vocabulary and uses the beginning consonant to spell other words. Lexi often struggles when identifying new words, because she does not know enough letter-sound associations to fully translate words into speech. Her story reads: I want to go to the park. I want to go for swim. I want to play on the playground.

children may know the sounds of frequently occurring single consonants, like *m*, *n*, *p*, and *s*, they do not have much, if any, knowledge of vowel letter patterns like the *oa* in *boat* or the *a* in *pat*; consonant clusters like *bl*, *tr*, and *st*; or consonant digraphs (two letters representing one sound), like *th*, *sh*, and *ch*. Lexi often struggles when reading new words because she does not know enough about letter-sounds and does not have enough phonemic awareness to associate sounds with all the letters in new words.

Lexi and children like her frequently guess at words using the context cues, picture cues, and beginning and/or ending letter-sound cues. As long as context and picture cues are robust, these children may successfully read new words. Context has a strong effect on the word identification of these children: high context, especially text that tells a predictable story and uses excellent, descriptive pictures related to the story, is most conducive to accurate word identification; weak context and weak picture cues may result in guesses that do not make sense in the story.

Just as Lexi uses partial alphabetic cues when reading, so does she use partial alphabetic cues when spelling. She spells semiphonetically; that is, she uses letters to represent some, but not all, of the important sounds in words (Gentry, 2006). From Lexi's writing in Figure 3-5, we observe that she uses consonant letters such as *w* to represent *want* and *swim*, and *p* to represent *park*. Lexi conventionally spells words in her reading vocabulary (*I, to, go, the, play*). Notice how she spells *playground*: *play* is among the words she fluently recognizes. The portion of this compound word that she does not know how to read, *ground*, she represents with the letter *g*, resulting in *playg*.

Alecia has moved further than Lexi toward developing a rich reading vocabulary. Alecia writes about her favorite things, as shown in Figure 3-6, using a blend of conventionally and semiphonetically spelled words that are not yet in her reading vocabulary. In comparing Lexi's and Alecia's writing, we see that Alecia has more known words in her story (*I, have, green, and, blue, a, my, is, love, dog, see*), and she typically uses two or three consonants for words she unconventionally spells (some examples are *bn* for *brown*, *sdr* for *sister*, and *lk* for *like*). Alecia's use of letters to represent some of the sounds in words (for example, *clr* for *color*, *fd* for *food*, and *rt* for *restaurant*) suggests that she is carefully thinking about letter-sound relationships.

Further evidence comes from her use of the vowel letter *i* in *pink* (spelled *pik*). In contrast to Lexi who uses only beginning sounds to spell, Alecia frequently writes both beginning and ending sounds and includes some middle sounds as well (*sdr* for *sister* and *clr* for *color*). We have additional evidence that Alecia is looking carefully at print in the way she uses hyphens to spell her favorite restaurant, Chick-Fil-A®—spelled as *C-F-a*. From her story, we can infer that Alecia is phonemically aware of beginning and ending sounds, that she is developing awareness of the middle sounds in words, and that she is moving toward using more complex letter-sound relationships than simple partial alphabetic cues.

Figure 3-6   Alecia is phonemically aware of beginning and ending sounds and is developing awareness of middle sounds. She uses letters to represent the beginning and ending sounds, as well as some middle sounds in words. She is moving into the use of more sophisticated letter and sound relationships. Her story reads: I have green and blue eyes. I have brown hair. I have a twin sister. My favorite color is pink. My favorite food is corn. My favorite restaurant is Chick-Fil-A®. I like to see my friends.

Best Practices for Teaching Partial Alphabetic Word Learners

Partial alphabetic word learners will move further toward becoming good readers with a rich reading vocabulary when you follow these best teaching practices:

1.   **Teach phonemic awareness of all the sounds in words—first, middle, and last** (National Reading Panel, 2000). At this point in their development as readers, children have some awareness of the sounds in words, but lack sufficient awareness to separate words into each and every sound. Use the activities in Chapter 2 to develop the ability to separate words into sounds and to blend sounds together. And, when teaching phonemic awareness, combine instruction with activities in Chapter 5 that teach phonics letter-sound patterns.

2.   **Teach both consonant and vowel letter-sounds.** While partial alphabetic word learners and semiphonetic spellers are developing a working knowledge of single consonant letter-sounds, most children have little knowledge of vowel

patterns. Vowels usually occur in the middle of English words, sandwiched between the consonants. Additionally, vowel letter-sound patterns are more complex than consonant letter-sound patterns, which makes vowels more challenging to learn. However, since every English word contains at least one vowel sound, children cannot become expert readers and accomplished spellers without learning how vowel letter combinations represent sounds.

Children cannot read or write words if they have not learned the vowel sounds. Teach one sound for each vowel. Most teachers teach the short sound first, as the *a* heard in *apple*. The short vowel pattern, as illustrated by *can*, *bed*, *sit*, *mop*, and *tug*, is the easiest to learn because this pattern is less complicated than long vowel patterns, *same*, *boat*, *seed*, and *rain*, for instance. Additionally, short vowels often appear in words spelled with the same letter pattern, such as *fat*, *hat*, *sat*. (You will learn more about this in the next chapter.) In learning about both consonant and vowel letter-sound patterns, children will become capable of reading and spelling any new word that is spelled as it sounds.

3.   Have children read easy, meaningful text. Surround children with print in your classroom and then use that print to engage children in reading. For example, you might use shared reading with big books to familiarize children with words and letters and help to develop comprehension strategies. Shared reading occurs when the teacher reads aloud, and children follow along and participate when they recognize words, phrases, or sentences. Encourage children to read the small versions of big books, to read and reread familiar books with a buddy, and to read for pleasure. Have children read familiar text together in chorus. Put labels in prominent places in your room and, as children become familiar with the labels, ask one child to bring you a label and another child to put it back. Keep a storehouse of books available and encourage children to read them in their spare time and to take books home to share with their families.

4.   Ask questions that help children demonstrate and extend their knowledge of written language. It is important at this stage of children's development to give them opportunities to demonstrate and extend their knowledge of written language and to actively participate in reading aloud. While reading aloud, ask children to use their word and letter knowledge to do things like find words, point to letters, and find letter-sound patterns in familiar words. Before going to first grade, every child should know a name and at least one sound for each letter, be able to write the letters, be aware of beginning and rhyming sounds, and be able to segment the first and last sounds from words (Phillips & Torgesen, 2006), though many children will know much more than this.

5.   Explore words. Call attention to the vowel-consonant combinations at the ends of words (the *op* in *hop*, *shop*, and *drop*, explained in Chapter 4) and to letter-sound relationships (explained in Chapter 5). Make lists of rhyming words that share a similar spelling (*time-dime*, not *time-climb*) and lists of words with the same beginning, middle, or ending letter-sounds. Select some of these words to add to your classroom word wall; have children keep personal boxes of words they want to learn or words they need when writing; talk about how letters represent sounds in the words that children see on the word wall, in books, and in children's personal word boxes. You also might ask children to sort words according to particular letter-sound patterns and to build words from the letter-sounds they know (as explained in Chapter 5).

6.   Have children write every day and ask them to think about letters and sounds when spelling new words. When children cannot conventionally spell a word they wish to write and cannot find the word on the word wall, encourage them to write letters that represent the sounds they hear in the word. This helps children focus on sound, which enhances phonemic awareness, and also helps children focus on letter-sound relationships, which enhances phonics knowledge.

7.   Read aloud to children. Reading aloud to children has a long-lasting, beneficial effect on reading achievement. Read to children every day and read a variety of genres. When you read aloud, pause occasionally to ask questions that prompt children to interact with the book by doing or saying something (Justice, Weber, Ezell, & Bakeman, 2002). For instance, you might ask children to find words in text or to point to letters in familiar words, or you might engage children in discussing the structure of stories, including the setting, the characters, the problem, and the solution in the story.

As children read and write in your classroom, they will pay more and more attention to words. Instead of looking at just one or two letters in words, children will begin to look at the unique letter combination in each word. In due course, children will begin to look for cues in unfamiliar words that are present in familiar words. When children do this, they use existing information to construct and acquire new knowledge. Using parts of known words to identify unknown words that share some of the same letters is the key to reading new words with analogy-based phonics, which is the topic of the next chapter.

REFERENCES

Adams, M. (1990). *Beginning to read.* Cambridge, MA: MIT Press.

Bastien-Toniazzo, M., & Jullien, S. (2001). Nature and importance of the logographic phase in learning to read. *Reading and Writing: An Interdisciplinary Journal, 14,* 119–143.

Brown, M. (1982). *Arthur's Halloween.* Boston: Little, Brown.

Cronin, V., Farrell, D., & Delaney, M. (1999). Environmental print and word reading. *Journal of Research in Reading, 22,* 271–282.

Ehri, L. C. (2005). Learning to read words: Theory, findings, and issues. *Scientific Studies of Reading, 9,* 167–188.

Gentry, J. R. (2006). *The new science of beginning reading and writing.* Portsmouth, NH: Heinemann.

Justice, L. M., Weber, S. E., Ezell, H. K., & Bakeman, R. (2002). A sequential analysis of children's responsiveness to parental print references during shared book-reading interactions. *American Journal of Speech-Language Pathology, 11,* 30–40.

Lafferty, A. E., Gray, S., & Wilcox, M. J. (2005). Teaching alphabetic knowledge to preschool children with developmental language delay and with typical language development. *Child Language Teaching and Therapy, 21,* 263–277.

National Reading Panel. (2000). *Teaching children to read: An evidence-based assessment of the scientific research literature on reading and its implications for reading instruction: Reports of the subgroups* (NIH Publication No. 00-4754). Washington, DC: U.S. Government Printing Office.

Phillips, B. M., & Torgesen, J. K. (2006). Phonemic awareness and reading: Beyond the growth of initial reading accuracy. In D. K. Dickinson & S. B. Neuman (Eds.), *Handbook of early literacy research, volume 2* (pp. 101–131). New York: Guilford Press.

Schatschneider, C., Fletcher, J. M., Francis, D. J., Carlson, C. D., & Foorman, B. R. (2004). Kindergarten prediction of reading skills: A longitudinal comparative analysis. *Journal of Educational Psychology, 96,* 265–282.

Share, D. L. (2004). Knowing letter names and learning letter sounds: A critical connection. *Journal of Experimental Child Psychology, 88,* 213–233.

Treiman, R., Kessler, B., & Pollo, T. C. (2006). Learning about the letter name subset of the vocabulary: Evidence from U.S. and Brazilian preschoolers. *Applied Psycholinguistics, 27,* 211–227.

CHAPTER 4

Analogy-Based Phonics

Using the Predictable Patterns in Known Words to Read New Words

This chapter describes how children strategically use the parts in known words to read and learn new words, and the cross-checking, self-monitoring, and self-correction strategies for making sure that identified words make sense in the reading context. As you read this chapter, you will learn how syllables consist of onsets and rimes and how we teach analogy-based phonics. You also will learn how to encourage readers to cross-check for meaning, monitor their own word identification, correct their own miscues, and why this is important for successful word identification. You will find the best teaching practices for teaching analogy-based phonics as well as activities for teaching children to use the analogy strategy to read and learn new words.

KEY IDEAS

- Syllables have a two-part structure, consisting of an onset, which is the consonant that comes before the vowel, and a rime, which is the vowel and all the letters thereafter.
- In analogy-based word identification, children use parts of familiar words to read unfamiliar words.
- Cross-checking helps readers make sure that the words they identify fit the reading context.
- Readers monitor their own reading to detect probable word identification miscues.
- When readers realize that an identified word does not make sense, they use a self-correction strategy to fix their word identification miscue.
- Successful word identification depends on cross-checking, self-monitoring, and self-correcting, regardless of the strategy used to read new words.

KEY VOCABULARY

Cross-checking

Onset

Phonogram

Rime

Self-correcting

Self-monitoring

Word family

Look at the following sets of words:

rain	dish	sore
train	swish	store
sprain	finish	before
explain	furnish	explore
maintain	astonish	pinafore

A quick glance is all it takes to realize that the same letter patterns occur in many different words. Once readers discover that the words in each of these three word sets share a common pattern, they have a way to organize their thinking to use parts of known words to identify unknown words. The analogy-based approach to phonics teaches children how to find a shared letter pattern in words, such as the *ain* in *rain,* and then to use this similarity to identify unfamiliar words with the same pattern, such as *train* and *sprain.*

LOOKING INSIDE SYLLABLES

Lucy sets a decidedly lighthearted tone as she ruminates about school in the poem in Figure 4-1. Lucy repeats words and rhymes words. What's more, all the words

Figure 4-1 Some of the one-syllable words in Lucy's poem consist of an onset and a rime; others consist of a rime only.

she uses have only one syllable. Looking inside the syllables in Lucy's poem reveals a two-part structure that consists of an onset and a rime (Goswami, 1997). *Onsets* are the consonants that come before the vowel in a syllable or one-syllable word, such as the *sch* in *school*. Similarly, the *s* in *sit*, the *sl* in *slit*, and the *spl* in *split* are onsets. Onsets are always consonants; there can be as many as three clustered together in *common* words (*sch* and *spl*, for example).

Rimes are the vowel and everything thereafter. The *ool* in *school* is a rime. Correspondingly, the *ent* in *tent* is a rime consisting of the vowel (*e*) and the consonants that follow it (*nt*); the rime in *scream* is *eam*; in *black*, it is *ack*. We can see, then, that in dividing one-syllable words into onsets and rimes, we split the beginning sound(s) from the part of the word that begins with the vowel (*s - at; sl - at; spl – at*). Two-syllable words are divided the same way. For example, *pencil* would be divided into *p-en* and *c-il*; habit is *h-ab* and *it*. Some words and syllables do not begin with an onset. Words like *at*, *it*, and *in* consist of a rime but no onset. Similarly, a syllable in a multisyllable word may not begin with an onset. The first syllable in both *em-ber* and *ap-ple* is a rime. Remember, too, that the rime has one and only one vowel sound. Although a rime may have more than one vowel letter in spelling, we hear just one vowel sound. For instance, *ice* has two vowels, the *i* and *e*, but only one sound /i/. Likewise, *heat* has two vowel letters, *e* and *a*, but only one vowel sound, /ē/.

Rhyming words like *school* and *cool* share a rime—in this case the rime *ool*. When rime is common to two or more words, then the words usually share a rhyming sound. However, this is not always the case, as we see in *know* and *now*,

TABLE 4–1		*Onsets and Rimes in Lucy's Poem*		
Onset	+	Rime	=	One-Syllable Word
sch	+	ool	=	school
c	+	ool	=	cool
	+	is	=	is
l	+	ike	=	like
f	+	un	=	fun
n	+	eat	=	neat

which share the *ow* pattern but do not rhyme. And, of course, sometimes rhyming words do not share a common letter pattern (*sheep* and *leap*). In this case, the words rhyme, but the rhyming sound is spelled differently (*eep* versus *eap*). In this chapter we are interested in words that both rhyme (*sheep—deep*) and have the same vowel and ending letter pattern (*eep*). Table 4–1 shows the onset-rime structure of the one-syllable words in Lucy's poem. When using the analogy strategy, readers connect onsets and rimes in words they already know how to read with the same onsets and rimes in words they do not know how to read. The analogy-based method teaches children to associate the onsets and rimes in known words with the onsets and rimes in new words.

TEACHING ANALOGY-BASED PHONICS

Analogy-based phonics is taught in late kindergarten and first grade. This method involves teaching children (1) the sounds that onsets and rimes represent, (2) how to identify rimes in words, and (3) how to substitute onsets. Children must be skilled at (1) separating spoken words into beginning sounds (onsets) and rhyming sounds (rimes) and (2) blending beginning sounds and rhyming sounds together to pronounce meaningful words. Refer to Chapter 2 for teaching ideas.

Children typically learn to associate one sound with each letter in kindergarten. Therefore, children should already know the sounds that single consonants (onsets) represent. The main teaching focus is on the rimes. The premise is that if words share onsets and rimes, then words must share similar pronunciations. Rimes are taught in the context of known words, such as the *ap* in *map*. When generalizing the rime in one word (*map*) to the pronunciation of another word with the same rime (*cap*), teachers show children how to look for shared letter patterns. Once children realize that *at* says /at/, children are taught how to read and spell words that are spelled with that rime.

Think aloud as you demonstrate the analogy strategy. You might say something like, "I know the word *find*. The *ind* in *find* says /ind/. So to read this new word (pointing to *kind*), I will change the *f* (/f/) to a *k* (/k/), which makes /kind/. Now you try it with me." Encourage children to reflect on their own strategy by asking, "What word do you already know that can help you figure out this new one?" It turns out that even young readers are sensitive to the shared patterns, or the rimes, in written language and use this knowledge to read new words (Goswami, 1997), which is the topic of the next section.

HOW CHILDREN USE THE ONSETS AND RIMES IN KNOWN WORDS TO READ NEW WORDS

Readers who remember the sounds associated with onsets and rimes will tell you, their teacher, that *ap* represents /ap/ in *map, tap,* and *nap.* Likewise, children will tell you that *m* represents /m/, *t* represents /t/, and *n* represents /n/. Since children make analogies from known to unknown words, the more words in children's reading vocabularies, the more potential there is for children to use words they know to read words they do not know.

Suppose that Tamara, a first grader, does not automatically recognize the word *tent* in the sentence *Jane saw a large tent in the campground.* Suppose further that Tamara cannot figure out *tent* from picture cues, word order cues, meaning cues, or her own background knowledge. However, Tamara brings to reading the knowledge of onsets and rimes in words she already knows. Here is how Tamara uses the analogy strategy:

1. Tamara notices a familiar onset and a familiar rime in *tent.* She recalls that the *t* represents /t/ and that the *ent* in *went* (a familiar word) represents /ent/.

2. Tamara now substitutes (Chapter 2) the /w/ in *went* for the /t/, which leaves /t/ + /ent/.

3. Tamara then blends /t/ + /ent/ to pronounce /tent/.

Substituting Beginning Sounds

If you notice that . . .
children know the sounds associated with onsets and rimes but struggle to decode with analogy-based phonics, in all likelihood children are not yet skilled at substituting one beginning sound for another.

The thing to do is . . .
to give children more instruction and more practice with sound substitution. Look in Chapter 2 for ideas on how to develop this phonemic awareness skill.

4. Last, Tamara checks to make sure that /tent/ is a good fit for the sentence. She asks herself: "Does *tent* sound and look right? Does *tent* make sense in the passage? Do I know what the author means?" If the answers to these questions are yes, Tamara continues reading. If the answers are no, Tamara tries once again to figure out *tent*.

SELF-MONITORING, CROSS-CHECKING, AND SELF-CORRECTING FOR MEANING-FOCUSED WORD IDENTIFICATION

Word identification works best when it serves comprehension. The new words children read absolutely must make sense in the reading context. So, in addition to using specific word identification strategies to read new words, children also use strategies to keep word identification meaning focused. There are three strategies children use to do this: cross-checking, self-monitoring, and self-correcting. Readers use these three strategies to make sure that the new words they read are consistent with passage meaning.

Cross-Checking

In the example, the last thing Tamara did was to verify that *tent* made sense in the sentence. Readers *cross-check* to make sure that the words they identify fit the reading context. Cross-checking is a strategy all by itself, and the last step in word identification. Good readers always cross-check, regardless of whether they identify words with the analogy strategy or some other strategy.

Cross-checking ensures that word identification supports comprehension. When cross-checking, readers actively think about meaning, taking into account the overall sense of the surrounding phrases, sentences, and paragraphs, as well as sentence structure, letter and sound cues, and their personal reasons for reading. Cross-checking may involve rereading a phrase or sentence to accept or reject the identified word. Once satisfied that the newly identified word makes sense in the reading context, children immediately focus their attention back on reading and understanding the text. Cross-checking gives readers valuable feedback on their own decoding efforts. Thus, one consequence of cross-checking is a metacognitive—or conscious—awareness of the success of word identification (*metacognition* is explained in Chapter 1). Readers know whether an identified word is acceptable or unacceptable for the reading passage. An acceptable outcome is a real, meaningful word that makes sense in the context; an unacceptable outcome is either a nonsense word or a word that does not fit the context. The following prompts may help children develop and use the cross-checking strategy:

- "Reread it and think about what would make sense."
- "What's wrong with _____ (rereading what the child read)?"

- "Does _____ look right and sound right?"
- "Does what you just read sound like a real word?"
- "Try reading that again."
- "Could it be _____? What makes you think so?"
- "You read _____. Can we say it that way?"
- "Does _____ make sense?"
- After the child successfully cross-checks, ask, "How did you know this is _____?"

Readers who cross-check put only as much energy into word identification as is necessary to identify a word that is consistent with the author's message. These readers know when to stop word identification and proceed with textual reading, and when to give word identification another try. When a word makes sense, word identification stops and comprehension moves forward unimpeded by the confusion created by an unknown or misidentified word. On the other hand, if an identified word does not make sense, then cross-checking lets readers know that they have not constructed a meaningful message.

Self-Monitoring

Self-monitoring is self-regulating one's own reading. Readers use self-monitoring to determine when they need to use the cross-checking strategy and when they do not. Self-monitoring assures that readers stop to cross-check only when an identified word does not fit the context. In monitoring their own reading, readers pay attention to comprehension, stopping to cross-check when they discover that text does not make sense. Use these prompts to encourage children to self-monitor:

- "Take another look at _____."
- "You read _____. Are you right?"
- "You made a mistake in this sentence (paragraph or page). Can you find it?"
- "Why did you stop?"
- "What's wrong with _____?"
- Pointing to the word, ask, "Could it be _____?"
- "You read _____. What did you notice?"
- "You read _____. Does it make sense?"

Self-Correcting

Self-correcting is the process of rereading to correct a miscue. Readers self-correct when, through cross-checking, they determine that the message does not make sense. Children go back into the text and reread to make the words fit the context. In so doing, children change or correct a misidentified word. Use these prompts to support readers as they self-correct:

- "What's the tricky part in this word?"
- "What is another word that begins with _____ (ends with _____ or has _____ in the middle) and makes sense?"

- "You were almost right. See if you can figure out what you need to fix."
- "Take another look at _____ (point the vowel pattern). What sound does the vowel make in this pattern?
- "You read _____. Try it again and think about _____."
- Pointing to the word, ask, "How did you know that was _____? Is there another way to tell?"
- Cover up all but the first letters and ask, "What would make sense that begins with _____?"

Encourage children to look at the letters, think of the context, and reread to confirm meaning. Then reinforce self-correcting, saying, "I like the way you went back to fix that word," or "You did a good job going back (rereading) to make sense."

When readers cross-check, self-monitor, and self-correct, they pay attention to meaning. Readers use self-monitoring to decide if they should cross-check. Readers cross-check to see if the identified word makes sense. If readers determine through cross-checking that an identified word does not fit the context, they self-correct their own miscue. Before returning to the text, readers once again cross-check to make sure that the self-corrected word makes sense in the reading context. If so, readers turn their attention back to reading and understanding the text. If not, then readers try once again to self-correct the miscue in order to re-create a meaningful message.

UNDERSTANDING RIMES, PHONOGRAMS, AND WORD FAMILIES

Rimes, phonograms, and word families are related terms. *Rimes* and *phonograms* refer to the vowel and any letter that comes after it in a syllable (the *at* in *cat*). *Word families* are word groups that share the same rime or phonogram (*cat, rat, fat, sat, bat*). Sometimes *phonogram* is used when referring to the shared letter patterns in word families. The essential points for you to keep in mind are (a) rimes and phonograms both refer to the vowel and any letter thereafter (*un*), and (b) word family refers to word groups that share the same phonogram (*run, sun, fun*).

Some popular teaching materials in the 1960s clustered words into "families" where every family member shared a common rime or phonogram. When these materials were first published, they were dubbed "linguistic" because their authors were linguists, not educators, and the materials were supposed to reflect linguistic principles. The Merrill Linguistic Reading Program (1986) and Programmed Reading (Phoenix Learning Resources, 1994) are contemporary examples of this approach. The sentences in linguistic materials are jam-packed with word family words like *The man has a tan pan in the van.* Text for beginning readers has minimal variation among words, with many words differing only in the onset. Though the objective of linguistic materials is to teach word identification, children do not learn the "rules" of phonics. Words are taught by sight, not by

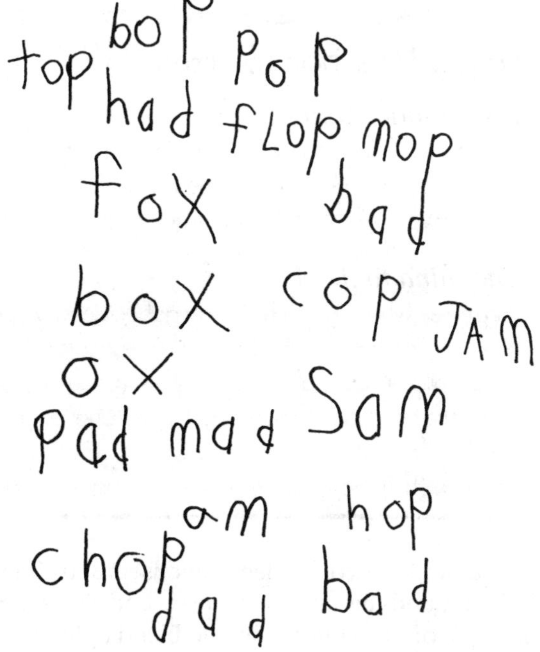

Figure 4-2   When Anna's teacher asked her to write as many words as she could, Anna wrote 20 words using only four rimes—*op, ox, ad,* and *am.*

sounding and blending as in traditional letter-sound phonics programs. Readers abstract their own generalizations about letter-sound correspondences as a consequence of reading words from the same families.

Anna wrote the word list in Figure 4-2 when her teacher asked her to write as many words as she could. We can infer from Anna's list that she thinks about the rime in words, for the 20 word family words are made up of only four rimes: *op, ox, ad,* and *am.* Anna's teacher emphasizes phonograms, so it is no surprise that Anna thinks of word family words when she writes. Anna knows how to substitute onsets, or beginning consonants, to make new words, so we would expect that she will also be able to read and write words like *drop, stop, sad, lad, ram,* and *ham,* provided that she recognizes the *op, ad,* and *am* phonograms (or rimes).

Why Some Children Use Onsets and Rimes to Read and Learn New Words

Identifying words by their analogous onsets and rimes is easier than decoding words letter-sound by letter-sound. First, learning that *ent* represents /ent/ is far less taxing than learning that the *e* represents the sound of /e/, *n* the sound of /n/, and *t* the

Paying Attention to Rimes

If you notice that . . .

children can figure out words spelled with the same rime (cat, rat, fat, mat) but struggle to identify words spelled with the same onsets but different rimes (rat, run, rag, ring), in all likelihood children do not pay enough attention to rimes.

The thing to do is . . .

vary rimes when giving children practice decoding, especially when reading words in lists (f<u>at</u>, f<u>an</u>, f<u>in</u>, t<u>in</u>, t<u>ub</u>). In order to successfully read or build words from a single family, children may pay attention to only the onset, as this is the only portion of each word that changes (<u>c</u>at, <u>r</u>at, <u>f</u>at, <u>m</u>at). Changing rimes helps children think about the sounds associated with both onsets and rimes and gives children the type of decoding practice they need in order to use analogy-based phonics while reading.

sound of /t/. Second, blending onsets and rimes is much easier than blending individual sounds because with onsets and rimes there are only two items to blend. In the example of *tent*, children would blend only /t/ + /ent/ in comparison with the four phonemes /t/ + /e/ + /n/ + /t/ associated with individual letters. Having fewer items to blend, in turn, decreases the probability of reversing sounds, deleting sounds, or adding sounds during blending. Consequently, readers who might not be successful sounding out and blending *tent* as /t/ + /e/ + /n/ + /t/ may be able to read *tent* when it is divided into /t/ + /ent/.

As Lilly writes about her pet cat (see Figure 4-3) she conventionally spells words in her reading vocabulary and spells other words by adding different onsets to the *at* rime. We can infer from her story that Lilly is thinking carefully about speech-to-print relationships, resourcefully combining her knowledge of onsets and rimes, her memory for known words, and her understanding of letter-sound associations. When Lilly reads, she uses frequently occurring rimes, as well as the letter-sound patterns of phonics, to identify new words.

It is quite typical for readers like Lilly to use both analogy-based decoding and letter-sound decoding. Children like Lilly look for consistency in written and spoken language relationships. They learn and remember words by paying attention to recurring letter patterns, and hence they can write and read words that consist of onset-rime combinations they already know (*p* + *et* = *pet*), as well as the letter-sound patterns of phonics (*p* + *e* + *t* = *pet*). Bear in mind that the beneficial effect of rimes may be more important in English than in other languages that have more consistent sound-letter matches (Booth & Perfetti, 2002).

English does not match only one letter to only one sound. There are many more English sounds (43 or so) than English letters (26). The same sounds are represented by different letter patterns (the long /o/ in *toe*, *boat* and *know*), and the same letters represent different sounds (the *e* in *be*, *bet*, and *her*). In presenting

my cat is fat
is your cat
fat? my cat is
fat his name
is o marf

Figure 4-3   When writing, Lilly uses her knowledge of rimes and her ability to substitute beginning consonants (onsets).

readers with consistent sound-letter matches, rimes make our English spelling system somewhat simpler for beginning readers.

Onsets and rimes are reasonably dependable maps for sound, so readers can justifiably place a certain amount of confidence in them. Onsets consist exclusively of consonant letters. As it turns out, consonant letters are far more reliable representations of sound than vowels. When combined with rich context cues, onsets give readers considerable insight into a word's identity. Upon seeing the word *track* for the first time in the sentence *The train rolled down the track,* a reader who knows the onset, *tr,* and who is sensitive to context and picture cues might logically assume that this never-seen-before word is *track.*

Though consonants are relatively dependable, this is not true for vowels. Each vowel represents more than one sound, as with the *a* in *track, bake, saw,* and *car.* Vowels are more easily remembered and decoded when learned as part of frequently recurring rimes (Goswami, 2001a). When syllables, in this example the one-syllable word *track,* are divided into onsets and rimes, the tricky vowels are not quite so troublesome. Because the vowels in rimes are learned as part of a chunk of letters and sounds, readers do not have to understand why the *a* in *track* is pronounced one way and the *a* in *bake* another way. Instead, readers remember that the *ack* in *track* represents /ack/ and the *ake* in *bake* represents /ake/.

Remembering the rimes in word family words sidesteps the need to learn exceptions to the conventional way letters represent sounds in English words. Take the *ind* in *find*, for example. The *i* in *find* should represent the same sound as the *i* in *dish*, since there is only one vowel (the *i*) in a short word followed by consonants (*ind - ish*). This is not so, of course. Children would be confused if they tried to read *find* as though the *i* represented the sound in /dish/. However, the sound represented by the *i* in *find* is not at all troublesome when remembered as part of the whole rime *ind*. Children who know how to read the rime in *find* have a cue to the identification of any word in the *ind* word family, for example, *mind*, *kind*, *blind*, and *bind*. The net effect is that even vowels that stand for a variety of sounds are more easily remembered and decoded when learned within the context of word family words. Therefore, it is not surprising that children who are taught to use analogous rimes are better at reading words that require attention to the rime, such as *sight* and *hold*, as compared with children taught only predictable letter-sound patterns, such as *bat* and *bit* (Walton, Walton, & Felton, 2001).

Best Practices for Teaching Analogy-Based Phonics

If you teach children like Lilly, you can expect them to recognize and use the rimes in word family words when you directly teach analogy-based phonics and when you provide reading and writing activities like those described later in this chapter. Even children in second grade benefit from analogy-based phonics when it is taught in a comprehension-focused reading program (White, 2005).

When you help children notice onsets and rimes in new words that are also part of familiar words, you are teaching analogy-based phonics and helping children use the analogy strategy. Suppose that a child sees the new word *kind* in a sentence in the text. You might guide the child in making an analogy to the rime in a familiar word, *find*, by saying, "Look at this word (pointing to *kind*). Now, look at this word (pointing to *find*). If this is /find/, what do you think this word might be (pointing to *kind*)?" Another way to guide readers as they apply analogy-based phonics is to say, "Can you think of another word that ends with *ind*?" It is also important to help children develop a metacognitive, or conscious, awareness of their own ability to use the analogy strategy. Give children opportunities to reflect on their own strategy by asking, "What word do you already know that can help you figure out this new one?" Along with asking questions like these, use the following best practices to ensure that instruction is effective and meets children's needs:

1. Use clue words (Goswami, 2001b). Readers are more inclined to use the analogy strategy when they learn clue words that contain rimes. A clue word is a familiar word that contains an often-used rime in word family words. Examples include *cat* for the *at* word family, *pig* for the *ig* word family, *fan* for the *an* word family, *jet* for the *et* word family, *sun* for the *un* word family, and *night* for the *ight* word family. Clue words like these help children remember the sounds and spellings of word family rimes. Make sure readers can readily refer to clue words by putting them on the word wall, writing them on charts, taping them to the tables where children read and write, or writing them on the board.

   2.   Show children how to use the analogy strategy. We cannot assume that children will naturally begin to use analogous onsets and rimes. Significantly, while some children may be able to figure out the identity of words with known onsets and rimes without their teachers' help, most children need guidance from their teachers and structure in learning (Goswami, 2001a; Savage, 2001).

   3.   Teach rimes from large, often-used word families. From a practical perspective, we want to teach children those rimes that are the most helpful—that is, the more common rimes that make up many different word family words. The rimes in Appendix A are part of almost 500 words in books for beginning readers.

   4.   Teach rimes along with the letter-sound relationships within rimes. (Juel & Minden-Cupp, 2000). Children who know the sounds that the individual letters in rimes represent are better able to use analogy-based phonics than children who do not understand the letter-sound relationships within rimes. For example, the reader who knows that *at* represents /at/ and who also knows that the *a* in *at* represents /a/ (the short *a*) and the *t* represents /t/ is more likely to effectively use the analogy strategy than the child who knows only that *at* represents /at/. In fact, readers may need to know something about the manner in which individual letters represent sound before they can successfully use analogy-based phonics (Ehri & Robbins, 1992). Good readers use several word identification strategies and change strategies, going between analogy and letter-sound decoding, depending on the reading circumstances (Walton et al., 2001).

ACTIVITIES FOR TEACHING ANALOGY-BASED PHONICS

The following activities help children learn the sounds that onsets and rimes represent and how to use the analogy decoding strategy. You can use these activities to teach any rime you think beneficial for the children in your classroom. Be sure to adapt the activities so that they are compatible with your teaching style. Combine these activities with reading aloud books that include the rhyming words listed in Appendix A. In addition to the following activities, look in Chapter 5 for activities to teach letter-sounds. Provide clue words to help children make analogies from known to unknown words and include in your balanced classroom reading program a generous amount of time devoted to reading and writing, including the reading and writing of word family words.

Activities

4.1 *Pocket Chart Word Building*

Skill: Use onsets and rimes to build words.

In this scaffolded activity, the teacher supports children in building words by lining up small cards with onsets and rimes on them. This activity is suitable for children working in small groups.

Things You'll Need: One set of large 3-inch-by-5-inch onset and rime cards that combine to build often-seen and often-used word family words; sets of small onset and rime cards; a pocket chart.

Directions:

1. Use a pocket chart (a hanging chart with lines of clear compartments to hold cards) and the large onset and rime cards to demonstrate word building, as shown in Figure 4-4.
2. Put an onset and a rime card side by side in a pocket chart (*s* and *at*, perhaps) and push the cards together to build a word family word (*sat*).
3. Use a different onset and the same rime to build another word from the same family (*fat*, for instance). Line up word family words, thus

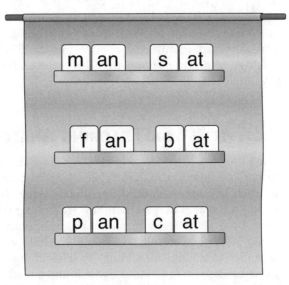

Figure 4-4 The use of a pocket chart to build words helps readers gain insight into the sound that analogous onsets and rimes represent in word family words.

creating opportunities to compare and contrast the rimes in words and to develop an understanding of how word family words sound alike and look alike.

4. Once the children understand how to build word family words, they are ready to try the next activity, Word Family Word Building, which entails less teacher support than Pocket Chart Word Building.

4.2   *Word Family Word Building*

Skill: Use onsets and rimes to build words.

Use this activity with small groups of children who are ready to build words with slightly less teacher guidance than present in the Pocket Chart Word Building activity.

Directions:

1. Give children onset-rime cards and ask them to work individually or with a partner to build the word family words you specify.
2. Once children are familiar with word family word building, you may wish to ask them to build as many words as they can from the same set of onset-rime cards. Have children share the word family words they build, write the words on the board, and compare and contrast word family words.

4.3   *Paper Plate Word Families*

Skill: Use onsets and rimes to build words.

Children working in centers combine onsets and rimes to build word family words and write the words on word family paper plates, which are then put on the bulletin board and sent home for children to share with their families.

Things You'll Need: Sets of onset-rime cards; inexpensive *paper* plates.

Directions:

1. Put onset-rime cards and paper plates in a learning center. Children visiting the center combine onset-rime cards to build word family words.
2. Children then write the word family words on the paper plates.
3. Put the word family paper plates on the bulletin board, discuss the word families, and send the plates home with children to share with their own families. Table 4–2 has onsets and short vowel rime combinations for word family word building and other activities in this chapter.

TABLE 4–2 Onsets and Short Vowel Rimes for Word Family Word Building and Other Activities

Rimes				Onsets						
ap	at	ad	an	c	m	h	r	s	t	b
ed	en	et	ell	b	n	y	p	l	w	m
ig	id	in	ip	b	d	h	l	p	w	r
op	ob	og	ot	c	h	d	r	m	p	l
ug	um	un	ub	b	g	h	m	r	s	t
ap	ip	op	ot	s	t	l	n	c	m	d
ell	est	ill	in	b	f	p	w	t	s	d
ack	ash	ick	ock	s	t	l	p	r	st	sm

Word Family Words Built From the Onsets and Rimes

ap, at, ad, an

cap, map, rap, sap, tap

cat, mat, hat, rat, sat, bat

mad, had, sad, tad, bad

can, man, ran, tan, ban

ed, en, et, ell

bed, led, wed

yen, pen, men

bet, net, yet, pet, let, wet, met

bell, yell, well

ig, id, in, ip

big, dig, pig, wig, rig

bid, did, hid, lid, rid

bin, din, pin, win

dip, hip, lip, rip

op, ob, og, ot

cop, hop, mop, pop, lop

cob, rob, mob, lob

cog, hog, dog, log

cot, hot, dot, rot, pot, lot

ug, um, un, ub

bug, hug, mug, rug, tug

bum, gum, hum, mum, rum, sum

bun, gun, run, sun

hub, rub, sub, tub

ap, ip, op, ot

sap, tap, lap, nap, cap, map

sip, tip, lip, nip, dip

sop, top, cop, mop

tot, lot, not, cot, dot

ell, est, ill, in

bell, fell, well, tell, sell, dell

best, pest, west, test

bill, fill, pill, will, till, still, dill

bin, fin, pin, win, tin, sin, din

ack, ash, ick, ock

sack, tack, lack, pack, rack, stack, smack

sash, lash, rash, stash, smash

sick, tick, lick, pick, stick

sock, lock, rock, stock, smock

4.4 *Rewrite Familiar Poems*

Skill: Read and write words with the rimes children are learning.

Children in small groups predict rhyming words in familiar poems and then use their knowledge of rimes to add their own new and creative endings to the poems.

Things You'll Need: Sticky notes; familiar poems written on large charts. Use only poems with words that both rhyme and share a rime (*might-light* not *might-write*).

Directions:

1. Use a sticky note to cover up one or more rhyming words in a familiar poem. Have children read the poem aloud.
2. When the children come to a covered-up word, have them predict the word under the sticky note.
3. Once children make their prediction, take off the sticky note to reveal the word family word.
4. After children are thoroughly familiar with the poem, ask them to write their own versions by adding new endings. The endings in Figure 4-5 were written by first graders after their teacher shared the big book *Oh, A-Hunting We Will Go* (Langstaff, 1989).
5. Once children share their poems with the class, you may want to bind the poems together to make a class poetry book.

4.5 *Sticky-Note Word Family Books*

Skill: Read and write word family words.

Children working in small groups or in learning centers use sticky notes to make their own word family word books, such as those in Figure 4-6.

Things You'll Need: Sticky notes; pencils; stapler.

Directions:

1. Have children join you in making lists of word family words.
2. Give each child a few sticky notes. Ask children to write one word family word on each sticky note.
3. Children put their sticky notes together to form a book; staple the pages to keep them together (see Figure 4-6).
4. Children flip the pages to read their sticky-note word family books.
5. Children take the books home to read with their families.

Figure 4-5 Writing new endings for familiar poems helps readers gain insight into words that share letter and sound patterns.

Figure 4-5 (*continued*)

Figure 4-6   Sticky-Note Word Family Books. Children make sticky-note word family (or beginning letter-sound) word books and then flip the pages to read their books.

4.6 *White Board Riddles*

Skill: Use onsets and rimes to solve riddles.

Small groups of first, second, and third graders use their knowledge of rimes and beginning letter-sounds to solve riddles and then write their answers on small white boards. In writing solutions to riddles, children think about how to spell words and cross-check for accuracy, which helps children remember the words.

Things You'll Need: As many small white boards (or small chalk boards) as there are children in a small group; dry-erase markers (or chalk); paper towels for erasers.

Directions:

1. Begin by demonstrating how to solve riddles. Write two clue words on the board, *rice* and *bug*, perhaps. Explain that children are to use the clue words to solve a riddle. For example, you might say something like, "The word starts like *rice* and rhymes with *bug*. It is something you walk on. What is it?"
2. Show children how to substitute the beginning letter-sound (the onset) in the first word (the *r* in *rice*) for the beginning letter-sound in the

second word. This substitution creates b+ug to solve the riddle (*rug*). (Look in Chapter 2 for more information on the phonemic awareness skill of sound substitution.)

3. Give each child a small white board, a dry-erase marker, and a paper towel for an eraser. Make up easy riddles with onset and rime clue words. Children write their answers on the white boards and then hold up the boards to show their solutions.

4. Everyone in the group responds, thus giving you valuable insight into how children use their knowledge of onsets and rimes, as well as children's ability to substitute initial consonants.

   When you use this activity for the first time, give children an extra clue by telling them something important about the answer, such as "It barks." Later, when children are more confident, they may not need the extra clue. In considering only the clue words (the word begins like *box* and rhymes with *tell*), children must depend completely on their knowledge of onsets and rimes and on their ability to substitute beginning sounds.

5. Examples of riddles include
   - What begins like *dip* and rhymes with *hog*? Extra clue: It barks.
   - It begins like *pink*, rhymes with *big*. What is it? Extra clue: It lives on a farm.
   - The answer to this riddle begins like *cat* and rhymes with *rake*. Extra clue: You eat it, or you eat it at birthday parties.
   - What begins like *fan* and rhymes with *box*? Extra clue: It is a forest animal.
   - It begins like *jar*, rhymes with *wet*. What is it? Extra clue: It flies.
   - What begins like *rat* and rhymes with *sing*? Extra clue: It is something we wear on our fingers.
   - This word begins like *girl*, rhymes with *cold*. What is it? Extra clue: It is a color.
   - What begins like *bat* and rhymes with *fox*? Extra clue: This is a container we put things in.
   - It begins like *tan* and rhymes with *sail*. What is it? Extra clue: It's something dogs wag.
   - What begins like *box* and rhymes with *tell*? Extra clue: It rings.

4.7 Word Family Muffins

Skill: Use onsets and rimes to build words.

This word-building activity is especially good for learning centers and yields a permanent record of the words children build with onsets and rimes.

Things You'll Need: A muffin tin; small cards with onsets and rimes (or small tiles with onsets and rimes); muffin word guide. Put an assortment of onset-rime cards in each compartment of the muffin tin. Tape a small label above each compartment to tell which onset or rime cards are inside. If you prefer to use tiles and would like to make your own, buy small tiles from a home improvement store and write on them in permanent ink the onsets and rimes children are learning in your classroom. Tiles also are available commercially through retail stores and education catalogs.

Make a muffin word guide (see Figure 4-7) by drawing several circles on a sheet of blank paper to simulate a row on a muffin tin. Write a word family clue word above each of the simulated muffins. The clue words on the muffin word guide should be the same clue words that help remind children of word family rimes, consistent with best practice. Underline the rime in each word family clue word.

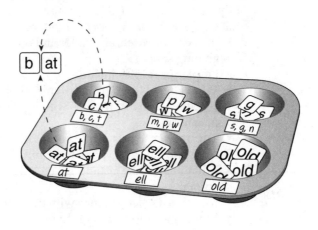

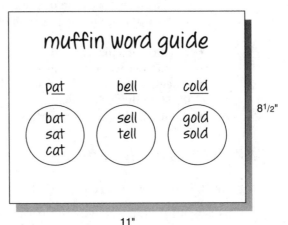

Figure 4-7   The muffin word guide that children fill in when they combine onset with rime cards placed in a muffin tin is a permanent record of the words that children build.

Directions:

1. Children in centers read the word family clue words on the muffin word guide and use onset and rime cards to build word family words (see Figure 4-7).
2. Then children write the words they built in the "muffins." If children build more words than fit in the blank muffins on the muffin word guide, ask them to write the extra words underneath the muffins.

4.8 *Word Family Fishing*

Skill: Substitute onsets.

Children fish for words in a bucket "pond." Instead of simply reading words, as is the procedure in the traditional version of the word fishing activity, children substitute one beginning letter-sound for another to read words with familiar rimes. This activity is suitable for small groups of first graders and second graders who need extra help in learning how to read word family words by substituting beginning sounds.

Things You'll Need: A plastic bucket to serve as a pond; a pole (a ruler works well); string; paper clips; a magnet; fish made of laminated construction paper; a marker. To make the fishing pole, tie a string to a ruler and fasten a small magnet to the end of the string. To make the fish, cut colored construction paper into fish shapes. Write a different word with a familiar rime on one side of each fish—the word *band*, for instance. On the other side, write an onset that creates a word when substituted for the beginning letter in the word on the reverse, such as the letter *s*. Laminate the fish. Last, fasten a large paper clip to each fish and dump all the fish in the pond (the plastic bucket).

Directions:

1. Children catch a fish, read the word on one side (*band*), substitute the beginning sound written on the reverse side (*s*), and then make a new word (*sand*), as shown in Figure 4-8
2. Correctly identified words are removed from the pond.
3. If the word is not correctly identified, the fish is thrown back into the pond for another try later in the game.

4.9 *Hink Pinks*

Skill: Write word family words.

Hink pinks are two-word rhymes consisting of an adjective and a noun that share a rime.

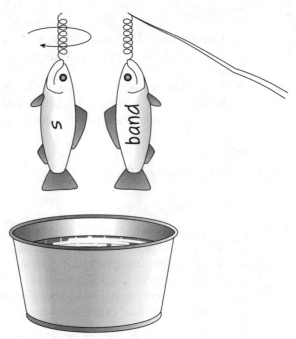

Figure 4-8 Children substitute one beginning sound (onset) for another to discover the words they catch in a "pond" made from a bucket or pail.

Things You'll Need: Paper; pencils; crayons or markers.

Directions:

1. Ask children to think of adjectives with the same rimes as the nouns they describe, such as *dairy fairy* or *smelly belly.*
2. Write examples on the chalkboard to serve as illustrations. Children create and illustrate their own hink pinks. Figure 4-9 shows hink pinks and pictures created by a multi-age group of second and third graders.
3. You may want to ask children in second grade and above to write definitions for their hink pinks. For example, "a drippy pet" and "a wet pet" are definitions for the hink pink *soggy doggy.*
4. You also may want to prop the definitions on the chalk tray and have children match the definitions with the hink pinks and pictures.

4.10 *Tongue Twisters*

Skill: Read and write short sentences with the same onset.

Tongue twisters are sentences in which all (or nearly all) the words begin with the same letter-sound. Use this activity with first, second, and third

foggy doggy

STUPID CUPID

Figure 4-9   Children think about rime and word meaning when they create and illustrate pairs of words that share the same rime.

graders who need practice paying attention to onsets and extra practice in fluently reading short sentences.

Things You'll Need: Tongue twisters remembered from childhood or a good book with lots of twisters, such as *World's Toughest Tongue Twisters* (Rosenbloom, 1986) or Charles Keller's *Tongue Twisters* (1989).

Directions:

1. Write a tongue twister on the board and have children read and reread the twister in chorus for fluency.
2. Ask a volunteer to underline the words with the same beginning letter-sound (onset).
3. Children are now ready to write their own tongue twisters. You may designate the onset each child is to use in writing the tongue twister, or children may decide for themselves which beginning sound they would like to use.

happy
pappy

Figure 4-9 *(continued)*

Horribal Harry hits hippos on a hill on a happy holiday in Hairballville.

Figure 4-10 Writing and illustrating tongue twisters gives children opportunities to identify the onsets in words and to creatively use this knowledge.

4. Share the alliterative tongue twisters children write (see Figure 4-10); read twisters aloud in chorus; put them on wall charts.
5. To develop fluency, have children tape-record tongue twisters. Follow the example of Rosenbloom and fasten together children's alliterative sentences and illustrations to make a book of playful, alliterative language created by the readers and writers in your classroom.

4.11 *Eggs*

Skill: Use onsets and rimes to build words.

Children working in centers build words by putting together two halves of colorful plastic eggs—one half with an onset written on it and the other with a rime.

Things You'll Need: A permanent marker; plastic eggs; a basket (optional).

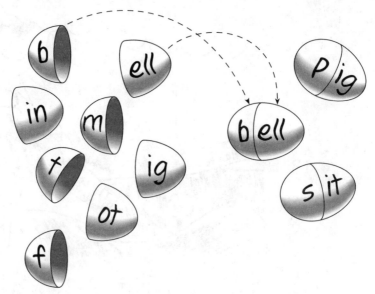

Figure 4-11   Children build words by putting the halves of plastic eggs with onsets on them together with the halves that have rimes written on them.

Directions:

1. Write an onset on one half of a plastic egg and a rime on the other half. Put the eggs in a basket; separate them into halves; scramble the halves.
2. Have children fasten together two halves of colored plastic eggs with a rime and an onset (See Figure 4-11).
3. Have children write the words they build.

4.12 *Chains*

Skill: Read and write word family words.

Children make brightly colored paper chains of word family words. They may instead make chains of words that begin with the same letter-sound, depending on which aspect of print (onsets or rimes) you wish to emphasize.

Things You'll Need: Colorful construction paper cut into strips about 1 inch wide; stapler or tape.

Directions:

1. Children look for word family words (or words with the same beginning letter-sound) on the word wall, on charts, and on bulletin boards.

2. Children write word family words or words with the same beginning letter-sound on construction paper strips. Make a list of the words children write.

3. Tape or staple the ends of strips into a circle, linking the circles with one another to form a giant chain.

4. Before hanging the chains, count the number of words children chained together. Drape chains over bulletin boards; hang them from one corner of the room to the other; tape them to desks, windows, and walls.

4.13 *Rime Pick-Up*

Skill: Think of word family words.

In this game-like activity, children pick up sticks—either the kind found in popsicles or used as tongue depressors—with rimes on them (see Figure 4-12). This activity works best when two or three children play together and fits nicely into learning centers.

Things You'll Need: Popsicle sticks, craft sticks, or tongue depressors with rimes on them.

Directions:

1. Scatter sticks on a table or floor. Taking turns, children pick up a stick, read the rime, and think of a word family word spelled with the rime.

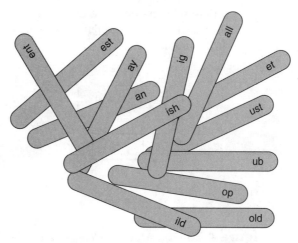

Figure 4-12   Children get lots of practice thinking of the recurring rime in words when they pick up craft sticks with rimes written on them and then think of a beginning sound to make a word.

2. If the child says a real word, the child puts the stick in his or her own personal pile. Each stick is worth one point. The player who gets the most sticks (the most points) wins.

4.14 *Tic-Tac-Toe*

Skill: Read and write word family words.

This old standby works well in learning centers and is played much like the original version of the game, except word family words are written in tic-tac-toe squares instead of Xs and Os.

Things You'll Need: Oak tag tic-tac-toe cards; markers. Make tic-tac-toe cards by drawing on sturdy oak tag the traditional nine-box design and writing two word family clue words with different rimes above the boxes. Underline the rime in each word family clue word (*cat, ran*). Laminate tic-tac-toe cards and have players use erasable markers when they play.

Directions:

1. Two children play. Each writes a word with the same rime as that at the top of the playing card (see Figure 4-13). In this example, one player writes *at* family words, while the other writes *an* family words. The traditional rules hold—any three words joined in a horizontal, vertical, or diagonal direction win.
2. Children can use this game for letter-sound patterns (Chapter 5), prefixes (Chapter 6), or suffixes (Chapter 6) by writing two words with different letter-sound patterns (such a *boat* and *tail* for long *o* and long *a*), prefixes (*unhappy* and *replay*), or suffixes (*playing* and *looked*) at the top of the tic-tac-toe cards.

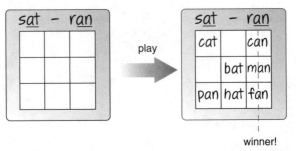

Figure 4-13   Tic-tac-toe challenges children to think of words that share the same rime. This activity can also be adapted for often-used prefixes and suffixes (chapter 6), or for words that have specific letter-sound patterns, such as long vowels or r-controlled vowels (chapter 5).

Figure 4-14   Getting on board this train calls for writing word family words (or words with the same beginning letter-sounds) and putting them inside the proper car. When the train leaves the station, all the cards are read and returned to the children, who then take them home for additional practice.

4.15 *Train Tickets*

Skill: Read and write word family words.

Children make their own train tickets by writing word family words on cards and then putting them inside train cars that have the same word family rime on them.

Things You'll Need: An engine and train cars made of colorful construction paper; large envelopes. Staple a large envelope with a word family rime, flap side out, to each car. Fasten everything to a bulletin board (see Figure 4-14).

Directions:

1. Children make their own "tickets" by writing word family words on index cards. Children then put the "tickets" inside the car with the word family clue word on it.
2. When the train is ready to leave the station, take out the tickets, read and discuss the words, and return tickets to their makers so children can take them home to share.

4.16 *Silly Sentences and Stories*

Skill: Read and write word family words or words that begin with the same onset.

Children write sentences or stories that have many word family words or words that begin alike. Using many words that share the same rime or beginning letter-sound results in silly, often humorous, sentences and stories. This activity is appropriate for children working in small groups, individually or in pairs with your guidance.

Things You'll Need: Nothing special.

Directions:

1. Review onsets or rimes, as appropriate for the focus of the activity.
2. Children write silly sentences or stories that predominantly feature either the same rimes or the same onsets. For instance, using the Minnie

Moo books (Cazet, 2000) as an inspiration, a child wrote a silly story that features the *m* onset: *One morning Mr. Moo and Mr. Moo's mooing wife (Mrs. Moo) mooed, "Moove over" to their little son Minnie Moo Jr. Minnie Moo Jr. yelled, "Mooomy, I want some m-m-m-ilk and coookie crisps." "I have some cookie crisps, but you will have to make your own m-m-m-ilk," said Mrs. Moo.* Then again, children might write silly sentences with the same rime, such as *Save brave Dave from the deep, dark cave* or *The fat cat sat on a hat and squashed it flat.*

4.17   *Slides*

Skill: Read and write word family words.

Children pull a strip of oak tag through a device to reveal one word family word at a time, as shown in Figure 4-15. This activity fits nicely into learning centers.

Things You'll Need: While slides can be purchased, they are extremely easy to make. Write onsets on a strip of oak tag. Then cut a medium-sized shape out of another piece of oak tag to serve as the body of the slide. Write a rime on the slide and cut a window (two horizontal slits) beside the rime. Make the window large enough so that the strip with onsets can be threaded through it.

Figure 4-15   Word family slides give children practice identifying word family words that are formed when different onsets are combined with the same rime.

Directions:

1. Children pull the strip through the slide. As children do this, different words are formed.
2. Ask children to read the word family words.
3. For a more permanent record of the word family words, have the children write the words they make and then later include these words in the word family word building activities described earlier.

4.18 *Binders*

Skill: Read and write word family words.

Children save important word family words in binders and then consult the words either when writing or when participating in other word family activities.

Things You'll Need: One binder for each child; paper for the binders.

Directions:

1. As a group, children make a list of words in the same family—the *at* family, for example. Children then put the *at* family list in their personal word family word binders.
2. Children add to their binders other word family words they meet in reading or need for writing. The words children put in their binders may come from the word family lists in your classroom, from the word wall, from poems, and from reading and writing activities.
3. Put lists in binders alphabetically according to the vowel in the rime, *am, an, at, et, ig, im, ip, it,* and so forth.

4.19 *Towers*

Skill: Read word family words or words that begin with the same onset.

Children build towers of word family words by reading words written on blocks. Alternatively, children make towers of blocks with words that have the same beginning letter-sound.

Things You'll Need: Blocks with word family words or words with some of the same beginning letter-sounds. To make blocks, you need square tissue boxes; tape; sticky shelf or drawer liner paper; a permanent marker. Cover the boxes with drawer liner paper, write words on the blocks. It is easier to make towers when blocks have words on only four sides, more difficult when words are on all six sides.

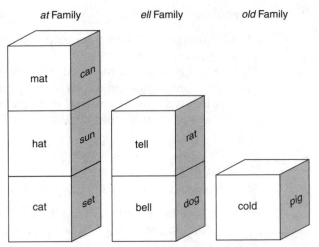

Figure 4-16   When children make word towers, they have opportunities to read and reread the same words, which helps familiarize children with onsets and rimes and, additionally, helps to develop fluency reading often-used words.

Directions:

1. Children read the words on each block, decide which word belongs to the family (or has the same beginning letter-sound), and then stack the blocks one on top of the other (see Figure 4-16). In reading different words on the blocks, children get repeated practice reading the same words, which helps to develop fluency reading word family words.
2. Count the number of blocks children stack up; ask children to suggest other words that share the same rime or beginning letter-sound; add some of the words to your classroom word wall.

4.20   *Word Family Hunts*

Skill: Identify and read word family words.

Children search for word family words. In the process, children learn to look for, recognize, and read words with the rimes you are teaching.

Things You'll Need: Nothing special.

Directions:

1. Have children scour the room and familiar books for word family words.
2. Children then write the words they find and share them with the class. If children are keeping their own word family binders, ask them to add the word family words to the binders.
3. Count the words children find. Make a simple bar graph showing how many words belong to the same word family.

SPARE MINUTE ACTIVITIES FOR TEACHING ANOLOGY-BASED PHONICS

4.21 *Buddy Words*

Skill: Use onsets and rimes to build words.

Tape an onset or a rime to individual children. Children find a buddy who is wearing an onset or rime that, when combined with the onset or rime worn by both children, makes a word family word.

4.22 *Duck, Duck, Goose*

Skill: Write word family words.

Give each child sitting cross legged in a circle a white board and marker. One person is "It." It has two cards, each with a word from a different family, such as *got*, and *run*. It walks around the circle tapping each child gently on the shoulder while saying "duck." Without warning, It stops in front of a child, taps the person on the shoulder, says "goose," and shows the tapped child the two cards. The tapped child then has a few seconds to read and write both words. If successful, the tapped child becomes the new It. Give the new It a different set of word cards.

4.23 *Beach Ball Roll*

Skill: Use onsets and rimes to build words.

Use a permanent marker to write onsets on a beach ball. Children sit in a circle and gently roll a beach ball with onsets on it. The child who catches the ball pronounces a word by blending the consonant closest to his or her right hand with one of several word family rimes you have written on the board.

4.24 *Word Building Race*

Skill: Use onsets and rimes to build words.

Give each child or pair in a small group an envelope containing onset and rime cards. At the word "Go" children combine onsets and rimes to make words. For a competitive game, the first child or pair to use all the onset-rime cards wins.

4.25 *Word Family Lists*

Skill: Read and write word family words.

Children make long lists of words that begin with the same onset or end with the same rime. Encourage children to actively participate in list making, to help write the words, and, additionally, have children read and reread the lists to develop instant word recognition.

4.26 *Theme-Based Lists*

Skill: Read and write word family words.

Children think of words that share rimes with food names, holidays, animals, community places, games, or toys. For example, word family words for an animal, say a *cat*, might include *hat, bat, fat, sat, rat*, and *mat*; a list for an outdoor toy, say a *swing*, might be *ring, king, bring, sing*, and *thing*. Fasten lists to walls, bulletin boards, and doors. Compare and contrast words; use words for writing poetry, for studying word spelling, and in games.

4.27 *Celebrate Onsets*

Skill: Read and write words with the same onsets.

Explore onsets with an old-fashioned celebration, an alliterative feast with all sorts of things that begin alike, such as *paper, paint*, and *pencil*. Make a list of these words. Write poems and stories about the experience, using lots of words from the alliterative list.

4.28 *Alliterative Shopping List*

Skill: Think of, read, and write words that begin with the same onset.

Make a game of creating imaginary shopping lists. Say "I am going to the store to buy a *pizza*." Then ask each child to add something to the list that begins with the same letter and sound as *popcorn, potatoes, pineapple, pie, pretzels*. Make a list on the chalkboard. Discuss onsets and the sounds they represent; invite children to create their own imaginative shopping lists.

LOOKING BEYOND THE ANALOGY STRATEGY

The number of words children can identify with the analogy strategy depends on the onsets and rimes readers remember in words, the frequency with which rimes occur in often-read words, and the size of children's reading vocabulary. As a consequence of typical reading and writing experiences, some children may look inside rimes to figure out the sounds that individual letters represent (Peterson & Haines, 1998), but not all readers do this, unless their teachers call attention to the individual letter-sound associations. Whereas some words consist of often-used rimes, many do not. This explains why beginning readers who *only* use rimes to make analogies are less proficient at decoding than their classmates who consider letter-sounds (Bruck & Treiman, 1992).

Furthermore, although the analogy strategy with onsets and rimes is a helpful and productive tool, it is not entirely suited to unlocking the complete range of words in our alphabetic writing system. Children who learn the sounds that letters represent have an advantage when spelling new words (Christensen & Bowey, 2005). One reason for this advantage is that our alphabet is a written map for the sounds in words, not the rimes in syllables.

Anyone who reads and writes a language written in an alphabet must understand how letters represent sounds. Since children develop the analogy strategy and the letter-sound strategy at about the same time, and these two strategies are beneficial for reading new words, teach children how to use both strategies. Use the activities in this chapter to increase children's strategic use of onsets and rimes, and the activities in Chapter 5 to increase their use of letter-sound combinations. After all, word identification is more than one strategy. It is many different strategies; the more strategies readers have at their fingertips, the better they read.

REFERENCES

Booth, J. R., & Perfetti, C. A. (2002). Onset and rime structure influences naming but not early word identification in children and adults. *Scientific Studies of Reading, 6,* 1–23.

Bruck, M., & Treiman, R. (1992). Learning to pronounce words: The limitations of analogies. *Reading Research Quarterly, 4,* 374–388.

Cazet, D. (2000). *Minni and Moo and the musk of Zorro.* New York: Dorling Kindersley.

Christensen, C. A., & Bowey, J. A. (2005). The efficiency of orthographic rime, grapheme-phoneme correspondence, and implicit phonics approaches to reading decoding skills. *Scientific Studies of Reading, 9,* 327–349.

Ehri, L. C., & Robbins, C. (1992). Beginners need some decoding skill to read words by analogy. *Reading Research Quarterly, 27,* 12–28.

Goswami, U. (1997). Rime-based coding in early reading development in English: Orthographic analogies and rime neighborhoods. In C. Hulme & R. M. Joshi (Eds.), *Reading and spelling: Development and disorders* (pp. 69–86). Mahwah, NJ: Erlbaum.

Goswami, U. (2001a). Early phonological development and the acquisition of literacy. In S. B. Neuman & D. K. Dickinson (Eds.), *Handbook of early literacy research* (pp. 111–125). New York: Guilford Press.

Goswami, U. (2001b). Rhymes are important: A comment on Savage. *Journal of Research in Reading, 24,* 19–29.

Juel, C., & Minden-Cupp, C. (2000). Learning to read words: Linguistic units and instructional strategies. *Reading Research Quarterly, 35,* 458–492.

Keller, C. (1989). *Tongue twisters.* New York: Simon & Schuster.

Langstaff, J. (1989). *Oh, a-hunting we will go.* Boston: Houghton Mifflin.

Merrill Linguistic Reading Program (4th ed.). (1986). Upper Saddle River, NJ: Merrill/Prentice Hall.

Peterson, M. E., & Haines, L. P. (1998). Orthographic analogy training with kindergarten children: Effects on analogy use, phonemic segmentation, and letter-sound knowledge. In C. Weaver (Ed.), *Reconsidering a balanced approach to reading* (pp. 159–179). Urbana, IL: National Council of Teachers of English.

Programmed Reading (3rd ed.). (1994). New York: Phoenix Learning Resources.

Rosenbloom, J. (1986). *World's toughest tongue twisters.* New York: Sterling.

Savage, R. (2001). A re-evaluation of the evidence for orthographic analogies: A reply to Goswami (1999). *Journal of Research in Reading, 24,* 1–18.

Walton, P. D., Walton, L. M., & Felton, K. (2001). Teaching rime analogy or letter recoding reading strategies to prereaders: Effects on prereading skills and word reading. *Journal of Educational Psychology, 93,* 160–180.

White, T. G. (2005). Effects of systematic and strategic analogy-based phonics on grade 2 students' word reading and reading comprehension. *Reading Research Quarterly, 40,* 234–255.

CHAPTER 5

Letter-Sound Phonics

The Strategy of Using Letter-Sounds to Read and Learn New Words

This chapter explains how children use letter-sound associations to read new words. Here, you will learn about the letter-sound relationships of phonics. You will learn why the left-to-right sequencing of letters in words is important for word identification. You will discover how the strategy of associating sounds with letters to read and learn new words corresponds to full use of the alphabetic principle. In reading this chapter, you will also learn how to sequence phonics instruction, the appropriate place for decodable books in your classroom reading program, the best practices for teaching phonics, and activities for teaching letter-sound relationships.

KEY IDEAS

- Letters that routinely appear next to one another, such as the *oy* in *boy* or the *er* in *her,* form patterns that represent sound. Our writing system has many letter patterns.

- Readers who use phonics associate sounds with letters and then blend sounds together to pronounce words that make sense in reading contexts.

- Readers use phonics to teach themselves new words; they do this independently without help from better readers.

- Decodable books—books that include the same letter-sound patterns you are teaching in your classroom—may give some children beneficial practice using phonics when used as supplementary reading.

- Phonics is taught in the kindergarten, first, and second grades. We expect children to be able to read and learn new words on their own when they begin third grade.

KEY VOCABULARY

Alphabetic word learners

Consonant

Consonant cluster

Decodable books

Digraph

Diphthong

Invented spelling

Letter-sound pattern

Phonetic spellers

Phonetically regular word

Vowel

Unlike the turtles in Wen Ting's drawing in Figure 5-1, the alphabet is not a jumble of topsy-turvy letter-sound combinations. Readers do not aimlessly tumble as they learn how letters represent sounds, nor do they stand on their heads when using letter and sound patterns to read unfamiliar words. For readers who do not automatically recognize *topsy, turvy,* and *turtles,* the strategy of using letter-sounds is a quick and sure route to pronunciation. Letter-sound-based phonics instruction teaches readers how to take advantage of the alphabetic principle—the principle that letters of the alphabet represent the sounds in words.

The children in your classroom are likely to be successful readers only when they understand and use this principle. Children who learn phonics early and well are better readers and better comprehenders than children who do not learn phonics (Blachman et al., 2004; Christensen & Bowey, 2005; Connelly, Johnston, & Thompson, 2001; National Reading Panel, 2000). This is true regardless of children's social or economic background (Armbruster, Lehr, & Osborn, 2001). What's more, the children you teach will make faster progress when they decode by associating sounds with letters rather than associating sounds with only onsets and rimes (Johnston & Watson, 2004).

Good readers use their in-depth knowledge of letter and sound patterns with strategic flexibility and resourcefulness. They *think* while using the letter-sound strategy. They always focus on meaning. Children apply their knowledge of phonics letter-sound patterns to read new words and build large reading vocabularies. They use this strategy to support comprehension.

Topsy Turvy Turtles

Figure 5-1   Unlike the jumbled turtles in Wen Ting's drawing, letters represent sounds in predictable ways and are, therefore, a useful pathway to word identification.

Phonics and Fluency

As discussed at the beginning of this book, there is a link between phonics and oral reading fluency. Children who are good at phonics read with greater fluency and more closely approximate fluent adult readers than children with poor phonics skills (Schwanenflugel, Hamilton, Kuhn, Wisenbaker, & Stahl, 2004). Because instant word recognition is related to decoding ability, children develop larger reading vocabularies when they have already developed decoding skills (Aaron et al., 1999). In turn, instant word recognition makes it possible to read fluently. Knowing phonics does not make a child a fluent reader. Rather, phonics makes it possible for the child to build a large vocabulary of instantly recognized words. A large sight vocabulary is necessary for fluent reading. Children cannot develop fluency until they instantly recognize the words in text. Instant word recognition is necessary for fluent reading because it frees the reader from dealing with disruptions caused by unknown words and allows the reader to focus instead on reading with expression, in phrases, and at an appropriate pace.

Using letter-sounds to read and learn new words requires a sizable amount of attention, phonemic awareness, and letter-sound knowledge. Like so many things in life, the extra time and energy invested in a worthwhile activity is more than offset by the rewards. One reward is that children can read a large number of new words with a relatively small number of letter-sound patterns. Another reward is that letter-sound-based phonics helps children build a large vocabulary of words they instantly recognize. And finally, the use of letter-sound-based phonics is a pathway to the identification of a large number of unfamiliar words, which supports the comprehension of increasingly more challenging text.

PHONICS LETTER-SOUND PATTERNS

The 26 letters in our alphabet are a hardworking bunch. This small group of 26 is systematically arranged, rearranged, and sequenced to build tens of thousands of words. With all this arranging and sequencing, it is inevitable that certain letters routinely appear right next to one another in spelling. This creates a type of spelling context in which certain letters are frequently and predictably adjacent to other letters. With many fewer letters (only 26) than sounds (as many as 43), English spelling contains a host of letter and sound patterns. As children become familiar with the letters that appear together in spelling, they associate sounds with those letters and hence begin to use the letter-sound patterns of phonics.

Letter-sound patterns may represent one or more sounds in words, such as the *t* in *tap*, the *th* in *this*, and the *thr* in *three*. The letter and sound patterns of phonics represent sound at the phoneme (sound) level, which is the same level used by the alphabet to connect speech with print. Therefore, readers can use their knowledge of letter and sound patterns to pronounce any word that is spelled like it sounds. For instance, though the vowels and consonants in the *VC*[1] (vowel-consonant) pattern may differ from word to word, this pattern generally represents a short vowel sound. Consequently, with a relatively small amount of letter-sound knowledge, readers have a good idea as to the vowel sound in many words that include the *VC* pattern in spelling. We can see this in the short vowel words *it, an, jam, back, fled, best, hit, pitch, shop, clock, luck,* and *scrub.*

The left-to-right order of letters is immensely important because letter order affects the sounds that the letters represent. Let us use the letter *a* as an illustration. The *a* represents one pronunciation when followed by a consonant and an *e* in the word *made*, a different pronunciation when followed by a consonant letter in *mad*, yet another pronunciation when followed by the *l* in *malt*, and still another when followed by an *r* in *mart*. If we were to look at only the first two beginning letters, *ma*, we might conclude that the *a* in each of these four words—*made, mad, malt,* and *mart*—is pronounced the same. On closer inspection we notice that the letter following the vowel, the letter to the right of the *a*, provides the cue to sound. In reading English words, we must look to the right of the vowel, in this example the letter *a*, to figure out the sound that *a* represents. This is why it is so important to encourage your students to look all the way through new words, beginning with the first letter and ending with the last.

Because there is almost always more than one way to group the letters in a new word, readers must consider which letters combine to form patterns and which do not. For example, *me* forms a *CV* long vowel pattern in *me*. This same sequence (*me*) does not constitute the letter-sound pattern in *met* because the *e* belongs to the *VC* short vowel pattern. Experienced readers know this and therefore look for predictable and frequently occurring patterns in words they have never seen before. Table 5–1 summarizes letter-sound patterns; Appendix B gives more detailed explanations of letter-sound patterns and also gives lists of words that include these patterns.

---

[1] For brevity, C stands for consonant; V for vowel.

TABLE 5–1   *Summary of Letter-Sound Pattern**

Consonant Letter-Sound Patterns	Examples
Single Consonants Usually represent the sounds associated with the italicized letters in the key words.	*b*oat, *c*at and *c*ity, *d*og, *f*ish, *g*oat and *g*em, *h*at, *j*eep, *k*ite, *l*ion, *m*oon, *n*ut, *p*ig, *q*ueen, *r*ing, *s*un, *t*urtle, *v*an, *w*agon, *f*ox, *y*o-yo, *z*ipper
Qu Qu represents /kw/ as an onset and in the middle of words, and /k/ when it is a final sound.	*qu*een, fre*qu*ent, anti*qu*e
Double Consonants Double consonants usually represent only one sound, and that sound is the same as the single consonant.	ra*bb*it, ri*dd*le, wa*ff*le, wi*gg*le, do*ll*, ha*mm*er, di*nn*er, co*pp*er, ca*rr*ot, go*ss*ip, mi*tt*en, da*zz*le
Consonant Clusters Two or three consonant sounds are blended when pronounced. Some teachers' manuals refer to this pattern as a consonant blend. Two-letter cluster consist of *bl, cl, fl, gl, pl, sl, br, cr, dr, fr, gr, pr, tr, sc, sk, sm, sn, sp, st, sw,* and *tw.* The three-letter clusters are *scr, spl, spr, squ,* and *str.* The following three-letter clusters represent only two sounds and consist of a digraph plus one other letter: *chr, sch,* and *thr.*	*bl*ack, *cl*ay, *fl*ag, *gl*ass, *pl*ay, *sl*ip, *br*oom, *cr*ib, *dr*ess, *fr*og, *gr*ass, *pr*etty, *tr*ain, *sc*arf, *sk*ate, *sm*ile, *sn*ail, *sp*ider, *st*ar, *sw*eep, *tw*ig, *scr*een, *spl*ash, *spr*ing, *squ*irrel, *str*eet, *chr*ome, *sch*ool, *thr*ow
Consonant Digraphs The letters in a digraph represent a different sound than the letters represent individually. *Th* represents two sounds: the voiced sound (*that*) and the unvoiced or voiceless sound (*thumb*).	*ch*air, *ph*one, *sh*oe, *th*umb, *th*at, *wh*ale
The Letter S As an onset *as* represents the /s/ heard in *sack*, never /z/. Only two alternatives, /s/or/z/, are possible when *s* is the middle or the last letter in a syllable.	Onset /s/ in sack and save. Middle /s/ in basic and hassle. Middle /z/ in cousin and closet. Final /s/ in bus and toss. Final /z/ in rose and his.
Ca, co, and cu *Ca, co,* and *cu* usually represent /k/. Teachers' manuals call the /k/ a hard sound.	*ca*mel, *co*lor, *cu*te

*Look at Appendix B for more detailed explanations and examples.

(continued)

TABLE 5–1   *Summary of Letter-Sound Pattern* * *(continued)*

Consonant Letter-Sound Patterns	Examples
Ce, ci, and cy *Ce, ci,* and *cy* generally represent /s/. Teachers' manuals call the /s/ a soft sound.	*cent, city, cycle*
Ga, go, and gu *Ga, go,* and *gu* usually represents the /g/. Teachers' manuals refer to /g/ as the hard sound.	*game, got, gum*
Ge, gi, and gy *Ge, gi,* and *gy* generally represent the /j/ as in /jelly/. Teachers' manuals refer to the /j/ as the soft sound. The *ge* and *gi* patterns are not as dependable as the *ga, go,* and *gu* patterns.	*gem, giant, gym*

Vowel Letter-Sounds Patterns	Examples
Short Vowel Patterns	
Examples of Short Vowel Sounds We hear short vowel sounds in the key words.	*apple, edge, igloo, octopus, umbrella*
*VC** Short Vowel Pattern* One vowel in a syllable that ends in a consonant usually represents the short sound. We can represent the vowel and consonant as *VC*-vowel-consonant.	*cat, bed, hit, top, bug*
VCCe Short Vowel Pattern A vowel followed by two consonants and a final *e* (*VCCe*) usually represents its short sound.	*chance, fence, bridge, bronze, fudge*
Long Vowel Patterns *Examples of Long Vowel Sounds* We hear long vowel sounds in the key words.	*apron, eraser, ice, overalls, unicorn*
VCe Long Vowel Pattern A vowel followed by a consonant and a final *e* usually represents the long sound and the *e* is silent.	*bake, gene, bike, bone, cute*
CV Long Vowel Pattern The vowel may represent the long sound when a word or syllable ends in a vowel sound.	*later, be, tricycle, no, cucumber, cycle*
Y in a Short Word or Single Syllable When *y* is the only vowel in a short word or syllable, it generally represents the long *e* sound. At the ends of words with no other vowels, *y* typically represents the long *i* sound.	Long *e*: an*y*, bab*y*, bod*y* Long *i*: b*y*, sk*y*, wh*y*

** V = vowel, C = consonant

TABLE 5–1 *Summary of Letter-Sound Pattern* *(continued)*	
Vowel Letter-Sounds Patterns	**Examples**
VV Long Vowel Patterns In the patterns *ai, oa, ay, ee, ey,* and *ea,* the first vowel is generally long and the second is silent.	ch*ai*n, b*oa*t, pl*ay*, tr*ee*, hon*ey*, b*ea*ch
Other Vowel Patterns	
Double *oo* The *oo* usually represents either the sound heard in *book* or the sound heard in *school.*	b*oo*k, st*oo*d, br*oo*m, sch*oo*l
Vowel Diphthongs *Ow* and *ou* often represent the sounds heard in *cow* and *out,* while *oi* and *oy* represent the sounds heard in *oil* and *boy.*	br*ow*n, d*ow*n, cl*ou*d, p*ou*t c*oi*n, s*oi*l, b*oy*, t*oy*
Vr Pattern *R* affects pronunciation so that vowels cannot be considered short or long.	f*ar*m, h*er*, b*ir*d, c*or*n, h*ur*t
Au and aw Patterns *Au* and *aw* usually represent the sound in *fault* and *straw.*	h*au*l, s*au*cer, l*aw*n, j*aw*
Ew and ue Patterns These patterns generally represent the sound in *blew* and *blue.*	ch*ew*, gr*ew*, bl*ue*, tr*ue*

As children have experiences reading and writing, they become sensitive to the letter and sound patterns that recur in many different words. Sensitivity increases as readers move up in the elementary grades (Juel, 1983) and is significantly related to reading ability (National Reading Panel, 2000; Tunmer & Chapman, 2002). The more opportunities children have to strategically use letter-sound-based phonics, the more they will know about how letters represent sounds and how to use their knowledge of letter-sound patterns to read and spell.

TEACHING LETTER-SOUND PHONICS IN YOUR CLASSROOM READING PROGRAM

Letter-sound phonics is taught from kindergarten through the second grade. All the letter patterns in Table 5–1 and Appendix B are taught from kindergarten to the end of second grade. Because there is no established, research-documented teaching sequence for phonics, classroom programs vary considerably in when different patterns are taught. Generally speaking, kindergarten teachers spend about 30 minutes a day teaching phonics and phonemic awareness. First-grade teachers devote approximately 30 to 35 minutes to instruction. Second-grade teachers spend a bit less time, say around 25 to 30 minutes. Bear in mind that these are general guidelines. The classroom reading programs in your school may set aside more or less time for teaching phonics in these grades. Regardless, some children will require extra help, and you must consider their needs when planning spare-minute activities.

Kindergarten

Kindergarten teachers usually teach phonics, phonemic awareness, and perhaps high-frequency words during the time set aside for word study or word work. Generally speaking, kindergarten classroom reading programs usually apportion about 30 minutes a day for direct instruction in word work, although this may vary depending on the classroom reading program, the daily schedule, and the teacher's philosophy. If you teach kindergarten, you will teach letter names and a sound for each letter, including a sound for each vowel letter. Your classroom reading program may also include teaching beginning and ending consonants, the VC short vowel pattern, and rimes or phonograms in word family words. The kindergarten teachers in your own school may teach more phonics or less phonics, depending in large measure on the needs of the kindergartners in their classrooms. At the end of kindergarten, the children in your class should know all the letter names; associate a sound with each letter; recognize some onsets and rimes; and read and spell some word family words. Some children will understand the VC short vowel pattern. In addition, children should bring to first grade a cache of words known by sight, the ability to spell some words conventionally, and the ability to spell new words by associating letters with sounds.

First Grade

First-grade teachers spend a bit more time for word work (or word study), usually over 30 minutes, depending on the classroom schedule. Word work or word study in first-grade classroom reading programs usually includes direct instruction in phonics, phonemic awareness, spelling, and high-frequency words. First-grade teachers integrate phonics throughout and across subjects, so first graders get much more instruction and have many more opportunities to use phonics while reading and spelling than is provided in the time set aside for word work.

If you teach first grade, you will begin with the VC short vowel pattern. If children learned this pattern in kindergarten, you may review the pattern for a short time to refresh memory and then move on to teaching the long vowel patterns, usually beginning with the VCe pattern (*cap – cape*). You will continue teaching consonant letter-sounds, picking up where the kindergarten teacher left off. You will teach nearly all the digraphs (*thing*, *charm*, *shell*) and all of the consonant clusters, including digraphs clusters at the end of words (*blast*, di*sh*). Once children know how to spell the high-frequency words they need for writing, you will connect letter and sound patterns to spelling. By the end of first grade, the children will have been introduced to almost all of the letter-sound patterns in Table 5–1 and Appendix B.

Second Grade

Second-grade teachers spend slightly less time teaching phonics and spelling each day, perhaps around 25 minutes or so. Phonics and spelling are taught during this time in second-grade classroom reading programs, and, depending on children's development as readers, programs also may teach high-frequency words. If you are a second-grade teacher, you will continue to teach the letter-sound patterns covered in first grade. You will review and reteach the vowel and consonant patterns throughout the year. By the end of the second grade, the children in your classroom will have learned a great deal about phonics. Children will know all the vowel and consonant patterns; their reading vocabulary will be growing rapidly; and they will be independent readers. At the end of the year, average second graders *only* sound out words they do not know; they read words instantly; their reading vocabularies are growing by leaps and bounds; and they read faster and more efficiently than ever before. Additionally, children will be developing, or on the brink of developing, the ability to recognize many different multiletter chunks in word structure (explained in Chapter 6).

Third Grade

Third-grade teachers spend about 15 minutes a day on word work. The 15 minutes or may be devoted to phonics, spelling, structural analysis (see Chapter 6). Phonics is not taught every day. Most third-grade classroom reading programs provide for reteaching, reviewing, and revisiting selected phonics letter patterns. Reviewing and reteaching ensure that the children have ample opportunities to master any phonics letter-sound they did not completely master by the end of second grade.

If you teach third grade, your classroom reading program may teach phonics and spelling together. To teach phonics and spelling together, teachers ask children to spell words that include the letter-sound patterns children are reviewing. However, it is fair to say that more time is spent on structural analysis than on phonics letter-sound patterns. As a matter of fact, teachers build on children's knowledge of vowel patterns to develop knowledge of syllables in longer words, as explained in Chapter 6. By the end of the year, the average third graders in your classroom use letter-pattern knowledge to read and spell new words with minimal effort. Added to this, children are well on their way to using the multiletter chunks in word structure to read and spell new words (explained in Chapter 6).

Fourth, Fifth, and Sixth Grades

If you teach fourth, fifth, or sixth grade, you will not set aside specific time during the school day to teach phonics. You will fold phonics into the teaching of spelling. In teaching spelling, you will remind children of the letter-sound patterns they already know and then have children spell words with those patterns. This helps children appreciate how knowing phonics makes it easier to spell and read long words. Classroom programs in the fourth through sixth grades focus on teaching the structure of long words (explained in Chapter 6). By the time children go to the seventh grade, they are good spellers and good readers. They have a large and growing reading vocabulary and read independently. These children do not need further review or reteaching of any of the letter-sound patterns, whether that review is through spelling or direct instruction.

Classroom reading programs vary, of course, so your program may have different expectations than the sequence described. We expect some flexibility in teaching phonics. Instead of being tied to a specific grade-by-grade teaching sequence, we want to consider children's individual needs and then adapt and adjust phonics instruction to meet those needs. Some children will learn phonics early, well ahead of the expectations for their grades. Other children will make good, average progress, while still others will fall behind. We would teach children with excellent phonics skills how to use the multiletter chunks in word structure (Chapter 6); we would provide grade-level phonics instruction to average learners; we would provide extra instruction to children who struggle. The advantage of knowing the letter-sound patterns, understanding best practice, and having teaching activities at your fingertips is that you have the tools to be an effective phonics teacher for all children.

How Children Use Letter-Sound Patterns to Read New Words

Readers who use the letter-sound strategy have the full strength and power of the alphabet at their fingertips. Thanks to their constant self-monitoring, self-correcting, and cross-checking, readers identify and pronounce real words that match the reading context. Children who use the letter-sound strategy have good phonemic awareness. They can tell you, their teacher, all the individual sounds in spoken words, and children can blend separate sounds into meaningful words. And, of course, children have a solid working knowledge of letter-sound patterns (Ehri, 2006; Snow, Burns, & Griffin, 1998).

As an illustration of this strategy, we will consider how Leslie decodes the new word *tree* in the sentence *Rosie and Rita sat under the tree.* In using the letter-sound strategy to read *tree*, Leslie reaps the full benefit of reading a language written in an alphabet, and here is how she does it:

1. Leslie groups the letters in *tree* into two different letter-sound patterns. She recognizes that *t* and *r* (*tr*) belong in one pattern (a consonant cluster) and that the *ee* is an example of the *VV* long vowel pattern. Noticing the VV pattern gives Leslie the clues she needs to figure out the vowel pronunciation.

2. Leslie then associates *tr* with /tr/ and *ee* with the long *e* sound.

3. Now she blends /tr/ + /e/ (long *e*) to pronounce /tree/.

4. Last, Leslie cross-checks to make sure that /tree/ fits the reading context. She asks herself: Does *tree* sound and look right? Does *tree* make sense in the passage? If the answers are yes, Leslie stops decoding and turns her full attention to *meaning,* finishing the page and reading the rest of the chapter. If the answers are no, she returns to decoding.

Interestingly, readers do not have to be segmenting and blending experts like Leslie to begin to use the letter-sound strategy. All readers need is just enough phonemic awareness to separate and blend the sounds in short words. Likewise, readers need just enough knowledge of letter-sound patterns to associate sounds with the letters in short, uncomplicated words.

Sounding out a short word like *big,* which has only three sounds and a predictable *VC* short vowel pattern, is far less taxing than sounding out a long word like *hippopotamus,* which has 12 letters, many letter-sound patterns, and a whopping five syllables. For this reason, it is quite possible, and indeed highly likely, that some children who have no difficulty sounding out short words like *big* will have trouble sounding out a long word like *crayon.*

The letter-sound strategy Leslie used (as well as all other strategies explained in earlier chapters) works when, and only when, readers connect the meaning of printed words with the meaning of spoken words. In the preceding example, *tree* is among the words Leslie recognizes in conversation. So, as soon as Leslie pronounces /tree/ when decoding, she knows what this word means. Connecting the written word (*tree*) with the meaning of a familiar spoken word (/tree/) makes it possible for Leslie to add *tree* to her reading vocabulary. But what would happen if *tree* were not among the words Leslie recognizes in everyday conversation?

If the words children sound out are not in their speaking vocabularies, sounding out will help with pronunciation, but not with meaning. So, when you teach letter-sound-based phonics (and previously described strategies), make sure that the words children identify are already in their speaking or listening vocabularies. If you suspect that children do not know the meanings of the words they are to identify while reading, help them build enough background knowledge so as to add these words to their speaking vocabularies before they decode them.

Leslie paid careful attention to the letter-sound patterns in *tree.* Close attention to letter-sound patterns and repeated experiences reading and writing *tree* will make it possible for Leslie to form a clear and easily accessible image of the word *tree* in her memory. Her memory for this word will include the letters in spelling, the sound (/tree/), and word meaning (Ehri, 2005). The letter-sound strategy is especially helpful for beginning readers like Leslie—say kindergartners, first and second graders. These children meet many new words, and the words tend to be less complex than those in text for older children.

Leslie successfully sounds out *tree* because the letter patterns in *tree* represent sounds in a predictable way. However, English spelling often strays from the sounds the reader expects. *Where* is an example of an often-used word that cannot be identified through associating sounds with letters. While the *wh* gives children a partial clue to identity, children will have to remember, through repeated reading and writing experiences, the print-to-speech connection between *where* and /where/. Some teachers call words like *where* outlaw words; others call them rule breakers. The point is to call the children's attention to the fact that the word cannot be sounded out with phonics and to emphasize the idea that these words have to be memorized; there is no letter-sound shortcut to fully pronouncing this type of word.

Difficulty Decoding Words with Letter-Sound Patterns Children Know

If you notice that...
children know the letter-sound patterns in a new word but cannot pronounce the word, in all likelihood children cannot successfully blend sounds into words.

The thing to do is...
assess and teach blending (see Chapter 2). Poor blenders struggle with decoding because they cannot combine the sounds they pronounce into contextually meaningful words.

Correcting Misidentifications

Readers who use the letter-sound strategy are experts at correcting their own misidentifications. Given the complexity of our English alphabetic writing system, there is no guarantee that the first try will result in a meaningful word. If the sounds Leslie blends together do not make a sensible word, self-monitoring and cross-checking (explained in Chapter 4) bring the misidentification to light. She then draws on her considerable storehouse of letter-sound patterns (and well-developed phonemic awareness) to fix mistakes and correct misidentifications. There are three ways Leslie might self-correct:

1. She might reblend the same sounds, perhaps gliding sounds together more smoothly, and then cross-check for meaning.
2. Leslie might associate different sounds with the same letter groups and then reblend to pronounce a new word that is then cross-checked for meaning.
3. Leslie could redo the entire process—regroup letters into letter-sound patterns, associate sounds with the letters in patterns, blend, and cross-check all over again.

The children whom you teach are bound to prefer easier, less attention-demanding ways to self-correct over energy-draining alternatives. You will notice that successful word identifiers often try reblending as their first attempt to correct mistakes. Then, if reblending does not work, they may try a different sound for a specific letter, often the vowel. For example, should a child misidentify *save* by pronouncing a short vowel (the sound we hear in *sat*), the child will reconsider the vowel sound, look again to notice the VCe pattern, and try the long sound. Only when all else fails do readers typically redo the entire process of re-identifying every letter-sound pattern.

Minor Mistakes

Readers may take minor mistakes in stride. Minor mistakes may not derail decoding because readers actively look for sensible connections between the words they recognize in everyday language and the words in the reading context. Accordingly, as readers self-monitor, self-correct, and cross-check, they find words in their speaking vocabularies that sound similar to minor decoding mispronunciations. When this happens, readers associate minor mispronunciations with real words that make sense in the reading context. Once plausible words are identified, readers automatically adjust mispronunciations so that the sounds in the words they decode match the words in their speaking vocabularies. The net effect is that slight letter-sound mistakes and minor blending miscalculations do not require a lot of extra special effort to repair.

Interestingly, not all misidentifications interfere with comprehension, so not all misidentifications need correcting. Readers have greater tolerance for misidentifications when they read a novel for pleasure than when they read a content subject textbook to learn new information. In this example, Leslie is reading for pleasure, so she is less concerned with absolute accuracy than when she reads a chapter in her science book. As a consequence, the misidentifications Leslie chooses to ignore as she reads for pleasure may well be, and in some cases absolutely ought to be, corrected if she were reading for technical information in a content subject.

BEST PRACTICES FOR TEACHING LETTER-SOUND-BASED PHONICS

You will be a more effective phonics teacher when you follow these best practices:

1. Teach letter-sound patterns early (Armbruster et al., 2001; National Reading Panel, 2000). Effective phonics instruction begins early and uses learning activities that are appropriate for a child's age and development. Introducing the letter-sound patterns of phonics early in the elementary school—kindergarten or first grade—is more effective than introducing instruction later in the elementary grades, say second grade and above.

2. Teach directly (Shankweiler & Fowler, 2004). Teaching phonics directly at the beginning of schooling is more effective in helping children learn and spell new words than teaching phonics indirectly or on an as-needed basis (Foorman, Francis, Fletcher, Schatschneider, & Mehta, 1998; Johnston & Watson, 2004; Shanahan, 2005).

3. Follow a logical, planful sequence. Teaching should be sequenced so that kindergarteners, first graders, and second graders learn the phonics patterns in Table 5–1 and Appendix B well enough to use them when reading and spelling new words.

4. Teach phonemic awareness, when needed. Programs that combine phonics with phonemic awareness are more beneficial for kindergartners and first graders than programs that teach these two skills alone (Christensen & Bowey, 2005).

5. Pace instruction to the needs of each child (Armbruster et al., 2001). Children learn phonics patterns at different paces. Some quickly grasp letter-sound patterns and how to use them, while others take more time, more instruction, and more reading and spelling practice. Move children along at a pace that is comfortable for them—fast enough to cover the letter-sound patterns children need to learn and slow enough to assure that children are competent users of the letter-sound strategy. Recognize, too, that the amount of time you devote to phonics is related to achievement. First graders are better readers when their teachers spend more time on phonics and phonemic awareness than on noninstructional and non-reading activities (Foorman et al., 2006).

6.   **Teach the same letter-sound patterns in spelling as you teach in reading.** Teaching the same letter-sound patterns in reading and spelling ensures that instruction in reading and spelling supports and reinforces each other. Children use their understandings of letter-sound patterns when they read and their understandings of sound-letter patterns when they spell. For example, in reading, children know that the *ck* in *back* represents /k/, and in spelling children know that the /k/ sound in /back/ is spelled *ck*. The more children learn about letter-sound patterns through spelling, the greater their insight into the use of these patterns while reading. And, of course, the more children learn to use patterns to read new words, the more likely they are to understand how to spell words with those patterns.

7.   **Integrate phonics into your classroom reading program.** Phonics is a means to an end, not the end itself. The goal of phonics instruction is to develop independent readers who are skilled at learning new words and who are fully capable of using reading as a learning tool. If we over-teach phonics by emphasizing letter-sound patterns at the expense of comprehension and reading for pleasure, we miss the mark. Make phonics part of your overall classroom literacy program, but not the predominant component or the most important component. Balance phonics teaching within your classroom program and measure success in many ways and by many barometers, such as the strategies readers use to read and spell new words, word learning, comprehension, the ability to use reading as a learning tool, love of reading, and interest in books.

A Sequence for Teaching Letter-Sound Patterns

A good working knowledge of letter-sound patterns contributes to comprehension and vocabulary alike, particularly in the early grades (Rupley & Wilson, 1997). We divide letters into consonants and vowels. Though we know it takes more reading and writing experiences to learn the vowel patterns than to learn the consonant patterns, you may be surprised to learn that research does not support the use of any one particular teaching sequence over another. There is no prescribed order in which the letter-sound patterns must be taught, no immutable learning hierarchy, and no sequence chiseled in stone.

You are free to teach letter-sound patterns in any order whatsoever, as long as children are successfully learning and using patterns. If you are using a commercial set of teaching materials that has already created a sequence for learning letter-sound patterns, follow that sequence. If you have some flexibility in how you sequence the teaching of letter-sound patterns and if you teach kindergarten, consider teaching vowels before you teach *all* the consonant letter-sounds. Teaching vowels before teaching all the 21 consonant letter-sounds makes it possible for children to begin to use phonics right away. Furthermore, your classroom reading program will be more effective when you teach often-used letter-sound patterns before you teach less-often used patterns. For example, children will see *sh* in far more words than *ph*. Wait to introduce less frequent patterns—*ph* and *aw*, for example—until children recognize and use the often-occurring patterns.

You also might wish to consider the relative difficulty of learning and applying patterns as a criterion for introducing letter-sound relationships. All things being equal, we find it useful to group letter patterns into those that are less challenging, more challenging, and most challenging for the children whom we teach. We begin with the less challenging patterns and then gradually move toward those that are the most challenging to learn and apply when reading and writing.

Less Challenging Patterns

- *Single Consonants.* The single consonant at the beginning of a word (the onset) is the easiest for children to learn and use (see Appendix B for an explanation). Beginning consonants are especially obvious and can be readily combined with sentence structure and meaning cues, which keeps decoding meaning based. It is not surprising, then, that many readers first pay attention to the single consonants at the beginning of words. As children gain more experience reading and writing, they notice this pattern at the end of words.
- *VC Short Vowel Pattern (Vowel-Consonant).* The children whom we teach find the *VC* short vowel pattern (explained in Table 5–1 and Appendix B) to be the least challenging of all the vowel patterns. The vowel in this pattern usually represents the short sound. The critical feature of the left-to-right letter order in the *VC* pattern is the consonant following the vowel. Therefore, we may have a short vowel pattern when only one consonant follows the vowel (*at, bat*), two consonants follow the vowel (*bath*), or three consonants follow the vowel (*batch*). Once readers know a few short vowel rimes, we encourage them to look inside the rimes they already know to discover how the *VC* short vowel pattern represents sound. In looking inside rimes, readers learn to recognize the *VC* pattern as a signal for a short vowel sound and then use this knowledge to pronounce many different words.

Somewhat More Challenging Patterns

- *Consonant Digraphs.* The children whom we teach usually find the consonant *digraphs,* such as the *sh* in <u>sh</u>ade and the *ch* in <u>ch</u>in, somewhat challenging to learn and apply. Perhaps the reason is that the letters in digraphs represent a totally different sound than the letters represent separately. Hence, readers cannot generalize, or transfer, what they already know about the sounds represented by single consonants to the consonant digraphs. However, many of the children we teach learn and use consonant digraphs more readily than consonant clusters. Learning something new, as in digraphs, may be somewhat less confusing than learning to pronounce familiar consonant sounds somewhat differently, which brings us to the consonant clusters.

- *Consonant Clusters.* The letters in consonant clusters (such as the *cl* in *clam* or the *st* in *stop*) represent the same sounds as the individual consonants. The only difference is that the sounds of letters in consonant clusters are pronounced by sliding them together rather than saying them separately. The consonants in clusters reliably represent sound. As a result, readers have practically no new information to learn to effectively use this letter sequence. However, many of the children whom we teach seem to stumble over blending the sounds in clusters. Some children try to pronounce the *cl* in *clock* as two separate sounds, /c/ + /l/, rather than two blended sounds, /cl/, and hence mispronounce this consonant cluster. For this reason, we find that consonant clusters take somewhat more time to learn and use than single consonants and the *VC* short vowel pattern. We first focus on two-letter clusters (*st*) and then move to three-letter clusters (*str*). Clusters that include a digraph (such as the *ch* portion of *chr* in <u>chr</u>ome) are left until after children know how consonant digraphs represent sound. Table 5–1 and Appendix B illustrate this concept.
- *VCe Long Vowel Pattern (Vowel-Consonant-e).* The *VCe* pattern is usually the easiest of the long vowel patterns (refer to Table 5–1 and Appendix B). Though the final *e* is a good visual reminder of the *VCe* long vowel pattern, as in *same* and *time,* some readers overlook the final *e,* thus treating letters as if they are in a *VC* short vowel pattern. As a consequence, these readers pronounce *same* as /sam/ and *time* as /tim/. Additionally, there are some obvious exceptions to the *VCe* pattern (see Appendix B for an explanation). My advice is to tell children to try the long vowel sound first and, if that does not make a sensible word that fits the reading context, to try a short sound.
- *VV Long Vowel Pattern (Vowel-Vowel).* The *VV* pattern is formed when the following two vowels are side by side: *ai* (s<u>ai</u>l), *ea* (cr<u>ea</u>m), *ee* (s<u>ee</u>d), *oa* (b<u>oa</u>t), *ay* (st<u>ay</u>), and *ey* (hon<u>ey</u>). For the most part, children pay attention to the middle of words when associating sounds with *ai* (tr<u>ai</u>n), *ea* (tr<u>ea</u>t), and *oa* (r<u>oa</u>d). Children usually look at the end of words when associating sounds with *ey* (hon<u>ey</u>) and *ay* (pl<u>ay</u>). When associating sound with the *ee*, children look at the end (s<u>ee</u>) or the middle of words (s<u>ee</u>d). The *VV* pattern usually represents the long vowel sound, with some exceptions (see Appendix B). Teach readers to try the long vowel sound and then, if necessary, to try the short vowel sound as a back-up.
- *CV Long Vowel Pattern (Consonant-Vowel).* The *CV* pattern represents a long vowel sound, as in <u>me</u> and <u>spi</u>der (refer to Table 5–1 and Appendix B). When this pattern comes at the beginning of words, it gives readers lots of excellent information to combine with context cues. The *CV* long vowel pattern has some exceptions (particularly in unaccented syllables) and hence takes more experience with print than patterns in the less challenging category (look for a detailed explanation of syllables in Chapter 6).
- *Double oo Pattern.* The *oo* pattern almost always represents one of two sounds: the sound heard in sch<u>oo</u>l or the sound heard in b<u>oo</u>k. Advise children to try

one sound first and, if that does not make a sensible word, to try the other sound. Look in Appendix B for examples of words with the *oo* pattern and a way to help readers manage the two options for its pronunciation.

- *Diphthongs.* The *ow, ou, oi,* and *oy* form *diphthong* patterns. The *ow* represents the sounds heard in c<u>ow</u>, *ou* the sounds in <u>out</u>, *oi* the sounds in <u>oil</u>, and *oy* the sounds in b<u>oy</u>. Diphthongs are different from the sounds that these letters represent in other patterns; readers must learn totally new letter-sound associations for them. Added to this, *ow* sometimes represents the long *o* sound, as heard in *crow.* For these reasons, diphthongs take more attention and more experience with print than letters in less challenging patterns.

Most Challenging Patterns

- *C or G Plus a Vowel.* As for the most challenging patterns, we find that letter-sound patterns made up of a *c* or a *g* plus a vowel (<u>cake</u>, <u>coat</u>, <u>cut</u>, <u>cent</u>, <u>city</u>, <u>cycle</u>, and <u>gate</u>, <u>go</u>, <u>gum</u>, <u>gem</u>, <u>giant</u>, <u>gym</u>) are quite challenging for children. Both of the consonants represent two sounds: the /s/ heard in *city* or the /k/ in *candy;* the /j/ heard in *gem* or the /g/ in *goat.* Not only do readers have to think very carefully about the left-to-right letter order, but they must also consider the exceptions, especially for the letter *g* plus a vowel. We suggest that you help children try more than one sound, if the first fails to produce a real, meaningful word. Look in Table 5–1 and Appendix B for more detailed explanations of the *c* and *g* plus a vowel patterns and examples of words with these letters.
- *Vr Vowel Pattern (R-Controlled Vowel).* The r-controlled pattern *Vr* is challenging to learn and use because the *r* changes the sound represented by the vowel letter. This is so regardless of which vowel precedes the letter *r.* This combination, *Vr,* may appear at first glance to be a *VC* short vowel pattern because, after all, *r* is a consonant letter. Readers must learn to pay special attention to the *r* and to anticipate its effect on the vowels it follows, as in c<u>ar</u>, h<u>er</u>, s<u>ir</u>, f<u>or</u>, and f<u>ur</u>. Do not be surprised if some end-of-year second graders still need practice and targeted instruction to efficiently and effectively use the *Vr* pattern.
- *VCCe Short Vowel Pattern (Vowel-Consonant-Consonant-e).* We also find it takes readers a while to develop competence reading and spelling words with the *VCCe* pattern, as in ch<u>ance</u>, f<u>ence</u>, br<u>idge</u>, br<u>onze</u>, and f<u>udge</u>. Perhaps the reason is that the *VCCe* short vowel pattern somewhat resembles the *VCe* long vowel pattern and is large, consisting of four or more letters. Unlike the *VCe* long vowel pattern, however, the first vowel in the *VCCe* pattern often represents a short vowel sound. This means that readers have to be especially careful to differentiate long vowel *VCe* words like *lane* from short vowel *VCCe* words like *lance.*
- *Au, aw, ue,* and *ew Patterns.* These four patterns, as in the words *haul, draw, due,* and *blew,* are quite challenging. They take a good bit of practice and, not surprisingly, emerge later in both reading and writing. Give readers lots of practice reading and writing words with these letter-sound patterns.

In the final analysis, the most challenging patterns typically require that children have much more practice reading all sorts of books, poems, articles, and stories, and many more opportunities to spell and write. So, if the children in your class take longer to figure out how to strategically use the most challenging letter-sound patterns, this is perfectly normal. Take opportunities during guided reading to point out and explore letter-sound patterns, help children become sensitive to these patterns through spelling, and use the activities described later in this chapter to support children as they use their letter-sound knowledge to read new words.

DO PHONICS RULES BELONG IN YOUR CLASSROOM READING PROGRAM?

Researchers have put tremendous energy into finding out which letter-sound patterns are dependable and which are not. In their quest, researchers investigated 45 phonics rules (Bailey, 1967; Clymer, 1963; Emans, 1967). Take the rule that says, "A vowel in the middle of a one-syllable word represents the short sound." Let us think about this middle vowel "rule," which is a way of explaining the *VC* short vowel pattern. We would agree that words like *man* and *red* are examples of the *VC* short vowel pattern and, coincidentally, follow the rule. Surprisingly, researchers find this rule to be relatively unreliable. In a sample of primary grade reading material, both Clymer and Emans report that the middle vowel rule applies only 62% and 73% of the time, respectively. Examining materials for Grades 1 through 6, Bailey reports that this rule is useful a mere 71% of the time.

Some of the examples these authors cite as exceptions to the middle vowel rule reflect a narrow interpretation of this "rule." Narrow interpretations make our alphabetic system seem more complicated than it really is. In this example, a narrow interpretation overlooks the fact that some vowels in the middle of one-syllable words are not in a *VC* short vowel pattern. Emans (1967) cites the word *hew* and Bailey (1967) the word *her* as examples of exceptions to the middle vowel rule. It is not reasonable to consider either word—*hew* or *her*—as an exception because the vowels in these words represent two different patterns: The *e* in *hew* is part of the *ew* pattern found in words like *jewel, chew,* and *threw* as explained in Table 5–1 and Appendix B. The *e* in *her* is perfectly regular, too, for the *e* in this word is part of an *r-controlled* pattern (*Vr*), and so the sound it represents is characteristic of this pattern, as in *germ* and *clerk,* as described in Table 5–1 and Appendix B.

While most readers cannot recite the "rules" of phonics word for word, they do have mental representations—mental images—of the way that phonics patterns represent sound. Their in-depth knowledge of letter-sound patterns gives them a powerful resource that, when combined with cross-checking, self-monitoring, and self-correcting, enables them to pronounce any word that is spelled like it sounds.

Perhaps you are wondering whether you should teach children the "rules" in your classroom reading program. Just because children recite rules does not mean that they know when and how to apply them. Children who memorize rules without connecting them to reading and writing may not be able to use them to support word identification or spelling. In fact, some children are quite skilled at reciting phonics rules yet do not have the foggiest notion of how to use the rules they put so much effort into memorizing. These children learn to "parrot" rules—they recite the wording of rules but do not relate the rules to the words they read and write.

Rather than focus on teaching the rules themselves, a more beneficial and balanced approach is to sensitize children to the way letter-sound patterns affect pronunciation and to ground patterns in the spelling of words children encounter as they read and write. Does this mean that you should never ever say a rule? Of course not. Sometimes it is helpful to tell children about a rule, especially when children need some clarification. In fact, explaining a rule from time to time can speed learning along, provided that the rule is solidly related to the words children read and spell. Encourage children to analyze left-to-right letter order and to learn how letter order affects the sounds letters represent. As a result, children will learn how letter-sound patterns look and sound in real words and create mental pictures of words in which the letter-sound patterns appear. This, in turn, contributes to word recognition and supports the development of a large vocabulary of instantly recognized words.

ALPHABETIC WORD LEARNERS AND PHONETIC SPELLERS

Whereas children who use partial alphabetic cues mainly look at beginning and ending letters, children who have full alphabetic knowledge analyze all the letter-sound relationships in words. As a consequence, these readers can identify any word that is spelled the way it sounds. Children enter into the alphabetic stage of word learning toward the end of kindergarten or, more typically, at the beginning of first grade when they begin to understand how consonant and vowel patterns represent sound (Ehri, 2005). The children in your classroom who use both consonant (*br*, *sh*) and vowel (*road*, *boy*) patterns have good phonemic awareness. They can tell you the number of sounds in spoken words and can blend sounds together. They are learning (or have learned) letter-sound patterns and use this knowledge to sound out words that are not already in their reading vocabularies. It is not surprising that these children learn words faster than children with low phonemic awareness and a poor understanding of letter-sound patterns (Stuart, 1995). Because they can read new words on their own, their reading vocabulary increases even when they are out of school on summer vacation, provided that they read over the summer break. These children learn many, many words, and they learn most of them on their own.

Awareness of the single consonant letter-sound pattern emerges early, as we see in Figure 5-2 in the note Roger taped to the gerbil cage in his first-grade classroom. Roger, who is just beginning to make the transition into alphabetic word learning, wrote this note to tell his classmates about the feisty habits of the resident pet, Biscuit. Roger's warning reads: *Biscuit bites. Don't bother Biscuit because he bites.* Roger spells words the way he hears them rather than the way letters are conventionally sequenced. He begins words with single consonants and ends words with consonant letters, too. Roger even includes consonants in the middle of words, as in *Biscuit* (spelled *Bekst*) and *bother* (spelled *brtr*). When we look closely at Roger's note, we can infer that he is beginning to discover the way that vowel

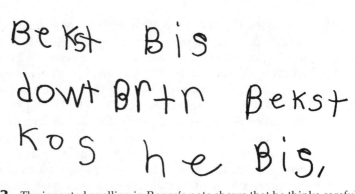

Figure 5-2 The invented spelling in Roger's note shows that he thinks carefully about the relationship between the letters in written words and the sounds in spoken words.

letters represent sound. In fact, it is this emerging use of vowels that tells us that Roger is moving out of the partial alphabetic and into the alphabetic word learning stage.

Although Roger seems to know that vowels are important, he is far from understanding all the vowel letter patterns. This is natural because there are several different vowel patterns and hence many choices for pronunciation. It then stands to reason that children need more time and more reading experience to use vowel letter-sound patterns than the consonant patterns (Zinna, Liberman, & Shankweiler, 1986). Of the 45 phonics rules researchers use to explain letter-sound correspondences, fully two-thirds pertain to vowels (Bailey, 1967; Clymer, 1963; Emans, 1967). Perhaps this explains why children misidentify the sounds represented by vowels far more frequently than the sounds represented by the consonants.

As children move further into alphabetic word learning, they become increasingly adept at learning words on their own and at spelling words in ways that others can read. Logan's story in Figure 5-3 shows that he knows more about letter-sound patterns than Roger. We can infer from Logan's spelling that he understands how many different patterns represent sound, including vowel letter-sound patterns. While Roger is just moving into alphabetic learning, Logan is solidly in this stage (Ehri, 2005). He has enough phonemic awareness and letter-sound knowledge to completely pronounce many new words, his vocabulary is rapidly expanding, he enjoys reading, and he can read easy books by himself without help.

Logan conventionally spells words in his reading vocabulary. And when he spells unconventionally, you and I can read what he writes. When Logan figures out the spelling of new words on his own, he represents all essential sounds in words, even though there may not be a correct match between letters and sounds (*drest* for *dressed,* for example). This type of spelling is called *phonetic spelling* (Gentry, 2006). *Phonetic spelling, invented spelling,* and *temporary spelling* all refer to an early problem-solving stance to spelling in which children write a letter for each sound heard in a word (*lisend* for *listened*).

Logan thinks carefully about the sounds in words and has enough phonemic awareness to associate letters with the sounds he wants to spell, as shown by *drest* for *dressed.* Logan's writing illustrates many characteristics of alphabetic word

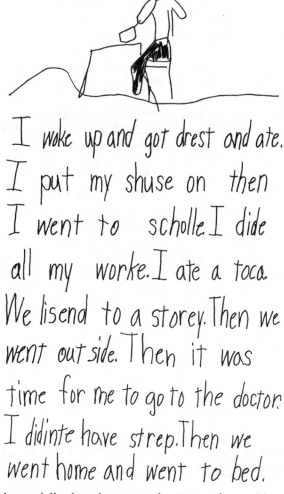

I woke up and got drest and ate.
I put my shuse on then
I went to scholle I dide
all my worke. I ate a toca.
We lisend to a storey. Then we
went outside. Then it was
time for me to go to the doctor.
I didinte have strep. Then we
went home and went to bed.

Figure 5-3   Logan thinks carefully about letter-sound patterns when writing. As he considers which letters represent sound, he sometimes substitutes incorrect letters for correct ones, adds incorrect letters after correct ones, and uses the letter-sounds he hears to represent past tense.

learners and phonetic spellers: Sometimes Logan uses letter names to spell (the *e* in *storey*), substitutes incorrect letters for correct ones (*scholle* for *school*), adds incorrect letters after correct ones (*dide* for *did* and *worke* for *work*), and matches letters with the sounds he hears to represent past tense (*drest* for *dressed*). Also interesting, children like Logan, who are learning how many different patterns represent sound, often use a pattern that could represent the sounds in words but is not the pattern we use in conventional spelling. For instance, Logan used the *VCe* pattern to spell *shoes* (*shuse*). This pattern, in fact, is a very good representation of sound even though it does not represent conventional spelling. Another interesting characteristic of children in this stage is that they sometimes overgeneralize. For example, Logan adds an extra *e* to *did* (*dide*), *school* (*scholle*), and *work* (*worke*). From this, we can assume that he is sensitive to the final *e*, but he is unsure of exactly when to use it in spelling and precisely what its function is in signaling sound.

Children like Logan try to figure out many more words in text than children who are not learning phonics (Connelly et al., 2001). Logan's teacher observes that sometimes he seems to move slowly through text as he focuses on the words. Slow, almost plodding, reading is frequently observed in children like Logan who are just beginning to develop some measure of competence using letter-sound patterns. For Logan and others like him, relatively slow reading is probably a consequence of dedicating a good bit of attention to identifying unfamiliar words, as well as trying to read exactly what the author wrote. As Logan's reading vocabulary grows and his ability to use the letter-sound strategy improves, he will pay less attention to figuring out the words and, consequently, have more attention left over to work out meaning.

Phonetic spelling, or invented spelling, has come under fire because some people fear that children will cling to inventions and, as a consequence, will not learn to spell conventionally. Phonetic spelling is a part of the natural course of learning to read and spell; it is helpful for writers who wish to express their thoughts and have only a small number of words they can spell from memory. In concentrating on the sounds in words, phonetic spellers have opportunities to increase their phonemic awareness. In thinking about how letters represent sound, phonetic spellers also have opportunities to develop greater sensitivity to letter-sound patterns. When children edit their own writing, they correct the unconventional spellings. This gives you, the teacher, opportunities to help children learn to conventionally spell often-used words. As children add words to their reading vocabularies, learn letter-sound patterns, and get practice spelling often-used words, they leave behind the unconventional phonetic spellings in preference for correct spelling.

DECODABLE BOOKS AND YOUR CLASSROOM READING PROGRAM

Books with unusually high numbers of words that sound like they are spelled are called *decodable* books. These books support word identification by using *phonetically regular* words; that is, words that can be pronounced by associating sounds with letters. For example, *pig* and *sweet* are phonetically regular words because readers can use their knowledge of letter-sound patterns to figure out pronunciation. *Have* and *cafe*, on the other hand, are not phonetically regular because readers cannot completely pronounce them by associating sounds with letters. Many decodable books emphasize one or two patterns by clustering together words that have the same letter-sound patterns, such as the long *e* spellings in *street*, *tree*, *bee*, *cream*, *leave*, and *real*.

Decodable books support word identification by directing readers' attention to the letter-sound patterns they are learning in your classroom and by allowing readers to actually use their letter-sound knowledge when reading (Mesmer, 2005).

These books are beneficial for three types of children: (a) partial alphabetic word learners moving into the use of the letter-sound strategy (b) alphabetic word learners who lack fluency using particular letter-sound patterns, and (c) readers who know letter-sound patterns but do not use them. The high number of phonetically regular words not only gives readers practice applying phonics knowledge, but also encourages them to use this knowledge to read new words (Juel & Roper-Schneider, 1985). When practice in reading decodable books is paired with supplemental phonics instruction, struggling first graders improve in word identification, comprehension, and fluency. This might be because they practice using the phonics they are learning while reading connected text (Vadasy, Sanders, & Peyton, 2005).

The amount and type of phonics instruction are likely to affect the contribution decodable books make to improving decoding ability. When a strong supplemental program for at-risk readers includes rich textbooks, a significant amount of reading practice, and a highly structured phonics program, spending more time or less time reading decodable books results in comparable growth in decoding (Jenkins, Peyton, Sanders, & Vadasy, 2004). Therefore, in deciding whether to make decodable books part of your classroom literacy program, consider the amount of structure in the phonics program and whether your students use the letter-sound patterns they are learning. If children do not use these patterns to read and spell, then consider decodable books for extra practice reading words spelled with the patterns children are learning.

The assumption underpinning the use of decodable books is that by reading many decodable words children will become convinced that the letter-sound strategy is worth trying and use this strategy to read new words in text. Thus, it stands to reason that the letter-sound patterns in decodable books should match the letter-sound patterns children are learning in your classroom (Mesmer, 2005). For example, if you are teaching the *VCe* pattern, a book that predominantly has *VC* short vowel words is not a good choice, because this book does not match ongoing instruction. In this example, you would want to find decodable books that feature many *VCe* long vowel words and make these books available to readers.

Decodable books serve a specific purpose at a specific time in children's development as readers. These books should never replace good quality literature in your classroom, and their presence in your classroom should not limit children's choices of the books they read. Decodable books are beneficial when they reinforce the letter-sound patterns children are learning, when they are used selectively, and when they are read by children who are transitioning into the alphabetic stage, lack fluency using letter-sound patterns, or know patterns but do not use them.

ACTIVITIES FOR TEACHING LETTER-SOUND-BASED PHONICS

The following activities help children develop knowledge of letter-sound patterns. You may adapt these activities to focus on the letter-sound patterns children are learning in your classroom, to meet the specific needs of the children whom you teach, and to your own individual teaching style. Some activities are appropriate for large, focused skill groups, others for small groups, still others for pairs or individuals, and still others for learning centers. You will be a successful teacher whether you teach to large groups, small groups, or individuals (Armbruster et al., 2001; National Reading Panel, 2000). What you teach is more important than the number of children whom you teach—large or small groups, or individuals—at one time.

As you use these activities, stop occasionally to ask children to explain how letter patterns represent sound, when to use letter-sound patterns to read new words, and how knowing letter-sounds helps in spelling. As children reflect on the letter-sound patterns in the words they read and spell, children become more metacognitively (consciously) aware of how, when, and why to use the letter-sound strategy, as explained in Chapter 1. As a consequence, children will learn to use this strategy on their own to read and learn new words.

Theses activities develop one or more of the following skills which are applied to different letter-sound patterns:

1. Associate sounds with the letter-sound patterns children are learning.
2. Spell words with the letter-sound patterns children are learning.
3. Read words spelled with the letter-sound patterns children are learning.

Activities

5.1   *Venn Diagrams*

Skill: Associate sounds with the letter-sound patterns children are learning.

Venn diagrams are overlapping circles with shared characteristics in the overlapping portion and unique characteristics inside each separate circle, as illustrated in Figure 5-4. Venn diagrams illustrate how some of the challenging patterns represent more than one sound.

Things You'll Need: Nothing special.

Directions:

1. Draw two overlapping circles and write a letter pattern that represents more than one sound (*ow*, for instance) in the overlapping portion.

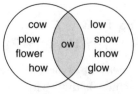

Figure 5-4   Venn diagrams illustrate how some of the more challenging letter-sound patterns represent more than one sound in words.

2. Write a word that represents one pronunciation (*cow*, perhaps) in one circle and a word that represents another pronunciation (*snow*, for example) in the other circle, as illustrated by Figure 5-4.
3. Ask children to think of words in which *ow* represents the sounds heard in *cow* and in *snow*; write those words in the appropriate circles. This gives children opportunities to think of words that fit the pattern and helps them become more sensitive to the two sounds that *ow* typically represents.

5.2   *Interactive Writing*

Skill: Associate sounds with the letter-sound patterns children are learning.

Interactive writing is a shared experience in which a small group decides what they wish to write and the teacher helps them match letters with sounds (McCarrier, Fountas, & Pinnell, 1999). While the focus is on writing meaningful messages, the interaction between the children and the teacher integrates phonics into the fabric of everyday writing, fosters phonemic awareness, and helps children productively use letter-sound knowledge.

Things You'll Need: Chart paper.

Directions:

1. Write sentences or short stories children dictate on large pieces of chart paper. Scaffold or support children by helping them (a) remember the words they dictated and (b) spell new words.
2. In assisting children with spelling, ask them to listen for sounds and connect letters with the sounds they hear in words they dictate. For instance, in writing *play* in the dictated sentence *We like to play ball*, the teacher begins by sound stretching /play/. A child from a small group (or the teacher) writes a letter for each sound heard. Children easily associate a *p* with the /p/ in /play/. When the teacher stretches /play/ a second time, the children associate an *l* with the /l/ sound. The third time the teacher stretches *play*, the children suggest writing an *a* for the /a/ (long a), thus spelling *pla*. The teacher then explains that, "In some words we use *ay* to show the /a/ (long *a*) sound." The teacher or a volunteer now writes the *y* to conventionally spell *play*.

5.3   *Build Words with Whole Letter-Sound Patterns*

Skill: Spell words with the letter-sound patterns children are learning.

Word building has definitely withstood the test of time because it has been around for decades in one form or another (Reed & Klopp, 1957). This activity is appropriate for children working in large, small, and flexible groups and for children in any grade. It also can be used with any letter-sound pattern. In this version of word building, children make words with the intact patterns (*oa, ee, ame, st*) they are learning.

Things You'll Need: As many cards with whole letter-sound patterns as there are children in a small group.

Directions:

1. Give children letter cards with a whole pattern on them. For example, you might distribute cards with the VV long vowel patterns *oa* and *ee*, and the consonants *b, t, f, l, m, d, p,* and *s*.
2. Ask children to arrange and rearrange the single consonants to build *boat, beet, feed, seed, feel, foam, seem, soap, peel, load, toad, seep*.
3. Talk about the patterns. Ask the children to explain how they know that *ee* represents long *e* and *oa* long *o*.

5.4 *Single-Letter Word Building*

Skill: Spell words with the letter-sound patterns children are learning.

In this version of word building, children build words that are spelled with two or more patterns. Use this version of word building with the letter-sound patterns that require a little extra practice before children effectively use them when reading and spelling new words.

Things You'll Need: Cards with letters on them.

Directions:

1. Give children letter cards that combine to make words that are spelled with the patterns children need to practice. For example, you might distribute cards with *r, t, b, s, a, e,* and *m* (see Figure 5-5).
2. Ask the children to use the letters to spell words. For example, you might ask children to build *me* and change it into *meat*, and then build *team, seam, sea, sat, same, tame, tar, star,* and so forth.
3. Have children explain in their own words why they spelled the words as they did and how the patterns represent sound.
4. Also ask children to tell how knowing the letter-sound patterns helps them read new words.

5.5 *Compare-Contrast Word Building*

Skill: Associate sounds with the letter-sound patterns children are learning.

This version of word building can be used to help children learn or better understand how different patterns represent different sounds and how to identify the patterns they use.

Things You'll Need: Word cards (or tiles) with single letters on them.

Figure 5-5 Building words helps children think about the way letters form patterns that represent pronunciation.

Directions:

1. Give the children cards with letters that combine to make words with two or more patterns. Ask children to first build a word with a pattern they already know.
2. Then have children build a new word with a pattern they are learning or need to practice. For example, if children already know the *VC* pattern and are learning the *VCe* pattern, you might give children cards with *t, r, c, n, p, a,* and *e* and ask them to build *cap - cape; can - cane; pan - pane; nap - nape; rat - rate; tap - tape.*
3. Compare and contrast the patterns. In this example you would demonstrate how adding an *e* (*cap + e = cape*) turns a short vowel word into a long vowel word. Table 5–2 is a list of *VC* words that, when the final *e* is added, make *VCe* pattern words (also see Figure 5-6).
4. Ask children to explain why they spelled the words the way they did and how the patterns represent sound. Also ask children to tell how knowing the letter-sound patterns helps them read and spell new words.

5.6 *Letter-Sound Pattern Hunts*

Skill: Associate sounds with the letter-sound patterns you are teaching.

Children look for letter-sound patterns in the familiar words on your classroom word wall, charts, and bulletin boards. This type of word hunting is suitable for large, small, or flexible skill groups of first and second graders.

Things You'll Need: Nothing special.

TABLE 5–2   *VC and Vce Words for Word Building and Other Activities*

VC	VCe	VC	VCe	VC	VCe	VC	VCe
bid	bide	fin	fine	man	mane	shad	shade
bit	bite	gal	gale	mat	mate	sham	shame
can	cane	gap	gape	mop	mope	slat	slate
cap	cape	glad	glade	nap	nape	slid	slide
cod	code	glob	globe	not	note	slim	slime
con	cone	grad	grade	pan	pane	slop	slope
cop	cope	grim	grime	pet	Pete	snip	snipe
crud	crude	grip	gripe	pin	pine	tap	tape
cub	cube	hat	hate	plan	plane	Tim	time
cut	cute	hid	hide	plum	plume	ton	tone
dam	dame	hop	hope	prim	prime	tot	tote
dim	dime	hug	huge	rat	rate	trip	tripe
din	dine	Jan	Jane	rid	ride	tub	tube
dot	dote	kit	kite	rip	ripe	twin	twine
dud	dude	lob	lobe	rob	robe	van	vane
fad	fade	lop	lope	rod	rode	wad	wade
fat	fate	mad	made	Sam	same	win	wine

Directions:

1. Write a few words with the same pattern on the board. Talk about the pattern and then ask readers to find word wall words with this pattern.
2. Then turn children loose to find as many words as they can that are spelled with the target pattern. In addition to hunting in your classroom, children might look for words on posters at your schools in the lunchroom or in the community.
3. Make a list of the words children find. Talk about the letter-sound patterns in words. Ask children why the pattern represents sound in the way that it does.

5.7 Board Search

Skill: Associate sounds with the letter-sound patterns children are learning.

In this activity children think of words with the same sound and then circle different patterns that represent the sound.

Things You'll Need: Colored chalk (or colored dry erase markers if your classroom has a white board).

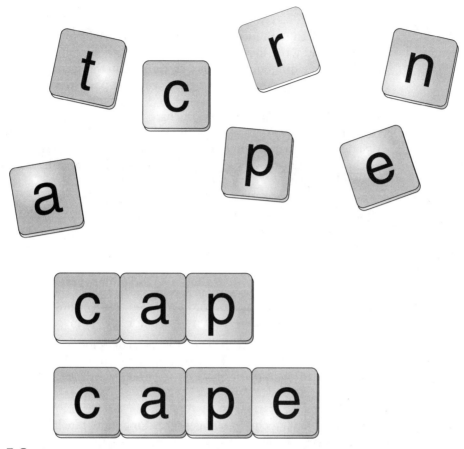

Figure 5-6 Comparing a known pattern with a new pattern helps children understand how to identify different patterns and associate sounds with them.

Skipping Middle Sounds

If you notice that . . .
children associate sounds only with the beginning or ending letter patterns in words, in all likelihood children are overlooking the middle letters.

The thing to do is . . .
focus children's attention to all the patterns in words. Show children how to begin with the pattern at the left and move through the word. Also use activities that call for using middle letter-sounds to build words and solve word puzzles, described in this chapter.

Directions:

1. Ask children to think of words that have a certain sound, such as the long *e*, and write these words on the board.
2. Discuss the different patterns (*see, be, team,* in this example). Draw children's attention to the different ways the pattern is spelled in the words.
3. Give children different colors of chalk, one color for each pattern. Children then take turns drawing lacy clouds around each different letter-sound pattern. In our example, all the *ee VV* (*see*) words might be circled in blue; the *ea VV* (*team*) words, in yellow; and the *CV* (*be*) words, in red.

5.8 Word Banks

Skill: Associate sounds with the letter-sound patterns children are learning.

Word banks are boxes with words children are learning or have already learned. Word banks are a ready resource for spelling words while writing.

Things You'll Need: A recipe-size box for each child; index cards that fit nicely into the boxes; ABC tabs for filing words alphabetically. Put ABC tabs on the top of index cards and use the tabs for filing words in alphabetical order.

Directions:

1. Begin by having children make cards for a moderate list of often-used words.
2. Children write one word on each card and file cards alphabetically in the bank. The benefit of beginning with a common group of words is that you, the teacher, know which basic words readers have at their fingertips.
3. Children then add words to their banks that contain the letter-sound patterns they are learning, words they need for writing, and words they are learning to recognize fluently. The word cards in boxes are excellent references for writing and letter-sound activities.

5.9 People Pattern Words

Skill: Spell words with the letter-sound patterns children are learning.

This is a whole body analog of the word-building activities described earlier. Only here, children wearing letter-sound patterns line up one pattern after another to build words with the letter-sound patterns they are learning, as in Figure 5-7. Use this activity with small, ongoing groups or flexible skill groups.

Figure 5-7   People pattern words. Children line up to build words that are spelled with the letter-sound patterns they are learning, read the words in chorus, and then add the words to their personal word boxes.

Things You'll Need: Large cards with letter-sound patterns on them.

Directions:

1. Distribute one card with one letter-sound pattern to each child. For example, one child might hold a card with *tr*, another a card with *ai*, still another a card with an *n*.
2. Children with letter-sound patterns line up to spell the words you pronounce (see the illustration in Figure 5-7). In this example children spell the word *train*.
3. Talk about the letter-sound patterns in words; read words in chorus.

5.10   *Picking What Works for Me: Letter Pattern Prompts*

Skill: Develop metacognitive awareness of how to use letter-sound patterns to read new words.

Children select prompts to guide them in reading and spelling new words. The prompts are cues or scaffolds for using the letter-sound strategy to read new words. This activity is useful for small, flexible skill groups.

Things You'll Need: One small plastic flower pot (or disposable container) per child or pair of children; popsicle sticks with flowers that prompt the child to look for different patterns (see Figure 5-8). On the side of the pot, in permanent marker, write "Does it make sense?"

Figure 5-8 Selecting prompts helps children reflect on their own use of the letter-sound strategy and become metacognitively (consciously) aware of how to use patterns to read new words.

Directions:

1. Give each child or pair of children a pot with flowers that serve as prompts or reminders for letter patterns they have already learned or are currently learning.

2. Demonstrate how to use flower prompts to guide decoding. Write a word on the board and then read all the flower prompts. Compare the prompts

with the letter patterns in the word. Select an appropriate prompt, take it out of the pot, and show children how to use it to guide decoding.

3. Model cross-checking by drawing children's attention to "Does it make sense?" on the side of the pot.
4. Leave flower pot prompts in an accessible place for general use or in a learning center for targeted practice. Encourage children to use the flower prompts on their own to help them look for patterns in new words.
5. Add or change flower prompts as appropriate for children's needs. Do this by removing prompts for patterns children already know and use; adding prompts for patterns the children are learning.

Examples of prompts:

- Do I see a part I know?
- What is the beginning sound?
- Do I see a silent *e*?
- Are two vowels together?
- Is there an ou or *ow*?
- Is there an oy or *oi*?
- Do I see *oo*?
- Do I see a vowel before an *r*?

5.11 *Compare-Contrast Charts*

Skill: Associate sounds with the letter-sound patterns children are learning.

Children working in small groups make large charts that show how several patterns represent the same sounds. Understanding how different patterns represent the same sounds, in turn, gives children valuable insight into word recognition and spelling.

Things You'll Need: As many large sheets of paper as there are pairs or small groups; colored markers.

Directions:

1. Begin by pronouncing a sound—the long *o* sound, for instance. Ask children to suggest words with this sound. Make a list of these words on the board. Call children's attention to the different letter-sound patterns that represent the long *o*.
2. Distribute chart paper and have children divide the paper into as many sections as there are different spelling patterns for the same sound. In our example, children would divide the chart into four sections, each for a different long *o* pattern.
3. In each section, children write words with one of the letter-sound patterns and draw a picture of one of the words (see Figure 5-9).

Figure 5-9 In making charts, children compare and contrast different letter-sound patterns that represent the same sounds in words.

5.12 *Letter-Sound Sort*

Skill: Associate sounds with the letter-sound patterns you are teaching.

Children working with a learning partner, individually, or in learning centers sort words into paper lunch sacks according to the sounds letter patterns represent.

Things You'll Need: As many sets of word cards as there are pairs or individual children; small paper sacks with a letter-sound pattern on them, as shown in Figure 5-10.

Directions:

1. Give children several small paper sacks and a group of word cards or leave the sacks and cards in a learning center. Children sort by putting words that have the same letter-sound pattern in the sack with that letter pattern on the front. For example, children might sort for long and short vowel patterns or digraphs and diphthongs.
2. When finished sorting, children empty each sack, cross-check with a partner to make sure that all the words inside are sorted correctly, and then write each word on the sack in which it belongs. This gives you a

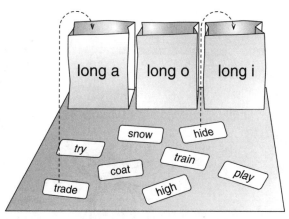

Figure 5-10   Sorting helps readers become sensitive to the letter-sound patterns that occur in many different words.

record of how children sorted and, additionally, gives children practice writing words that include the letter-sound patterns they are learning.

5.13   *Fly-Away Words*

Skill: Read words spelled with the letter-sound patterns children are learning.

Children read words on make-believe flies, bees, or mosquitoes and, as quickly as possible, read words and smack the insects with a swatter. Books like *The Giant Jam Sandwich* (Lord, 1972) and *Why Mosquitoes Buzz in People's Ears* (Aardema, 1975) are examples of stories that feature insects. The activity is appropriate for small groups.

Things You'll Need: Two fly swatters; tape; construction paper cut into flies, bees, or mosquitoes with words on them, as illustrated in Figure 5-11. Or you could use index cards and pretend they are flying away.

Directions:

1. Tape the fly-away words to the board, spacing them fairly far apart, as shown in Figure 5-11.
2. Divide players into two teams. Call one player from each team up to the board; give each a swatter. Say a word that is spelled with one of the letter-sound patterns children are learning in your classroom.
3. Each player finds and swats the word as fast as possible. Once the word is swatted, the player reads the word and explains or points to the letter-sound pattern you designate.
4. If the player is correct, the swatted word is taken off the board—it "flies away"—and the team gets a point. The team with the most fly-away words wins.
5. At the end of the game, hold up fly-away words and ask children to read them in chorus.

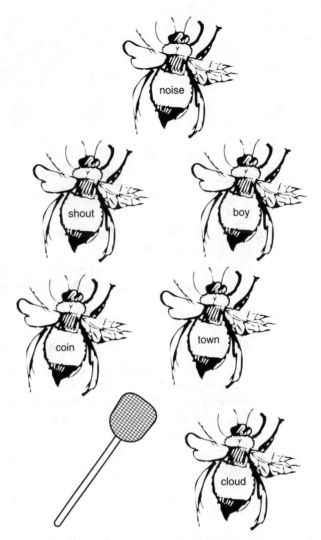

Figure 5-11   An example of fly-away words. In swatting words the teacher pronounces, children get practice rapidly reading words that contain the letter-sound patterns they are learning.

5.14 *Puzzles*

Skill: Read words spelled with the letter-sound patterns children are learning.

Children working with a partner, individually, or in a learning center solve puzzles with a clue word (like *steam*) and a set of instructions (– *ea* + *or* =) that transform the clue into a solution word (*storm*), as shown in Figure 5-12.

coin	–	oi	+	or	=	_____	steam	–	ea	+	or	=	_____
sheet	–	ee	+	ir	=	_____	house	–	ou	+	or	=	_____
coat	–	oa	+	ar	=	_____	dealing	–	ea	+	ar	=	_____

Figure 5-12   As children solve puzzles, they think analytically about the sounds that the letters in patterns represent in words.

Things You'll Need: Colored chalk; puzzles with the letter-sound patterns children are learning in your classroom.

Directions:

1. Demonstrate how to solve word puzzles. Do this by writing a puzzle on the board with a letter-sound pattern children are learning in your classroom. Use colored chalk to highlight the transformations children are to perform. For example, you might write *steam − ea + or =* _____. Show children that in subtracting the *ea* (*VV*) long vowel pattern and in adding the *or* (*Vr*) pattern in its place, children transform *steam* into *storm*.
2. Remind the children to cross-check to verify solutions by sharing them with a classmate. The examples in Figure 5-12 ask children to solve word puzzles with the *Vr* letter-sound pattern.
3. Children may also create their own puzzles and share them with other children.

5.15 *Mailbox Sort*

Skill: Associate sounds with the letter-sound patterns children are learning.

In this learning center activity, children sort words according to letter-sound patterns and then mail the words by slipping them into shoeboxes that look like mailboxes. This sort is appropriate for first graders at the beginning of the year or kindergartners who are learning words with a single pattern, such as the VC pattern in c<u>at</u> and c<u>ot</u>.

Things You'll Need: Two or more shoeboxes with tightly fitting lids for mailboxes; mock postcards with words that are spelled with the letter-sound patterns children are learning in your classroom; a few postcards with an extra line under the word for writing the name of a child in the class to whom the postcard might be sent. Cut a slit in the lid of the shoeboxes; cover each lid with construction paper or shelf paper. Above each slit, glue a picture of a word to represent a certain sound, such as a *boat* to represent a long *o* sound, or write a description of the letter-sound patterns children are learning, such as long vowel and short vowel, as shown in Figure 5-13.

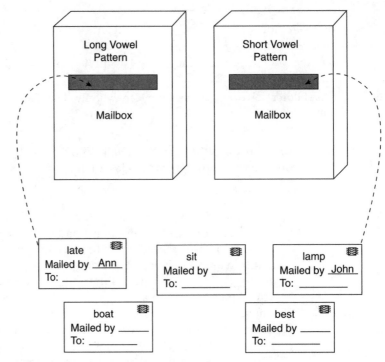

Figure 5-13   In this learning center activity, children sort "postcards" according to the letter-sound patterns in spelling and mail the postcards by slipping them into shoebox mailboxes.

Directions:

1. Place mailboxes and postcards in a center. Children sort the postcard words according to their letter-sound patterns by slipping each postcard word through the proper shoebox slot.
2. Tell children to be on the lookout for postcards with a line under the word. Children write the name of a classmate to whom they would like to send a special word.
3. Discuss the words children receive; talk about the letter-sound pattern.

5.16 *Letter-Sound Bingo*

Skill: Read words spelled with the letter-sound patterns children are learning.

An oldie but goodie for children of any age, bingo is a favorite activity that can be used with any letter-sound pattern children are learning. This version of bingo gives children practice reading words with the letter-sound patterns they are learning in your classroom.

Things You'll Need: Bingo cards; pencils. Make a model and duplicate it. Write words in squares, or write a word list on the board and ask children to select

same	bed	coat	seed	play
ham	cute	boat	time	slim
got	they	Free	mine	why
bead	slip	train	cut	bat
cap	tree	ship	Sam	cat

Figure 5-14   Bingo gives children practice reading words that are spelled with the letter-sound patterns they are learning.

words from the list and write them in squares. The words in Figure 5-14 feature the short vowel pattern and the long vowel patterns (*VV* and *VCe*).

Directions:

1. Pass out bingo cards. Say a word and ask children to listen for the sound that a pattern represents. Children then locate the word and cover it with a token.
2. Traditional rules hold: A child with any five consecutively covered squares lined up diagonally, horizontally, or vertically wins. Four corners or postage stamps (four squares in any corner) are fun to play, too. Coveralls are always challenging, but they take more time, so save them for days when there is plenty of flexibility in the schedule.

5.17 *Scrapbooks*

Skill: Associate sounds with the letter-sound patterns you are teaching.

Children working in a learning center make scrapbooks of words that are spelled with the letter-sound patterns they are learning. Scrapbooks are not only a record of the words and patterns children are learning, but also a resource for writing and phonics activities.

Things You'll Need: Magazines; markers; large pieces of light-colored construction paper with a letter-sound pattern or a word with an underlined pattern at the top; glue; a stapler.

Directions:

1. Place construction paper pages with a letter-sound pattern (*th*) or a word with an underlined pattern at the top (*thump*), scissors, glue, magazines, and other consumable print in a learning center.
2. Children look for words in magazines and other print that have a specific letter-sound pattern, cut the words out, and glue them onto a large page that has the targeted letter pattern written at the top.
3. As children learn new letter-sound patterns, have them make a scrapbook page for each one.
4. Staple pages together to make a large scrapbook. Use the words in scrapbooks when reviewing the letter-sound patterns and as resources for letter-sound activities.

5.18   *Wheels*

Skill: Read words spelled with the letter-sound patterns children are learning.

Wheels consist of two circles, each with one or more letter-sound patterns. To make and read words, children align the letters on the outer wheel with letters on the inner wheel. The key to success in using wheels is to create ways to ensure that children actually read the words on the wheels. Do this by having children work together in pairs, as explained in the directions.

Things You'll Need: Two oak tag circles, one larger than the other; a brad; a marker. Make one circle about 9 inches in diameter, the other about 6 inches. On the outermost portion of the large circle, write letter-sound patterns that come at the beginning of words. On the outermost portion of the small circle, write vowel patterns that come at the end of words. Poke a hole in the center of each and fasten them together with a brad.

Directions:

1. Children turn the circles to align letter patterns (see Figure 5-15).
2. Children then read the word to a partner who cross-checks to make sure that the combination forms real words. Have one of the children write down the real words they make.

5.19   *Phonics Cloze*

Skill: Read words by using letter-sound patterns and context clues.

A typical cloze sentence has a word deleted and replaced with a blank (*The ball rolled into the _____*). Only part of a word is deleted in phonics cloze sentences (*The ball rolled into the str_____t*). Children use sentence

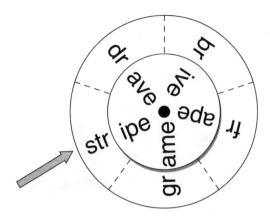

Figure 5-15 Children think about the sounds the letters in patterns represent and then turn wheels to form real words.

structure, meaning, and letter-sound cues to figure out the identity of the partially missing words and to write in the missing letters.

Things You'll Need: Modified cloze sentences. To make modified cloze sentences, delete portions of words so as to focus readers' attention on certain letter-sound patterns.

Directions:

1. Children read the sentences; consider sentence structure, meaning, and letter-sound patterns; and then write the missing letter patterns in the blanks.
2. For example, modified cloze sentences for practice using syntactic, semantic, and the *oy* and *oi* diphthong patterns would look like this:
   John got a t_____ car for his birthday. (toy)
   Nancy planted the seeds deep down in the wet s_____l. (soil)
   Glenda wanted to j_____n the club. (join)
   The b_____s like to play marbles during recess. (boys)

5.20 *Clothesline*

Skill: Associate sounds with the letter-sound patterns you are teaching.

Children working in small groups create a clothesline of words that share the same letter-sound pattern.

Things You'll Need: A rope for a clothesline; an assortment of clothespins; word cards (or construction paper in the shape of clothes with words written on each clothing article); blank cards (or pieces of construction paper in the shape of clothes); markers.

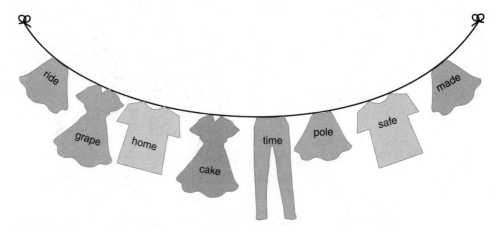

Figure 5-16　Pinning words that are spelled with the same letter-sound pattern to a clothesline gives readers opportunities to analyze the letter-sound patterns inside words and to draw conclusions about how the letter-sound patterns represent sound.

Directions:

1. String a clothesline (rope) across a corner of the room and give each child several cards (or pieces of construction paper cut in the shape of clothes).
2. After discussing the letter-sound pattern with the group, children read the words and then pin the cards to the clothesline, like the "clothes" in Figure 5-16. Children also may add their own words to the clothesline by writing words on blank cards. When finished, everyone reads the words in chorus.

5.21 *Small Group Chalkboard Sort*

Skill: Associate sounds with the letter-sound patterns you are teaching.

In this activity, children in a small group work together to sort words on cards according to the letter-sound patterns they are learning and then tape words to a chalkboard or white board, thereby making long chalkboard lists. This type of group sorting is especially useful to help children recognize letter-sound patterns that are easily confused, such as the *VC* and *VCe* patterns in m*ad* and m*ade*, or the *VC* and r-controlled patterns in *bun* and *burn*.

Things You'll Need: Word cards with masking tape loops on the back.

Directions:

1. Write several letter-sound patterns on the board, such as the long *a* in st*ay* (*VV*), *time* (*VCe*), and in *train* (*VV*).
2. Give children word cards with masking tape loops on the back. Children sort the words by putting them under the words on the board (*stay, time,* and *train,* in this example) that share the same letter-sound pattern.

3. When finished, read the words in chorus, point out the patterns, and ask children to explain why they pronounce each word as they do. If, on reading the lists, children find a few mistakes, simply move the words to the proper columns.

5.22 *Movies*

Skill: Spell words with the letter-sound patterns children are learning.

Children working in small groups use their prior knowledge, understanding of story structure, and knowledge of words spelled with important letter-sound patterns to produce "homemade" movies.

Things You'll Need: A cardboard box; two dowels; a knife; tape; butcher paper. Cut butcher paper into strips, one strip for each group. Partition each long piece of butcher paper into movie frames by drawing horizontal lines at equal distances. Make two extra frames, one at the beginning and one at the end of the movie. These extra frames are later wound around and fastened to dowels, as described next.

To make a movie projector, cut a rectangle in the bottom of a cardboard box to serve as a viewing screen. Cut two sets of holes on either side of the box. Cut one set toward the top of the box (one above the "screen"), the other toward the bottom (one below the "screen"). Make the holes large enough for a dowel to fit through. Slide each dowel through one set of holes. Now, working through the back of the box, tape the movie (which is written on the butcher paper) to the dowels. Wind the entire movie around one dowel; wind only the lead (the blank butcher paper that precedes the movie frames) around the other dowel. Turn the dowels to simulate a movie as the paper film moves from one dowel to another, as illustrated in Figure 5-17. Adjust the tension by turning either the top or bottom dowel. Advise children to

Figure 5-17 Children produce homemade movies and, in the process, get experience writing and reading words with the letter-sound patterns they are learning.

make the pictures and text a little smaller than the actual frame. This way, there is some leeway in case the frames drawn on butcher paper are not positioned quite right on the movie screen.

Directions:

1. Pairs or groups of three or four children write and edit a short story.
2. Working from their edited stories, children write one episode in each frame, draw an appropriate picture, and underline words with the special letter-sound patterns they are learning.
3. Fasten the butcher paper to dowels and insert it in the homemade projector. As the dowels are turned, different frames appear on the screen and children read their stories frame by frame.
4. Have children talk about the movies, the story structure, and some of the words with the letter-sound patterns they are learning.
5. Reread the movies for fluency. Have children read in chorus; share the movies with other classrooms.

5.23 *Vowel Pattern Sort*

Skill: Associate sounds with (vowel) letter-sound patterns you are teaching.

This small group activity is beneficial for any age reader who needs more practice identifying, and comparing and contrasting, long, short, and r-controlled vowel patterns.

Things You'll Need: A grid with spaces for long, short, and r-controlled vowel pattern words, as shown in Figure 5-18; pencils; cards with a variety of words with long, short, and r-controlled vowel patterns.

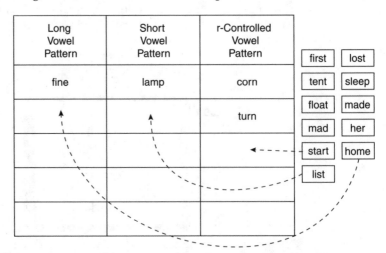

Figure 5-18 Sorting words by their vowel letter-sound pattern gives children opportunities to compare and contrast the sounds the letters in patterns represent.

Directions:

1. Ask children to work with a partner. Give each set of partners a piece of paper with a grid that has different letter-sound patterns and a stack of word cards.
2. Partners sort the words according to the vowel letter patterns—long vowel, short vowel, or r-controlled—and then fill out the grid by writing each word in the appropriate square.
3. Use the completed sort to compare and contrast the different vowel patterns and how they represent sound. Ask children to find or think of other examples of familiar words that include the vowel patterns. Make this activity easier by asking children to sort for only two letter-sound patterns.

5.24 *Baggie Books*

Skill: Spell with the letter-sound patterns children are learning.

Children use their knowledge of letter-sound patterns when writing stories, which are then edited and slipped inside plastic bags to make durable books. The Baggie Books activity is appropriate for first graders.

Things You'll Need: Gallon-size plastic bags that lock at the top; a hole punch; ribbon; paper and pencils; colored highlighters.

Directions:

1. Children write and edit stories on paper.
2. Put two pages of the story back to back. Slip them into a gallon-size plastic bag and seal the bag. When all the pages are inside bags, use a paper punch to make three holes on the far left of the bags, as shown in Figure 5-19.
3. Thread colorful ribbon through holes and tie the ribbon in a bow. This fastens the pages of the book together and adds a cheerful splash of color, too.
4. Share bag books with the class, and, when you do this, talk about story sequence, meaning, and the letter-sound patterns in words.

5.25 *Interactive Bulletin Boards*

Skill: Associate sounds with the letter-sound patterns children are learning.

Children in a small group sort words according to shared letter-sound patterns and then put the words on a bulletin board.

Things You'll Need: Construction paper; markers; word cards. Before introducing this activity, think of everyday objects (nouns are best) that are spelled with the letter-sound patterns children are learning. Cut construction paper

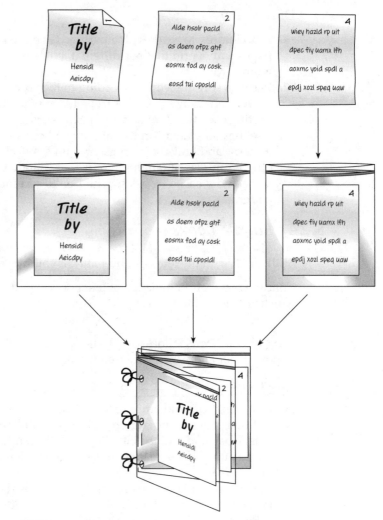

Figure 5-19 Writing stories that are then made into bag books gives children opportunities to use their knowledge of letter-sound patterns when writing.

into the shapes of the objects. For instance, if you are going to focus on consonant clusters and digraphs, you might make a *shoe* for *sh*, a *cloud* for *cl*, and a *truck* for *tr*. Make a word card for each cutout—*shoe, cloud,* and *truck*. Fasten the construction paper cutouts and accompanying words to the bulletin board.

Directions:

1. Read the words on the bulletin board, drawing attention to the letter-sound patterns children are learning.

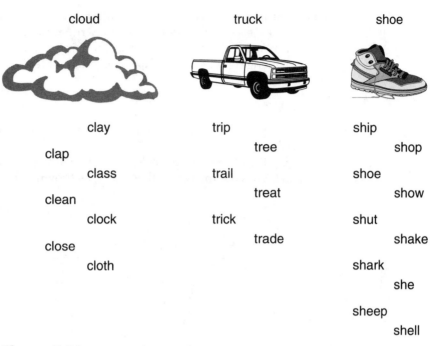

cloud   truck   shoe

        clay   trip   ship

clap   tree   shop

        class   trail   shoe

clean   treat   show

        clock   trick   shut

close   trade   shake

        cloth   shark

                                    she

                            sheep

                                shell

Figure 5-20   An interactive bulletin board. Children make colorful bulletin boards by sorting words according to their letter-sound patterns.

2. Give children word cards. You may wish to give children some cards with words that have the letter patterns on the bulletin board and some cards with words that do not include the targeted letter-sound patterns. If a word has the same letter-sound pattern as one of the bulletin board words (*shoe, cloud,* or *truck* in this example) children add it to the bulletin board, as illustrated in Figure 5-20.

3. You may wish to leave a few blank cards for children to add their own words and words they find on the word wall, on charts, and in the books they are reading in your classroom.

5.26 *Blocks*

Skill: Spell words with the letter-sound patterns children are learning.

Children working in small groups or in learning centers use blocks with letter patterns on them to build words.

Things You'll Need: Blocks with a letter-sound pattern on each side; markers. Purchase blocks at a craft store or make your own out of square tissue boxes covered with shelf paper. Each block has six sides, so you will want to think of three letter-sound patterns for each block and write each pattern twice per block. For instance, to build words with the *VV* pattern, children would use three blocks, each with the same pattern written twice: one block might have *tr, gr,* and *th;* the second, *ai, ee,* and *oa;* the third, *t, n,* and *p.* Block-building is more challenging when blocks have six different letter patterns, one pattern on each of the six sides.

Directions:

1. Place blocks in a learning center or distribute them to children in a small group.
2. Using the blocks you provide, children build as many words as possible and then write the words they build, as shown in Figure 5-21.

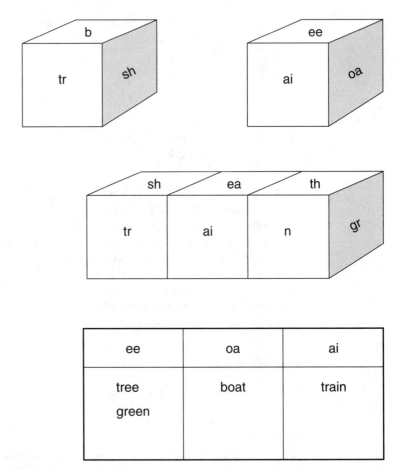

Figure 5-21   An example of block words. Children apply their knowledge of letter-sound patterns when building words with blocks that have letter-sound patterns on them and then writing the words they build.

5.27 *Catch-a-Word*

Skill: Read words spelled with letter patterns the children are learning.

Things You'll Need: Overhead projector; acetate for writing words with patterns the children are learning; gardening gloves.

Directions:

1. Turn the lights down. Have children take turns wearing the garden gloves.
2. Move the overhead fairly close to a white board or blank wall.
3. Write a word on the acetate. The child wearing the gloves "catches" the word by putting the glove in front of the projected word. The child then reads the word he or she caught and passes the glove to another child.

SPARE-MINUTE ACTIVITIES FOR TEACHING LETTER-SOUND PHONICS

5.28 *Silent Letter Cross-Out*

Skills: Recognize silent letters; read words with these letters.

Write several words with silent consonants on the chalkboard. Ask a child to pronounce one of the words and then to come to the chalkboard and draw a line through the "silent" consonant. For example, the second *b* in *rabbit* and the second *t* in *mitten* would be crossed off. You also might want to have individual children cross out silent letters on duplicate copies of grade-appropriate text.

5.29 *How Many Words Can You Make?*

Skill: Spell words with the letter-sound patterns children are learning.

Ask children to use the letters in a long word to spell as many short words as they can.

5.30 *Letter-Sound Pattern Dictation*

Skill: Write and read words spelled with the letter patterns children are learning.

Slowly spell a word letter-sound by letter-sound pattern. Children write each pattern and, when finished, read the word aloud. For example, you might spell "fl" as children write *fl*; "ow" as children write *ow*; "er" as children write *er*. Children then read the word—*flower*. Letter-sound dictation helps children focus on the patterns that form words and helps children use their letter pattern knowledge to read words.

5.31   *Color Vowel Patterns in Words*

Skill: Associate sounds with the (vowel) letter-sound patterns children are learning.

Give children two colors of crayons or markers, say green and red, and a short word list. Children mark long vowel patterns in red and short patterns in green. Read the words together in chorus; talk about the patterns children found.

5.32   *Change-a-Letter*

Skill: Spell words with the letter-sound patterns children are learning.

Write a word on the chalkboard, such as *team*. Children take turns changing one letter to make a new word, such as changing *pine* into *pin*, *pin* into *pen*, *pen* into *ten*, *ten* into *men*, *men* into *mean*, *mean* into *man*, *man* into *main*.

5.33   *Finger-Cued Vowel Sounds*

Skill: Associate sounds with the (vowel) letter-sound patterns children are learning.

If some of the children you teach have trouble remembering the sound of short and long vowels (short *a* says /a/, as in *apple;* long *a* says /ā/, as in *apron*), give them cues to make decoding smoother. Hold up two fingers to remind the children of how long vowels sound and one finger to remind children of how short vowels sound.

MOVING TOWARD USING THE MULTILETTER CHUNKS IN WORD STRUCTURE TO READ AND SPELL LONG WORDS

The letter-sound strategy takes advantage of the basic principle of alphabetic writing—the idea that letters represent sounds. Children who are skilled at using the letter-sound strategy have good phonemic awareness, know many different letter-sound patterns, and can read any new word that is spelled like it sounds. In addition, the letter-sound strategy paves the way for developing sensitivity to the large multiletter groups, or chunks, in the structure of long words, such as the *-ment* in *excitement*. The use of large multiletter chunks to identify words typically matures only after children have had lots of experience using letter-sound patterns to read and spell words. Not only does the use of large multiletter chunks make word identification quicker, but knowing the meaning of one or more of the large chunks in a word often gives readers insight into that word's definition, as you will learn in Chapter 6.

REFERENCES

Aardema, V. (1975). *Why mosquitoes buzz in people's ears.* New York: Dial Books for Young Readers.

Aaron, P. G., Joshi, R. M., Ayotollah, M., Ellsberry, A., Henderson, J., & Lindsey, K. (1999). Decoding and sight-word naming: Are they independent components of word recognition skill? *Reading and Writing: An Interdisciplinary Journal, 11,* 89–127.

Armbruster, B. B., Lehr, F., & Osborn, J. (2001). *Put reading first: The research building blocks for teaching children to read.* Washington, DC: National Institute for Literacy.

Bailey, M. H. (1967). The utility of phonic generalizations in grades one through six. *The Reading Teacher, 20,* 413–418.

Blachman, B. A., Schatschneider, C., Fletcher, J. M., Francis, D. J., Clonan, S. M., Shaywitz, B. A., & Shaywitz, S. E. (2004). Effects of intensive reading remediation for second and third graders and a 1-year follow-up study. *Journal of Educational Psychology, 96,* 444–461.

Christensen, C. A., & Bowey, J. A. (2005). The efficacy of orthographic rime, grapheme-phoneme correspondences, and implicit phonics approaches to teaching decoding skills. *Scientific Studies of Reading, 9,* 327–340.

Clymer, T. (1963). The utility of phonic generalizations in the primary grades. *The Reading Teacher, 16,* 252–258.

Connelly, V., Johnston, R., & Thompson, G. B. (2001). The effect of phonics instruction on the reading comprehension of beginning readers. *Reading and Writing: An Interdisciplinary Journal, 14,* 423–457.

Ehri, L. C. (2005). Learning to read words: Theory, findings, and issues. *Scientific Studies of Reading, 9,* 167–188.

Ehri, L. C. (2006). More about phonics: Findings and reflections. In K. A. D. Stahl & M. C. McKenna (Eds.), *Reading research at work: Foundations of effective practice* (pp. 155–165). New York: Guilford Press.

Emans, R. (1967). The usefulness of phonic generalizations above the primary grades. *The Reading Teacher, 20,* 419–425.

Foorman, B. R., Francis. D. J., Fletcher, J. M., Schatschneider, C., & Mehta, P. (1998). The role of instruction in learning to read: Preventing reading failure in at-risk children. *Journal of Educational Psychology, 90,* 37–55.

Foorman, B. R., Schatschneider, C., Eakin, M. N., Fletcher, J. M., Moates, L. C., & Francis, D. J. (2006). The impact of instructional practices in grades 1 and 2 on reading and spelling achievement in high poverty schools. *Contemporary Educational Psychology, 31,* 1–29.

Gentry, J. R. (2006). *The new science of beginning reading and writing.* Portsmouth, NH: Heinemann.

Jenkins, J. R., Peyton, J. A., Sanders, E. A., & Vadasy, P. F. (2004). Effects of reading decodable texts in supplemental first-grade tutoring. *Scientific Studies of Reading, 8,* 53–85.

Johnston, R. S., & Watson, J. (2004). Accelerating the development of reading, spelling, and phoneme awareness skills in initial readers. *Reading and Writing: An Interdisciplinary Journal, 17,* 327–357.

Juel, C. (1983). The development and use of mediated word identification. *Reading Research Quarterly, 18,* 306–327.

Juel, C., & Roper-Schneider, D. (1985). The influence of basal readers on first grade reading. *Reading Research Quarterly, 20,* 134–152.

Lord, J. V. (1972). *The giant jam sandwich.* Boston: Houghton Mifflin.

McCarrier, A., Fountas, I. C., & Pinnell, G. S. (1999). *Interactive writing: How language and literacy come together, K-2.* Portsmouth, NH: Heinemann.

Mesmer, H. A. E. (2005). Text decodability and the first-grade reader. *Reading & Writing Quarterly, 21,* 61–86.

National Reading Panel. (2000). *Teaching children to read: An evidence-based assessment of the scientific research literature on reading and its implications for reading instruction: Reports of the subgroups* (NIH Publication No. 00-4754). Washington, DC: U.S. Government Printing Office.

Reed, L. C., & Klopp, D. S. (1957). *Phonics for thought.* New York: Comet Press Books.

Rupley, W. H., & Wilson, V. L. (1997). Relationship between comprehension and components of word recognition: Support for developmental shifts. *Journal of Research and Development in Education, 30,* 255–260.

Schwanenflugel, P. J., Hamilton, A. M., Kuhn, M. R., Wisenbaker, J. M., & Stahl, S. A. (2004). Becoming a fluent reader: Reading skill and prosodic features in the oral reading of young readers. *Journal of Educational Psychology, 96,* 119–129.

Shanahan, T. (2005). *The national reading panel report: Practical advice for teachers.* Naperville, IL: Learning Point Associates.

Shankweiler, D., & Fowler, A. E. (2004). Questions people ask about the role of phonological processes in learning to read. *Reading and Writing: An Interdisciplinary Journal, 17,* 483–515.

Snow, C. E., Burns, M. S., & Griffin, P. (Eds.) (1998). *Preventing Reading Difficulties in Young Children.* Washington, DC: National Academy Press.

Stuart, M. (1995). Through printed words to meaning: Issues of transparency. *Journal of Research in Reading, 18,* 126–131.

Tunmer, W. E., & Chapman, J. E. (2002). The relation of beginning readers' reported word identification strategies to reading achievement, reading-related skills, and academic self-perceptions. *Reading and Writing: An Interdisciplinary Journal, 15,* 341–358.

Vadasy, P. F., Sanders, E. A., & Peyton, J. A. (2005). Relative effectiveness of reading practice or word level instruction in supplemental tutoring: How text matters. *Journal of Learning Disabilities, 38,* 364–380.

Zinna, D. R., Liberman, I. Y., & Shankweiler, D. (1986). Children's sensitivity to factors influencing vowel reading. *Reading Research Quarterly, 21,* 465–479.

CHAPTER 6

Structural Analysis

Using the Chunking Strategy to Read and Learn Long Words

This chapter describes how readers use the multiletter groups in word structure to read long and complex new words. You will learn about multiletter groups that indicate meaning and sound, and about syllables that indicate pronunciation. In reading this chapter you will learn the best practices for teaching prefixes, suffixes, and syllables. You will also learn ways to support readers as they use the multiletter chunk strategy and activities for teaching the multiletter chunks in word structure.

KEY IDEAS

- ▶ Chunks consist of large, intact letter groups that readers automatically recognize and pronounce in words.

- ▶ Many multiletter groups indicate meaning—for example, the prefix *un-* in *unhappy*, the suffix *-ly* in *friendly*, and the root word *sign* in *signal* and *signature*.

- ▶ Syllables indicate pronunciation, such as the syllables *dis, trib,* and *ute* in *distribute*.

- ▶ The strategy of analyzing long words to find useful multiletter chunks is more efficient than other word identification strategies.

- ▶ The structural analysis strategy, using large multiletter chunks in word structure, is the last word identification strategy to develop before readers reach the stage where they automatically recognize all the words they see in text.

KEY VOCABULARY

Accented Syllables

Affix

Automatic readers

Base word

Compound word

Consolidated word learners

Contraction

Derivational suffix

Greek and Latin roots

Inflectional suffix

Prefix

Structural Analysis

Suffix

Syllable

Transitional speller

Unaccented syllables

At a mere glance, you know how to pronounce *astroport* as used in Figure 6-1 and you know it is a noun. You recognize that it is most likely an interstellar station for the space traveling public and, if asked, could use *astroport* in a sentence. All this is quite interesting since *astroport* is not a real word—at least, not yet.

The way to unlock this word's pronunciation and get insight into its meaning is to divide *astroport* into the two large, meaningful multiletter chunks: *astro* and *port*. Each multiletter chunk is spelled the way it sounds and contributes to the word's definition, provided you know that *astro* means *star* and *port* means *to carry*. With this knowledge, you might logically infer that an *astroport* is a site to which space travelers are transported, just as an *airport* is a site to which airline passengers are transported.

After reading and writing the same letter sequences time and time again, readers perceive these groups as large, intact units (Stuart & Coltheart, 1988). In so doing, readers chunk, or join together, groups of letters in their minds. Multiletter chunks significantly reduce the energy readers put into word identification and, when readers know the meaning of letter groups, they have some insight into the definition of words as well. Readers who use multiletter chunks do not recall analogous onsets and rimes in known words to identify unknown words as do users of analogy-based phonics, nor do they sound out and blend letter-sound patterns as do users of letter-sound-based phonics. Instead, readers recognize and pronounce all at once entire groups of letters in words (*complete = com + plete; unworkable = un + work + able*).

astroport

Figure 6-1   Meaningful chunks give insight into pronunciation and word meaning. The student who drew this picture used knowledge of *astro* and *port* to show what they might mean if put together.

When you, the teacher, help readers use multiletter groups to read new words, you are teaching *structural analysis*[1]. Rather than focus on the sound level, which is the scope of phonics-based instruction, structural analysis focuses on teaching the large structural units that make up words. When you demonstrate how the meaning of *effort* changes when you add *-less* to make *effortless,* you are teaching structural analysis. You also teach structural analysis when you help readers understand how *isn't* consists of *is* and *not.* And when you help a fifth grader use a hyphen to divide the word *government* into syllables so as to write part of the word on one line (*govern-*) and part on another (*ment*), you are teaching structural analysis.

ROOTS OF THE MULTILETTER CHUNK STRATEGY

The strategy of analyzing word structure to find multiletter chunks is rooted in both the analogy and the letter-sound strategies. In fact, there is reason to believe

---

[1] Analysis of meaningful units in words is part of morphology, a specialized study in linguistics that concentrates on word forms and their connections to meaning. Prefixes, suffixes, contractions, compound words, base words, and root words are more accurately described as morphemic analysis because each deals with meaning. Syllables, accents, and other pronunciation units, such as rimes, represent sound and therefore are associated with phonic analysis. Combining meaningful and nonmeaningful chunks under the umbrella of structural analysis makes sense for the purpose of teaching inasmuch as readers recognize these letter groups as single, intact units.

that the origin of multiletter chunks in readers' minds comes from using rimes and letter-sound patterns to identify words (Ehri, 2005). Readers who use the analogy strategy learn to capitalize on large, predictable letter groups in spelling. This helps them develop a predisposition to look for and to use rime groups (the *ig* in *pig*). The use of analogous rimes presents early opportunities for readers to use multiletter chunks and constitutes a step toward the more sophisticated chunk strategy.

Readers using the letter-sound strategy think analytically about letter-sound patterns in words. In so doing, they have opportunities to form hypotheses about recurring letter sequences in word structure. As a consequence of reading and writing the same letter sequences, readers eventually fuse letters together to recognize common chunks (Stuart & Coltheart, 1988). Children refine their knowledge of multiletter chunks through further reading and writing experiences. As reading maturity increases, so too does the ability to take advantage of multiletter chunks (Santa, 1976–1977). The multiletter chunk strategy develops to coexist with the analogy and letter-sound strategies. As readers become sensitive to more and more multiletter chunks in word structure, they become much better at word learning (Ehri, 2005).

Seven Multiletter Chunks

In analyzing word structure, readers pay attention to the following seven multiletter chunks:

1. Prefixes. Prefixes are added to the beginning of words to change meaning (the *un-* in *unpleasant*) or to make meaning more specific (the *mid-* in *midweek*).

2. Suffixes. Suffixes are added to the end of words to clarify meaning (the *-s* in *cats*) or to change grammatical function (the *-able* in *drinkable*).

3. Base Words. Base words (also called morphemes) are the smallest meaningful units, or words, in English that can stand alone (*play, go, come, here, father*).

4. Greek and Latin Root Words. Greek and Latin roots are word parts we borrowed from these two languages (*astro* borrowed from Greek and *port* from Latin) that are combined to form English words.

5. Compound Words. Compound words are two base words that, when combined, make an entirely new word (*cow + boy = cowboy*).

6. Contractions. Contractions are shortcuts for writing two words together (*isn't, we're*).

7. Syllables. Syllables are the basic units of pronunciation in our English language (the *ta* and *ble* in *table*). All words have one or more syllables, and each syllable has one vowel sound.

Prefixes, Suffixes, and Greek and Latin Roots Help Children Infer Word Meaning

Prefixes, suffixes, and Greek and Latin roots tell readers something about word meaning, which in turn supports the understanding of text. Therefore, knowing the meaning of these structural units or chunks makes it possible for readers to infer word meaning. As children have experiences reading and writing, and as they learn about word structure from their teachers, children come to understand that some words consist of two or more meaningful units. Eventually, children become so familiar with the meaningful chunks in words they read words with more than one chunk, such as the suffix and base word *shady*, faster than words with only one meaningful chunk, as in *lady* (Carlisle & Stone, 2005).

Free and Bound Morphemes

Shady consists of two meaningful chunks or morphemes—*shade* (the base word) and *-y* (the suffix meaning full of or having). *Morphemes* are the basic meaning units in language. They can be free or bound.

Free morphemes represent meaning in and of themselves; they can stand alone. *Lady* is an example of a free morpheme. We do not need to add any other morpheme to associate meaning with *lady*. Furthermore, we cannot reduce *lady* to a smaller word. *Lady* is a complete, meaningful word all by itself.

Bound morphemes have meaning only when they are attached to another morpheme. *Shady* consists of two morphemes: one free morpheme (*shade*) and one bound morpheme (the suffix *-y*). For the *-y* to be meaningful, we need to add it to another morpheme, such as *baggy*, *chewy*, or *foamy*. Bound morphemes do have meaning, but that meaning is expressed only when these morphemes are attached to another morpheme. Bound morphemes include prefixes, suffixes, and root words borrowed from other languages to form English words. Examples of bound morphemes include the *pre*- in *prepay*, the *-ing* in *laughing*, and the Greek root *phon* in *phonics*.

Combining morphemes is a common way in which we form multisyllable words. One way to identify an unfamiliar long word is to identify free and bound morphemes in the word. For example, on seeing *laughable*, readers would find the bound morpheme *-able* and the free morpheme *laugh*. Having disaggregated the word into morphemic parts, readers now know how to pronounce this word and have insight into word meaning.

Interestingly, the use of large multiletter groups is not unique to reading, because we group—or chunk—together all sorts of information. Before we explore each of the seven important multiletter chunks, we will consider *why* readers use multiletter chunks in the first place.

WHY READERS CHUNK LETTERS TOGETHER

While there is a great deal of space to store information in long-term memory, the storage space in short-term memory is extremely limited. In fact, only five to seven thought units are held in short-term memory at once (Miller, 1956), and this information lasts only a few seconds before it is either forgotten or moved into long-term memory. A thought unit can be small (one letter, such as *p*) or large (a group of letters, such as *pre*-). A bottleneck occurs when there are so many separate thought units, or pieces of information, in short-term memory that some are forgotten before the information is sent to long-term memory.

When we combine small units, or bits, of information (a single letter, *p*) into a large chunk (a group of letters, *pre-*), we pack more information into a single thought unit. This prevents overcrowding and makes it easier to keep more information in short-term memory. It also makes it possible to get more information into long-term memory because a number of small bits of information are grouped in each thought unit.

Take *astroport* as an example. If we consider the nine letters separately ($a + s + t + r + o + p + o + r + t$), we are almost certain to overburden short-term memory. However, if we consider multiletter groups, we reduce information to just two thought units: *astro* and *port*. With only two thought units in short-term memory, we are less likely to forget the information. There is also room left over to make some sense of *astroport* before it goes to long-term memory. Added to this, the use of multiletter chunks decreases the number of spoken language segments to be blended. Blending a few large chunks—/astro/ + /port/—makes it less likely that individual sounds will be forgotten or reversed.

Given the advantages of multiletter chunks, it is not surprising that as readers increase the number of chunks they recognize, their efficiency in word identification improves (Invernizzi, 1992). Readers who use multiletter chunks put less mental attention and energy into reading new words than is the case with other forms of word identification. This means that readers who use large multiletter groups return to textual reading more quickly and that the disruption to comprehension created by new words is reduced.

TEACHING MULTILETTER CHUNKS IN YOUR CLASSROOM READING PROGRAM

First and Second Grades

If you are a first- or second-grade teacher, you will teach the mutliletter chunks that children need to be successful readers and spellers. As a first-grade teacher, you will introduce common suffixes like *-s/es*, *-ly*, *-ing*, *-ed*, *-er*, and *-est*; a few common prefixes such as *un-* and *re-*; compound words; contractions; and a few syllable patterns such as CVC, (*cap*), VCe (*cape*), CV (*he*), or C + *le* (*table*). In the second grade, children review the multiletter chunks taught in the first grade. As a second-grade teacher, you will introduce compound words and contractions that were not taught in first grade, and a few more common prefixes and suffixes, such as *mis-* (*mistook*) and *-less* (*useless*). Additionally, you might introduce easy-to-recognize and consistently pronounced syllables like the *-tion* in *nation* and *-ture* in *picture*. While word structure is taught in first and second grade, phonics is the main focus of first- and second-grade classroom reading programs.

Third, Fourth, Fifth, and Sixth Grades

Classroom reading programs emphasize word structure in the third, fourth, fifth, and sixth grades because the children in these grades have a reasonable grasp of phonics. They do not need focused phonics instruction. The classroom reading programs in these grades focus instead on the multiletter chunks in word structure, reflecting the fact that third through sixth graders read and spell long, complex words.

Third-, fourth-, fifth-, and sixth-grade teachers usually spend about 15 minutes a day on word work (or word study). If you teach third grade, your classroom reading program may use several approaches to teaching word structure. You may use (a) direct instruction, (b) reading text with long words, and (c) spelling words that include the multiletter chunks children are learning. If you teach fourth, fifth, or sixth grade, you will teach word structure through spelling. Spelling long words that contain the multiletter chunks children are learning is beneficial because it helps to develop in-depth knowledge of how (a) adding suffixes affects base word spelling, (b) prefixes and suffixes affect word meaning, and (c) syllables are spelled in long words. Teachers might, for example, ask children to learn to spell words like *supernatural* (five syllables) or *illogical* (four syllables).

The classroom program may include a review of prefixes and suffixes taught in previous grades such as *un-* and *-ly*. You will teach new prefixes and suffixes such as *over-* (*overdue*) or *-ive* (*creative*), words that sound alike but are spelled differently (*wait-weight*), and words that look alike but do not sound alike (*present-present*). Greek and Latin roots usually enter the curriculum in the fourth grade. Fourth-grade teachers introduce frequently used roots like *phon-* in *telephone* or *-port* in *transport*. Fifth-grade classroom reading programs usually include teaching Greek and Latin roots like *aud-* in *auditory* or *-logy* in *biology*. By seventh grade, the average reader recognizes a variety of prefixes and suffixes, knows how prefixes and suffixes affect word meaning, reads and spells multisyllable words, and infers the meaning of new words by analyzing Greek and Latin roots. The average reader is fully independent, confident, and skilled at learning new words in content areas and enjoys reading for pleasure.

How Children Use Multiletter Chunks in Word Structure

Reading new words by identifying multiletter chunks in word structure takes less mental attention than sounding out words with the letter-sound strategy and requires less time away from comprehending text. Readers who use multiletter chunks know that spoken and written words can be divided into a variety of units, some small and some large. Readers decode long words by breaking them into chunks. In this strategy, children identify known word chunks or parts first and then use these chunks to read the whole word. These readers know that the same chunks are part of many different words, such as the *ter* in *butter* and *terrific*. They recognize multiletter chunks that indicate pronunciation only (the *ter* in *butter*), as well as multiletter chunks that indicate meaning and pronunciation (the *ing* in *playing*). The more reading and writing experiences children have in school, the more they learn about the multiletter groups in language, and the more accomplished they become at using the multiletter chunks in word structure.

The multiletter strategy hinges on identifying chunks in long words. Let's look at an example. Peter comes across the new word *antiseptic* in this sentence from his science book: "Perhaps you recall getting a cut on your knee. Someone may have disinfected the cut with an antiseptic" (Hackett, Moyer, & Adams, 1989, p. 27). Peter's science class has already discussed *antiseptics* and their function, so this word is in his speaking and listening vocabularies. Peter also knows that *anti* means *against* or *preventing* when it is in common words like *antismoking* and *antitheft*. All things considered, Peter brings a good deal of prior knowledge to word identification. He knows (a) what the spoken word *antiseptic* means, (b) how *anti* contributes to a word's definition, and (c) how to recognize many different types of multiletter chunks in the words he reads. Here is how Peter goes about using this streamlined strategy:

1. Peter recognizes *anti* and, in so doing, instantly recalls its pronunciation and meaning.
2. He identifies two additional multiletter chunks: *sep* and *tic*. Peter now has divided *antiseptic* into three pronounceable groups: /anti/ + /sep/ + /tic/.
3. Peter blends /anti/ + /sep/ + /tic/ into /antiseptic/.
4. Last, he cross-checks to make sure that he pronounces and understands the word in the context in which it is used in his science book. He asks himself: Does *antiseptic* sound and look right? Does *antiseptic* make sense in the passage? If *antiseptic* makes sense, Peter continues reading.

In the way Peter separated them, the first group of letters is *anti*; the second, *sep*; and the third, *tic*. However, there are other ways Peter might have chosen to group letters. Though the *septic* in *antiseptic* is a meaningful multiletter chunk, it is not in Peter's speaking or listening vocabulary. Had he known the meaning of *septic*, Peter might have divided *antiseptic* into these two meaningful chunks: *anti* + *septic*. Or he could have divided *antiseptic* into *an* + *ti* + *septic*. Though the specific multiletter groups individual readers use will vary depending on each reader's background knowledge, all readers who use this strategy are sensitive to which letters form chunks and which do not, and which chunks are meaningful and which are not.

Take *ing* as an example. Readers know that *ing* represents meaning and sound in *playing* and only signals pronunciation (a rime) in *swing*. They also know that *ing* is not a viable multiletter chunk in *hinge*. When identifying multiletter groups, readers bring to bear their knowledge of the letter-sound patterns in a word. This explains why Peter did not identify the *ise* as a multiletter chunk in *antiseptic*. Though *ise* is a pronounceable multiletter group in *rise, wise*, and *revise*, it is not a viable chunk in *antiseptic* because it is not consistent with the surrounding letter-sound patterns of phonics. Peter and readers like him use their knowledge of letter-sound patterns to determine the letters in new words that are most likely to belong in groups. This kind of in-depth knowledge is not an overnight phenomenon. Rather, it develops gradually as readers strategically use the multiletter chunks in word structure to read and write.

Correcting Misidentifications

Readers who do not successfully identify words on the first try may choose from among the following four alternatives:

1. Rechunk letters (divide words into different multiletter groups and then reblend).
2. Fall back on either the letter-sound or analogy strategy.
3. Look up words in the dictionary.
4. Ask expert readers for help.

Rechunking and falling back on the letter-sound or analogy strategies are, of course, less efficient ways to identify never-seen-before words. With its dependence on an in-depth knowledge of multiletter chunks, the strategy of analyzing word structure does not come into its own until after readers have had experience using the analogy and letter-sound strategies. Readers like Peter who use the multiletter chunk strategy are in the *consolidated stage of word learning* and the *transitional stage of spelling,* as you will learn in the next section.

CONSOLIDATED WORD LEARNERS AND TRANSITIONAL SPELLERS

Readers who use the multiletter chunks in word structure are at the *consolidated stage of word learning.* These readers have insight into the letter-sound patterns of phonics and have consolidated, or grouped, letter sequences in memory (Ehri, 2005). Readers at the consolidated stage recognize meaningful letter chunks, such as the *un-* and *-ed* in <u>un</u>finish<u>ed,</u> as well as nonmeaningful syllables, such as the *cir* and *cle* in <u>circle</u>. While the transition into the consolidated stage comes toward the end of second grade for most readers, some will move into this stage during the third grade. Average third-grade readers quickly recognize multiletter groups in words. Because these readers automatically associate sounds with multiletter groups, they read words faster and with greater accuracy than their classmates who do not look for large chunks (Neuhaus, Roldan, Boulware-Gooden, & Swank, 2006).

Readers at the consolidated stage use the reading context to help them identify words and use cross-checking to determine whether words make sense in the passages they read. These readers know when to self-correct and, because their focus is on meaning, know when it is necessary to fix a word identification miscue. They do not sound out words letter-sound by letter-sound, nor do they think about analogous portions of known words to identify unknown words. Instead, these readers instantly recognize large intact letter groups in words. They recognize syllables, such as the *tion* in *nation,* and they also automatically recognize prefixes (the *pre-* in *preheat*), suffixes (the *-er* in *smaller*), base words (the *clean* in *cleaning*), compound words (*snowman*), and contractions (*she'd*).

Readers at the consolidated stage are at the *transitional stage of spelling.* Transitional spellers have insight into the structure of words and use this understanding when spelling (Gentry, 2006). When you look at the writing of transitional spellers, you will notice that they (a) conventionally spell common word endings (such as *-s, -ed, -ing,* and *-ly*), (b) include a vowel in every syllable, (c) put a vowel before the letter *r* (though not necessarily the correct vowel, *buttur* instead of *butter*), and (d) use the *VCe* long vowel pattern and the *VV* long vowel pattern (though not always correctly, *trale* instead of *trail*). You also will notice that the transitional spellers in your classroom sometimes substitute alternative spellings for the same sound; *naym* or *naim* for *name* is an example.

By late spring of second grade, Shania, a transitional speller, is sensitive to some of the meaningful multiletter chunks that make up word structure. She correctly spells common word endings (*lives, fishing,* and *lunches,* for instance), uses the *VV* long vowel pattern (*street* and *each*), and puts a vowel in every syllable, as you can see in Figure 6-2. She writes a vowel before the letter *r* (*together* and *over*), though she sometimes writes letters in the wrong sequence (*evrey*). And, of course, she conventionally spells most of the words in her reading vocabulary. When Shania misspells, she writes words the way she believes they sound (*comin* for *common*). From her misspelling of *snaping* for *snapping,* we can infer that Shania is still learning how to add endings to words that require doubling the last consonant. The more literacy experiences she has, the more sensitive she will become to

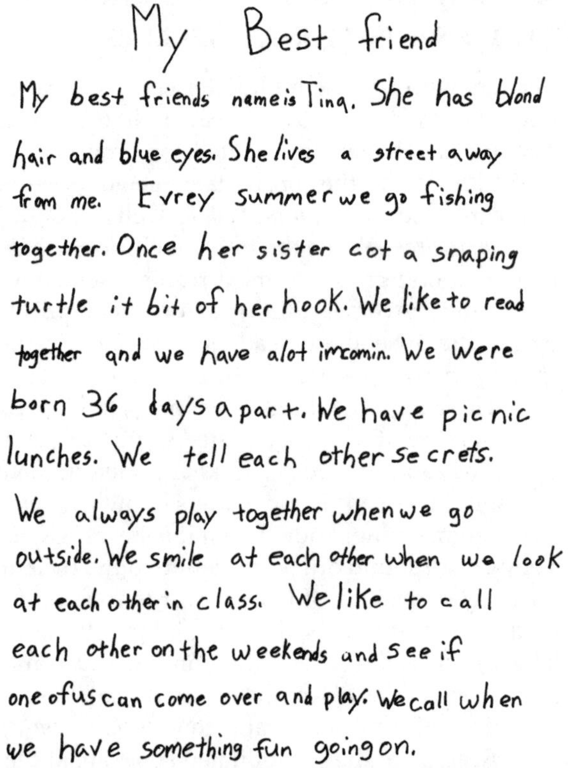

Figure 6-2 Shania recognizes the multiletter chunks in word structure and uses this knowledge when she reads and spells.

the multiletter chunks in words, and the more effectively she will use this knowledge when she reads and spells.

Fifth grader Kristen spells all words conventionally, with the exception of *restaurant*, which she spells *restarant* (see Figure 6-3). She has a large reading vocabulary and automatically identifies many words. When she does not instantly recognize a word, she is most likely to look for pronounceable multiletter chunks in its structure. Kristen's knowledge of multiletter chunks will continue to grow in middle and high school. This is important because she will rely on this strategy when she is challenged to learn the long, complex technical terms in high school textbooks.

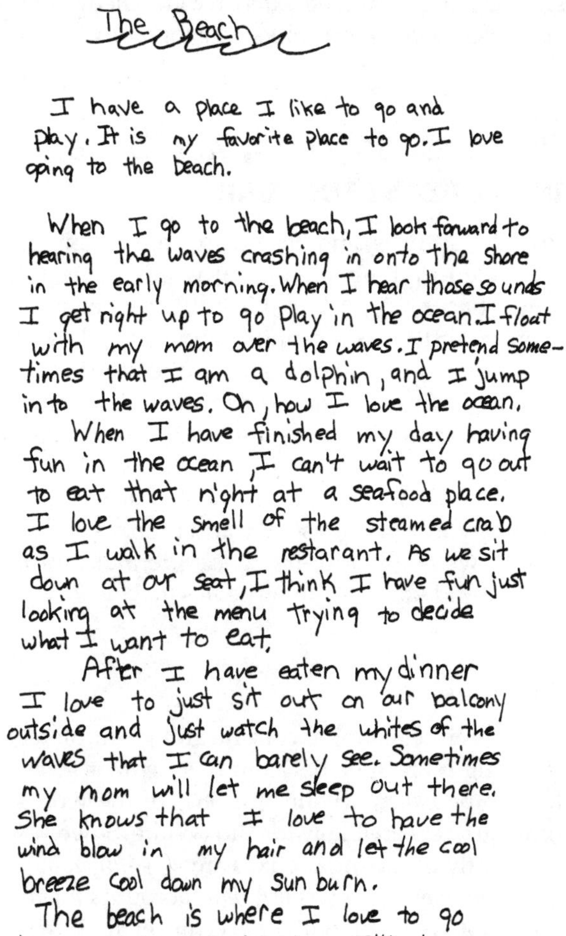

The Beach

I have a place I like to go and play. It is my favorite place to go. I love going to the beach.

When I go to the beach, I look forward to hearing the waves crashing in onto the shore in the early morning. When I hear those sounds I get right up to go play in the ocean. I float with my mom over the waves. I pretend sometimes that I am a dolphin, and I jump into the waves. Oh, how I love the ocean.

When I have finished my day having fun in the ocean, I can't wait to go out to eat that night at a seafood place. I love the smell of the steamed crab as I walk in the restarant. As we sit down at our seat, I think I have fun just looking at the menu trying to decide what I want to eat.

After I have eaten my dinner I love to just sit out on our balcony outside and just watch the whites of the waves that I can barely see. Sometimes my mom will let me sleep out there. She knows that I love to have the wind blow in my hair and let the cool breeze cool down my sun burn.

The beach is where I love to go because I love playing there. I'll always have fun at the beach.

Figure 6-3   Kristen, a fifth grader, conventionally spells the words in her fluent reading vocabulary. When reading, she looks for pronounceable multiletter chunks in the words she does not automatically recognize.

In due time, children's reading vocabularies become so enormous that they include all the words they typically see in text. Children who automatically recognize all the words they read are at the fifth and final stage: *automatic word recognition.* Now word recognition is completely automatic, with the exception, of course, of unusual words and some content subject words. These children spell known words conventionally, including irregular words; they know when words are not spelled right and fix their own misspellings (Gentry, 2006). Accomplished high school readers use many effective comprehension strategies and, because they automatically recognize words, they concentrate on comprehending and learning from their textbooks. When these readers encounter new words, they use the multiletter chunk strategy, calling on their extensive knowledge of multiletter groups to learn words in subjects like geometry, physics, geography, and American literature.

PREFIXES, SUFFIXES, AND BASE WORDS IN WORD STRUCTURE

Prefixes, suffixes, and base words are meaningful chunks or morphemes. *Prefixes* are added to the beginning of words (*prename*); *suffixes* are added to the end of words (*movement*). We will use *affixes* when referring to both prefixes and suffixes. Prefixes and suffixes cannot stand alone; they are bound morphemes and must be attached to words. For example, the word *like* can stand alone, but the prefix *un-* and the suffix *-ly* cannot. When *un-* and *-ly* are added to *like*, we create a word with a different meaning and grammatical function, *unlikely.* Prefixes and suffixes make words longer, as we see in *unlikely, reworked,* and *returnable.* Unlike prefixes and suffixes, base words stand alone. *Base words* are free morphemes and are the smallest real words in English. We add prefixes and suffixes to some base words. For example, we might add *-ing* to *learn* to make *learning, -able* to *train* to spell *trainable,* and *in-* and *-ive* to *act* to write *inactive.*

Prefixes

Prefixes either change word meaning completely, as in *non + fat = nonfat,* or make meaning more specific, as in *re + write = rewrite.* A mere smattering of prefixes, four to be exact, account for 58% of the words with prefixes that third through ninth graders are likely to read (White, Sowell, & Yanagihara, 1989). The four most frequently occurring prefixes are: *un-* (*unhappy*), *re-* (*rewrite*), *in-* (meaning *not* as in *inaccurate*), and *dis-* (*dislike*). *Un-* accounts for the lion's share: A full 26% of words with prefixes begin with *un-* (White et al., 1989). While *un-, re-, in-,* and *dis-* are certainly useful, older readers benefit from knowing more difficult prefixes, because these prefixes offer considerable insight into word meaning. The 20 prefixes in Table 6–1 are the most important prefixes to teach children in grades three through nine. When the prefixes in Table 6–1 have more than one meaning, the meaning listed is that given by White, et al., 1989.

TABLE 6–1	*The 20 Most Common Prefixes*	
Prefix	**Meaning**	**Examples**
anti	against	antitrust, antiknock, anticrime, antiglare, antitheft
de	from, away	debug, defog, decaf, defrost, deplane, derail
dis	apart from, not	disarm, disbar, disown, disuse, disable, dislike
en, em	in	enact, enclose, enable, embark, embark, embody, embattle
fore	in front of, before	foresee, forego, forewarn, foreground, foretell
in, im, ir, il	not	invisible, improbable, irresponsible, illogical
in, im	in or into	inborn, inflow, inward, immigrant, immoral
inter	between, among	interact, intermix, interlace, interlock, interplay
mid	middle	midair, midday, midway, midweek, midnight
mis	wrong, bad, not	misfit, misplace, mislay, misuse, misdeed
non	not	nonfat, nonskid, nonprofit, nonstick, nonstop
over	too much	overage, overdue, overeat, overlap, overlook
pre	in front of, before	precut, premix, prepay, predate, precook
re	back, again	rearm, retell, redo, renew, repay, rerun
semi	half, partly	semicircle, semisoft, semifinal, semisweet
sub	under, inferior	subplot, subzero, subset, submarine, substandard
super	above, in addition	superman, superfine, superhero, superheat, superstar
trans	across, through	transact, transport, transplant, transform, transpolar
un	not	uncut, unfit, unlit, untie, unzip, unhappy, unsure
under	too little	underage, underfed, underpay, underdone, underfed

Suffixes

Suffixes either clarify word meaning or change grammatical function. There are two types of suffixes: *inflectional suffixes* and *derivational suffixes*. Inflectional endings consist of *-s(es)*, *-ed*, *-ing*, *-er*, and *-est*. These suffixes change the number (*dog-dogs*), affect verb tense (*walk-walked*), or indicate comparison (*big, bigger, biggest*). Inflectional endings are the most frequently occurring of all the suffixes (White et al., 1989). Look in Appendix C for generalizations about adding these five suffixes to words.

Derivational suffixes affect meaning and grammatical usage, such as changing *dirt* (noun) to *dirty* (adjective), *history* (noun) to *historic* (adjective), and *agree* (verb) to *agreeable* (adjective). Children's knowledge of derivational suffixes increases from the third to the sixth grade (Mahony, Singson, & Mann, 2000; Singson, Mahoney, & Mann, 2000). You can expect older readers to more readily recognize

TABLE 6–2   *The 20 Most Common Suffixes*

Suffix	Meaning	Examples
al, ial	relating to	bridal, global, rental, burial, memorial, personal
ed	past tense	played, jumped, painted, hopped, kicked
en	relating to	liken, ripen, olden, frozen, waken, wooden
er, or	one who	painter, player, reader, worker, visitor, actor, sailor
er	comparative	quicker, higher, fatter, uglier, faster, slower
est	most (comparative)	biggest, slowest, highest, largest, fastest, nicest
ful	quality of	artful, joyful, beautiful, plentiful, careful, fearful
ible, able	able to, quality of	readable, eatable, fixable, defensible, divisible
ic	like, pertaining to	historic, scenic, acidic, atomic, poetic
ing	ongoing	reading, listening, running, jumping, helping
ion, ation, ition, tion	act or state of	action, addition, adoption, construction, donation
ity, ty	state or quality of	dirty, dusty, nutty, salty, fruity, oddity, activity
ive, ative, itive	tending to, relating to	creative, active, massive, formative, additive
less	without	joyless, aimless, fearless, endless, jobless, useless
ly	every, in the manner of	friendly, badly, kindly, dimly, boldly, calmly
ment	result or state of	payment, argument, judgment, excitement, shipment
ness	quality of	fitness, illness, happiness, madness, goodness
ous, eous, ious	full of, state of	studious, joyous, envious, furious, gaseous
s, es	plural	dogs, houses, boys, girls, ashes, boxes, teachers
y	quality, full of	ability, muddy, baggy, bossy, bumpy, chewy, jumpy

and understand suffixes like *-ment, -able,* and *-ic* than younger, less experienced readers. Table 6–2 is a list of the 20 most common suffixes (White et al., 1989).

Ross's story in Figure 6-4 illustrates how a precocious first grader uses common suffixes. Ross conventionally spells words with *-ed, -ing,* and *-s/es* and correctly forms contractions. Ross has learned these multiletter groups so well that they are second nature when he reads and writes. For example, he drops the final *y* in *try* and writes an *i* before adding *-ed* to spell *tried.* Notice the word *cutted,* which does not need an *-ed* to signal past tense. Ross writes the way he talks, and he sometimes says *cutted* when he means *cut.* Though Ross does not use *cut* conventionally, he shows us that he understands the convention of doubling the last consonant, the letter *t,* before adding the *-ed.* Ross's teacher thinks he will benefit from learning more about writing in complete sentences and using periods and capitals, so she has formed a small, flexible skill group to give Ross and a handful of his classmates extra help with punctuation.

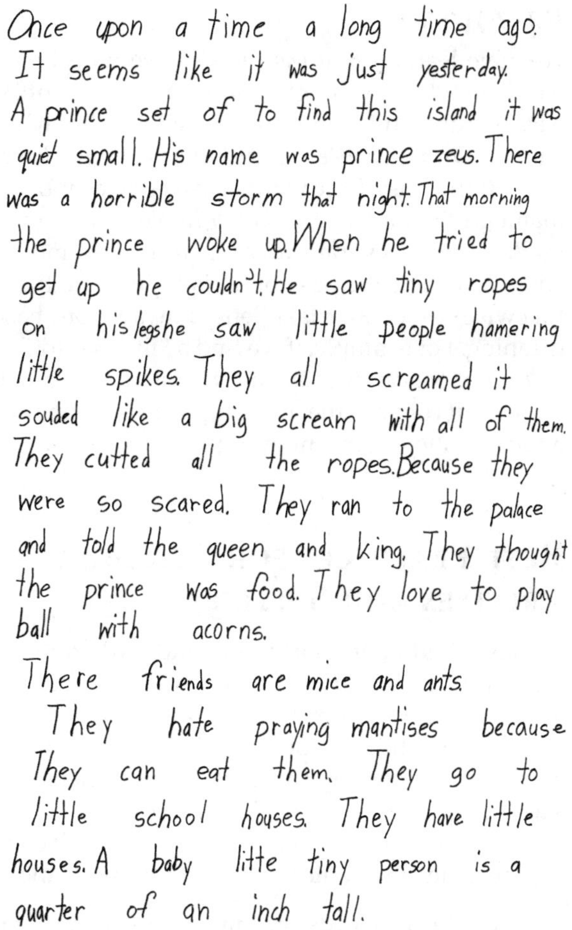

Once upon a time a long time ago.
It seems like it was just yesterday.
A prince set of to find this island it was
quiet small. His name was prince zeus. There
was a horrible storm that night. That morning
the prince woke up. When he tried to
get up he couldn't. He saw tiny ropes
on his legs he saw little people hamering
little spikes. They all screamed it
souded like a big scream with all of them.
They cutted all the ropes. Because they
were so scared. They ran to the palace
and told the queen and king. They thought
the prince was food. They love to play
ball with acorns.
There friends are mice and ants.
They hate praying mantises because
They can eat them. They go to
little school houses. They have little
houses. A baby litte tiny person is a
quarter of an inch tall.

Figure 6-4   Through his writing, Ross demonstrates that he knows how to correctly use and conventionally spell common suffixes and how to form contractions.

The number of words with affixes doubles from fourth to fifth grade and doubles again by the seventh grade (White, Power, & White, 1989). It is estimated that fifth graders may meet an average of 1,325 words a year that include the prefixes *in-, im-, ir-, il-* (meaning "not"), *un-, re-,* and *dis-*. Seventh graders may identify 3,000 words, and perhaps as many as 9,000 words, with these prefixes as well as a variety of suffixes. As readers move into higher grades, their knowledge of suffixes also increases (Nagy, Diakidoy, & Anderson, 1993), quite possibly as a consequence of increased grammatical awareness (Nunes, Bryant, & Bindman, 1997). So, it is not surprising that fourth, fifth, sixth, seventh, and eighth graders use their knowledge of suffixes to read new words in context, and that sixth, seventh, and eighth graders are better at this than fourth graders (Wysocki & Jenkins, 1987).

Base Words

We have learned that *base words* (free morphemes) are the smallest real English words to which we might add prefixes and suffixes. Unlike prefixes and suffixes, base words stand alone; they are what is left when we take away the prefixes and suffixes (*drinkable-able = drink; unhappy-un = happy*).

Butterfly is a base word because we cannot divide it into *butter* and *fly* and still maintain the meaning of *butterfly*. We can, however, add a suffix to *butterfly*. We might refer to several *butterflies*. In this example, the *-es* ending is not part of the base word. The purpose of *-es* is to indicate that there is more than one *butterfly*. Likewise, we cannot take letters away from base words and still preserve their meaning. For example, if we find a "little word," such as *wag*, in a "big word," such as *wagon*, we cannot say that *wag* is the base word for *wagon*. *Wagon* is the base word, as it conveys the meaning. *Wag* is an English word, to be sure, but it conveys a totally different meaning from that of *wagon*.

BEST PRACTICES FOR TEACHING PREFIXES AND SUFFIXES

Because children in fourth, fifth and sixth grade read longer, more complex words than children in earlier grades, understanding how prefixes and suffixes affect word meaning becomes increasingly important. Fourth, fifth and sixth graders who understand how prefixes and suffixes affect base word meaning have larger reading vocabularies and better comprehension than their classmates with less knowledge (Carlisle, 2000; Deacon & Kirby, 2004; Nagy, Berninger, & Abbot, 2006). In using the following best practices, you will effectively teach children how to recognize, read, and write words with prefixes and suffixes.

1. **Break words into meaningful parts, talk about the parts, and put the words back together again.** In following this teaching sequence, you show children how affixes combine with base words. This makes children more aware of affixes and, additionally, teaches children something about word meaning. For example, you might begin with *unfairly*, break it into parts—*un*, *fair*, *ly*—and talk about the meaning of each part, and then show children how the parts work together to make *unfairly*.

2. **Teach readers how to peel away prefixes and suffixes to reveal familiar base words.** Peeling prefixes and suffixes away from long words is helpful because this reveals base words that are already part of readers' reading vocabulary. We will use the word *unfriendly* as an illustration. Show readers those steps

   1. *Do I see a prefix?* Look for a prefix. Ask, "Do I see a prefix I know?" If so, peel it off: Peeling *un-* away from *unfriendly* (*unfriendly-un = friendly*) reveals *friendly*.
   2. *Do I see a suffix?* Ask, "Do I see a suffix I know?" If so, peel it off, too. Peeling *-ly* away from *friendly* (*friendly-ly = friend*) reveals the base word *friend*.

3. *Do I know this base word?* Ask, "Do I see a word I can read?" If so, "What does it mean?"

4. *Put the word back together.* The word is *unfriendly.* Now I can read this word.

3. Teach inflectional suffixes (-*s/es*, -*ed*, -*ing*, -*er*, -*est*) in the first and second grades. Though words with affixes do not make up the major portion of text in the storybooks for younger children (Ives, Bursuk, & Ives, 1979), it is wise to begin to explore meaningful multiletter chunks early, and suffixes are a better investment in learning than prefixes. Authors who write for young readers frequently use words that end with -*es*, -*ing*, and -*ed*, which makes these suffixes extremely important (Templeton, 1991). The comparative suffixes -*er* and -*est* are useful because they are important for understanding comparisons such as *quick, quicker,* and *quickest* or *large, larger,* and *largest.*

4. Give children practice reading and writing many different words with the same prefixes and suffixes. As children's reading ability increases, you can expect their knowledge of multiletter chunks to expand as well (Gibson & Guinet, 1971; Invernizzi, 1992; Santa, 1976–1977). In reading and writing words with the same prefixes and suffixes, such as the *re-* and -*ing* in *replaying, reloading, retelling,* and *rerunning,* children learn how these affixes contribute to word meaning. Prefixes and suffixes are significant features of syntax and therefore contribute to the strength of sentence structure cues. This is especially true for the inflectional endings. When children read and write in your classroom, take naturally occurring opportunities to ask them to find base words with affixes and to explain in their own words how the affixes affect word meaning.

5. Teach base word meaning. Children need to know the meaning of the base words to which the affixes are added. Once children understand base word meaning and recognize base words in text, then it is appropriate to teach them how affixes affect base word meaning.

GREEK AND LATIN ROOTS

Greek and Latin roots are word parts we borrowed from these two languages. When the scholars, philosophers, and authors of the Renaissance became interested in writing in their own language, English, they borrowed liberally from ancient Greek and Latin (Ayers, 1980). Just as the great thinkers and writers of the Renaissance used Greek and Latin words to make lots of new words, so too do we continue this tradition today. When we ventured into space in the middle of the 20th century, a new word was needed for space explorers. Rather than devising a whole new word from scratch, the term *astronaut* was coined by combining the Greek root *astro,* meaning *star,* with *naut,* meaning *sailor.* Considering the Greek origin, modern-day *astronauts* are *star sailors,* a term that suggests all sorts of engaging images.

Words that share the same Greek or Latin roots, such as the *aud* (meaning to hear) in *auditory, audible,* and *audience,* form meaning families (Henderson, 1990; Templeton, 1991). By organizing words into meaning families, readers have a platform for figuring out the meaning of unfamiliar words with the same Greek or Latin root. For example, *aqua* (of Latin origin) means *water*, and therefore words with *aqua* also have something to do with *water*, as in *aquarium, aquatic, aqueduct,* and *aquaplane*. Likewise, *magni* (from Latin) means *great* or *large*. Consequently, *magnify, magnificent, magnanimous,* and *magnitude* all pertain to conditions in which an object or action is great or large. From a practical standpoint, you can expect readers who recognize and appreciate Greek and Latin roots to learn a great many technical terms with relative ease, and to do so with less guidance from you than their classmates who do not understand the contribution Greek and Latin roots make to English words.

Generally speaking, fourth and fifth graders learn Greek and Latin roots. Teachers introduce the roots and their meaning and then show children how the roots give readers some insight into meaning. For example, the root word *phon* in *phonics* and *telephone* tells readers that these words pertain to *sound; microchip* and *microprocessor* refer to *small* because each includes the root *micro* from the Greek language. Readers are not likely to figure out the meaning of borrowed word parts from normal reading experiences. In part, the reason is that Greek and Latin roots are semihidden in words, and in part because each English word that includes them has a slightly different meaning. A*quarium* and *aquaplane* both pertain to *water,* but the meaning of the individual words is quite different. Consequently, to develop the ability to strategically use Greek and Latin roots, readers need explicit explanations of them and modeling of how to use them to unlock word meaning, as well as many opportunities to read and write words with them.

COMPOUND WORDS

Compound words are formed when two words—for example, *finger* and *print*—are glued together to create a third word—in this case, *fingerprint*. Compounds differ depending on how far afield meaning wanders from the definitions of the individual words that are put together. In the case of *fingerprint,* the general definition of each word is unchanged. A second sort of compound is made of words whose meanings are somewhat different than that of the combined form, such as *basketball, driveway, skyscraper,* and *spotlight*. In a third category, the meaning of the compound has practically nothing to do with the meaning of the individual words. Examples include *butterfly, fireworks, dragonfly, hardware, turtleneck,* and *peppermint*.

The first-, second-, and third-grade readers we teach find compound words to be relatively easy to learn. Perhaps this is because compounds are made of two whole words and thus are not overly challenging to identify. When the words that make up compounds are already in children's reading vocabularies, pronunciation is merely a question of saying the words together. As for the meaning of compounds, we find that readers are intrigued by the changes in meaning that occur when words are glued together. First graders enjoy finding words that are glued together in compounds. Older readers, on the other hand, have so much experience that the compounds they see in everyday text usually pose no challenge whatsoever. This said, some teachers may continue to introduce a few new compound words through the fifth grade, depending on the reading program. When compound words are part of fourth- and fifth-grade programs, they are usually taught through spelling.

CONTRACTIONS

Contractions are formed when one or more letters (and sounds) are deleted from words. Missing letters are replaced by an apostrophe, which is a visual clue telling readers that a word is abbreviated, as in *hasn't, he's, she'll,* and *let's.* Words mean exactly the same thing whether they are written as a contraction or individually. First and second graders meet contractions in everyday reading material, so it is important that these readers learn to recognize the contractions they see in storybooks. Older children may occasionally review how to form contractions and the words that contractions represent.

All children encounter contractions in reading and use them in writing, so teaching contractions is a good large group activity. Use a set of magnetic letters and a magnetic apostrophe to illustrate how contractions are formed. Ask first and second graders to use magnetic letters to change words like *she* and *will* into *she'll,* as well as to reverse the process by changing contractions (*she'll*) into two words (*she* and *will*). Then you write pairs of sentences on the board. In the first sentence, you underline two words that can be combined to form a contraction. In the second sentence, you leave a blank where the contraction should be:

1. The dog <u>did not</u> find the bone.
2. The dog _____ find the bone.

Children then read the first sentence, form a contraction from the two underlined words (*did* and *not*), and write the contraction (*didn't*) in the blank in the second sentence. Everyone then reads both sentences together in chorus while you sweep your hand under the words as they are read.

SYLLABLES

The *syllable* is the basic unit of pronunciation. Each syllable has one vowel sound, so the number of syllables in a word equals the number of vowels heard. Try saying *lilac.* How many vowels do you hear? /li/-/lac/ has two vowel sounds and hence two syllables. Now try *table.* When you pronounce the last syllable, *ble,* you do not notice a distinct vowel. You hear instead a vowel-like sound—/bul/. So when we divide words into syllables, we listen for vowel and vowel-like sounds. One vowel or vowel-like sound equals one syllable.

Readers can identify the syllables in unfamiliar written words by counting the vowel letter-sound patterns. Just as a spoken word has as many syllables as

Deconstructing Contractions

If you notice that . . .
children read contractions correctly aloud but miss the meaning of sentences with contractions, children may not know which words the contractions represent. Many children are quite good at "calling" contractions but are stumped when asked to say the two words that make up the contractions.

The thing to do is . . .
deconstruct contractions. Take them apart, show children which two words come together to make contractions, and then give children practice taking contractions apart. Instead of asking children to form a contraction—didn't from did not—begin with didn't in a sentence and then ask children to write the two words that make up didn't.

---

vowel sounds, so too is a written word divided into as many syllables as vowel letter-sound patterns. Words with one vowel pattern have one syllable: the *CVC* short vowel pattern in *got; CV* in *go; VV* in *goat; VCe* in *gave.* Words with two vowel patterns have two syllables: *ba - con* and *be-gin* each with a *CV* and *CVC* pattern, for example. Those with three vowel patterns have three syllables (*in-ter-nal*), four patterns have four syllables (*in-ter-nal-ize*), and so on.

By the time children are 11 years old, they are quite adept at reading two- and three-syllable words (Duncan & Seymour, 2003). These children appear to read words as complete, whole units, or they look for large letter chunks that correspond to sounds. New words they encounter tend to have more than one syllable, and so we see that in addition to looking for meaningful chunks, readers also look for pronounceable chunks.

The syllable offers an avenue for decoding when long words do not have meaningful chunks or do not have Greek or Latin roots that are obvious to readers. For example, there are no meaning chunks that would be obvious to fifth graders in words like *canyon* and *calendar.* In order to read these words, which, incidentally, the average fifth grader has in his or her speaking vocabulary, the reader turns to large, pronounceable syllables. In so doing, readers look for certain syllable patterns or structures that are clues to pronunciation. Analyzing the syllables in words is a more effective word learning method than simply remembering whole words without syllable analysis (Bhattacharya & Ehri, 2004). We will now discuss five such patterns.

Syllable Patterns

When we say words aloud, it is sometimes hard to decide where one syllable ends and another begins. When consulting the dictionary, we occasionally find that syllable division does not reflect pronunciation. Our goal is to help children read new long words by dividing them into pronounceable syllables, not to have readers memorize dictionary-style syllabication. Syllable patterns are guidelines for dividing words into pronounceable multiletter chunks, with some exceptions. The following five syllable patterns and clues to syllable division are intended to help you, the teacher, organize and focus instruction.

1.   *CV*-open, long vowel syllable. Open syllables end in a vowel that generally represents a long sound. You can easily recognize the open syllable because it is the *CV* long vowel pattern. The one-syllable word *go* is an example of this pattern. *Table*, a two-syllable word, begins with a *CV* long vowel pattern (*ta*-ble), as do *motor* (*mo*-tor), *major* (*ma*-jor), and *bugle* (*bu*-gle).

Clue to syllable division: When there is a single consonant between two vowels, as in *favor*, divide the word right after the first vowel. The second consonant frequently begins the second syllable, as in *fa - vor, be - gan,* and *si - lent*. Other examples of a single consonant between two vowels are *lo - cal, fe - ver,* and *si - lo*. The *Vr* vowel pattern is a logical exception to this syllable division pattern because the vowel is not separated from the *r* in the *Vr* pattern (*car - ol,* not *ca - rol; mer - it,* not *me - rit;* and *chor - us,* not *cho - rus*). There are other exceptions, so advise readers to first try the long vowel sound and then, if that does not work, try the short sound.

2.   *CVC*-closed, short vowel syllable. Closed syllables end in a consonant, and the vowel typically represents a short sound. The closed syllable includes the *CVC* short vowel pattern, as in the one-syllable words *cat* and *chin*. Examples of words with closed syllables include *button* (*but - ton*), *pencil* (*pen - cil*), and *cactus* (*cac – tus*).

Clue to syllable division: If there are two consonants between two vowels, as in the words *rabbit* and *napkin,* the syllable usually divides between the consonants (*rab-bit, pup-pet,* and *nap-kin*). Generally speaking, advise readers to avoid dividing between the letters of a digraph (*fash-ion*) and a consonant cluster (*se-cret*), although there are exceptions, of course.

3.   **Prefix and suffix syllables.** In general, prefixes and suffixes are separate syllables, with the exception of *-s*, which does not have a vowel sound and hence cannot be a syllable, and *-ed* when pronounced as /t/, as in *jumped*. In examining the prefixes in Table 6–1, you will notice that a few have more than one vowel sound, and hence more than one syllable, such as the *semi-* in *semisweet* (*sem-i*). Readers who already recognize these multisyllable prefixes will automatically know how to pronounce them, so the fact that a few prefixes represent two syllables should not deter readers from figuring out the pronunciation of these prefixes in long words.

Clue to syllable division: Divide the syllable after the prefix and before the suffix as in *non-stop-able, un-help-ful,* and *re-fill-able*.

4.   *C + le* - syllable. When a word ends in a consonant + *le* (*Cle*), the *Cle* usually forms a syllable, as in *table* (*ta-ble*), *title* (*ti-tle*), and *sprinkle* (*sprin-kle*).

Clue to syllable division: In words that end in *le* preceded by a consonant—*ble, cle, dle, fle, gle, kle, ple, sle,* and *zle*—the consonant usually begins the syllable.

Examples include *fum-ble, cy-cle, can-dle, ri-fle, bea-gle, wrin-kle, dim-ple, has-sle, ti-tle,* and *driz-zle. Ble* is pronounced as /bul/, *cle* as /cul/, *dle* as /dul/, *fle* as /ful/, *gle* as /gul/, *kle* as /kul/, *ple* as /pul/, *sle* as /sul/, *tle* as /tul/, and *zle* as /zul/.

　　5.　Compound word syllables. Compounds are divided between the two words—for instance, *pop-corn, snow-man,* and *cow-boy.*

　　Clue to syllable division: Divide compounds between the two words.

　　Looking at the five syllable patterns, we see that the closed syllable explains why we double the last consonant when adding suffixes to words ending with a *CVC* short vowel pattern like *hop* and *sit.* By doubling the last consonant in a *CVC* short vowel pattern, we spell *hopped* and *pinned,* thereby keeping the vowel in its proper pattern. When the final consonant is not doubled, this indicates a long vowel letter-sound pattern, as in *hoped* and *pined.* It takes a lot of reading and writing experience for children to learn when to double (or not to double) the last consonant. Anticipate spending extra time helping children edit their writing and, perhaps, form a flexible skill group to give special practice to those who need it.

Accent Patterns

The syllables in long words are given different stress. *Accent,* the stress given to syllables, is very important because it affects vowel pronunciation. There are three levels of stress: primary, secondary, and reduced (or unaccented). For simplicity, we will call the syllable with the most stress the primary accent. The vowels in accented syllables tend to follow the pronunciation we would expect from their placement in letter-sound patterns. Most vowels in *unaccented syllables* have a soft, or short, sound. We will therefore focus on the accented syllable and will put a (´) after the syllable to indicate primary stress.

　　When we shift the primary accent, we also shift pronunciation. Try saying these words by placing the primary accent on the first or second syllable, as indicated: *con'-tent* and *con-tent'; ob'-ject* and *ob-ject'; con'-vict* and *con-vict'.* In these examples, shifting the primary accent from the first to the last syllable changes word meaning. Reread *con'-tent, ob'-ject,* and *con'-vict.* What do you notice about these words? If you conclude that they are nouns, you are right. The primary accent tends to fall on the first syllable of a noun. Here are five guidelines to indicate where to place the primary accent:

1.　All one-syllable words are accented syllables.

2.　The primary accent most often falls on the first syllable of a two-syllable word (*ma'-ple* and *sal'-ad*), unless the last syllable includes two vowels (*con-ceal'* and *ap-proach'*) and then that syllable is stressed, with some exceptions.

3.　Prefixes and suffixes are ordinarily not accented. The base word receives the primary accent, as in *name'-less* and *ex-chang'-ing.*

4. The primary accent usually falls on the first word of compounds, such as *snow'-man* and *base'-ball*.

5. When a word has two like consonants, the primary accent generally falls on the syllable that closes with the first letter, as in *rab'- bit* and *ham'- mer*.

Two additional tips help with certain spellings: First, *Cle* (consonant-*le*) syllables are generally not accented, as in *tram'-ple* and *tur'-tle*. And second, syllables ending in *ck* are often accented, such as *buck'-et* and *nick'-el*. And when teaching readers about the manner in which dictionaries represent syllables and pronunciation, point out that the way we divide words in writing does not always correspond to the way we group sounds together when speaking. The boldface type in the dictionary indicates how we divide a word when writing; the type in parentheses shows how we pronounce words when speaking. It is the type in parentheses that shows where to place the accent.

BEST PRACTICES FOR TEACHING READERS ABOUT SYLLABLES

1. **Use clue words to illustrate syllable patterns.** Clue words illustrate syllable patterns and help readers remember how to pronounce the five syllable types. Examples of clue words include

1. Open syllable clue words (*CV*): *go; he*.
2. Closed syllable clue words (*CVC*): *napkin* (*nap-kin*); *rabbit* (*rab-bit*).
3. Prefix and suffix syllable clue words: *replayed* (*re-play-ed*); *unlikely* (*un-like-ly*).
4. Consonant-le (*Cle*) syllable clue words: *table* (*ta-ble*); *maple* (*ma-ple*).
5. Compound word syllable clue words: *cowboy* (*cow-boy*); *popcorn* (*pop-corn*).

2. **Teach syllables and accent patterns only after readers have a good understanding of phonics letter-sound patterns.** Because syllables are multiletter chunks that include letter-sound patterns, readers first need to know how letter-sound patterns, particularly vowel patterns, represent sound. Combining a knowledge of letter-sound patterns with an understanding of syllable patterns helps readers decide which letters form syllables and which do not.

3. **Give readers opportunities to apply their syllable knowledge when reading and writing.** Asking children to engage in activities that are far removed from real reading and writing, such as memorizing lists of affixes, syllable patterns, or accent patterns is pointless because readers are unlikely to use the memorized lists.

After children have had a great deal of practice reading and writing long words, they automatically apply syllable and accent patterns. In fact, as an expert reader, you can read, with the proper accent, nonsense words that conform to English spelling, even though you may not be able to "say" the rules. To prove this, read and divide into syllables these two nonsense words: *quimlar* and *plygus*. Did you divide them into the syllables of *quim-lar* and *ply-gus*? And did you pronounce them with the accent on the first syllable—*quim'- lar* and *ply'-gus*? If so, you are doing what other good readers do, using your in-depth knowledge of our writing system, including syllable and accent patterns, to read and pronounce new words.

ACTIVITIES FOR TEACHING THE MULTILETTER CHUNKS IN WORD STRUCTURE

The following activities help readers learn and use the multiletter chunks in word structure. The more readers know about the multiletter chunks in word structure, the more effective and efficient they will be at reading and spelling new words, and the closer they will move toward the last word learning stage: automatic word recognition.

The objectives for activities are as follows:

1. Read words with prefixes and/or suffixes.
2. Read words with Greek or Latin roots.
3. Read contractions.
4. Develop insight into compound words.
5. Identify the syllables in long words.
6. Combine syllables into long words.

Select the activities that will be most beneficial for your students and adapt them to suit your own special classroom environment and teaching style.

Activities

6.1 *Fold-Over Contractions*

Skill: Read contractions.

This easy activity graphically demonstrates how we form contractions. It is manipulative and appropriate for working with children in large or small groups. Fold-over contractions look like accordions with deleted letters simply folded out of sight and replaced by a piece of masking tape with an apostrophe on it. The tape holds the fold-over contraction in place, as shown in Figure 6-5.

Things You'll Need: Construction paper strips about 2 inches wide and 6 inches long; markers; masking tape.

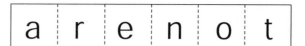

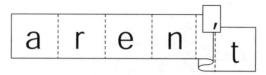

Figure 6-5   Fold-over contractions is a hands-on activity in which children fold deleted letters in contractions out of sight and replace them with an apostrophe.

Directions:

1. Give each child a paper strip and a small piece of masking tape. Children decide on the contraction they wish to make or follow your lead in making the contraction you designate.
2. Count the letters in the two separate words and fold a paper strip accordion style to make as many boxes as there are letters in the two words. For example, in turning *are not* into a fold-over contraction, children would make six boxes on the paper strip.
3. Children write the two words one after the other, putting one letter in each box. In this example, children write six letters: *a, r, e, n, o, t.* Children then write an apostrophe on the small piece of masking tape.
4. Turn the accordion into a contraction by folding the square with the letter to be deleted (*o*) under the square with the preceding letter on it (*n*), and putting the masking tape apostrophe at the top to hold the contraction together, thus forming *aren't*.
5. Encourage children to describe in their own words the purpose and placement of the apostrophe.

6.2 *Create Your Own Compounds*

Skill: Develop insight into compound words.

In this small or large group activity, first through third graders put everyday words together to create their own unique compounds.

Things You'll Need: Pencils; crayons or colored markers.

Directions:

1. Readers think of two words they use every day and then put those words together to make a brand-new compound word.
2. Have children illustrate their own compound words, as in Figure 6-6.

TooThCoat

A too th coat is a coat for your teeth

Seahouse

A seahouse is a house under the water

Sorry for using your roof for a ramp!

That's okay!

Figure 6-6 Coining new compounds gives children opportunities to creatively use their knowledge of word meaning and to write definitions for the unusual compounds they create.

3. Then have children look for compound words in text. Make a list of the words children find. Divide the list into two groups—one for compounds with meaning that can be inferred from the individual words and one for compounds with meaning that is removed from the meaning of the individual words.

6.3 *Prefix Binders*

Skill: Read and write words with prefixes.

Children collect words with the prefixes they are learning, put the words in binders, and then use the words as references when writing and participating in other classroom activities.

Things You'll Need: Each child needs a binder with tabs that have prefixes on them; notebook paper for the binder.

Directions:

1. Children write one prefix on each tab and put the tabs in the binder to separate pages with different prefixes.
2. Children then write one prefix at the top of each page of notebook paper followed by words to which the prefix is added. For instance, one page may have the prefix *un-* at the top and words like *unhappy, unkind,* and *unplugged* underneath.
3. Ask readers to be on the lookout for words with prefixes in everyday reading and to add these words to their prefix binder. Use the prefixes and base words as a ready resource for other word study activities.

6.4 *Graffiti*

Skill: Read words with prefixes and suffixes.

Here's a quick and easy opportunity for children to spontaneously express themselves while using prefixes and suffixes. This activity is appropriate for end-of-year second graders and above.

Things You'll Need: A large piece of newsprint; colorful markers.

Directions:

1. Fasten a large piece of newsprint to a bulletin board or put it on the floor. Write one or two affixes at the top of the paper. Over the course of several days, children write words on the newsprint that contain one or more of the affixes. Children may write in any color marker and may write words in any script, so long as the words are legible.
2. At the end of several days, ask the whole class to read the words in chorus and to find graffiti words with certain affixes. Add some of the

words to the word wall, or, if children are keeping personal binders for words with prefixes, add some of the words to the binders.

6.5   *Prefix Chalkboard Sort*

Skill: Read words with prefixes.

This activity, which allows children to move around as they compare base words with prefixes, is appropriate for second through sixth graders.

Things You'll Need: Two, three, or four cards with prefixes; cards with base words only; masking tape loops.

Directions:

1. Tape on the board two, three, or four cards with prefixes the children are learning (such as *un-*, *re-*, and *dis-*). Discuss how the prefixes affect word meaning.
2. Give each child one or more base word cards, each with a masking tape loop on the back. Children read the base words, find prefixes on the board to which their word might be added, and then tape the base words underneath the prefixes, thereby creating columns of words, as shown in Figure 6-7.
3. Children then analyze the chalkboard lists to answer the questions: Does every combination make a real word? Are there base words that might be combined with more than one prefix? Rearrange cards, when appropriate.
4. Give children blank cards; ask them to write their own base words on the cards and to add them to the chalkboard lists.

6.6   *Multiletter Chunk Cloze (Use for Prefixes and Suffixes)*

Skill: Read and write words with prefixes and suffixes.

In this activity, readers use context and their knowledge of word structure to fill in the missing words in sentences. This activity is suitable for readers working in small groups or in learning centers.

Things You'll Need: Three or four cloze sentences on a transparency for showing students how to fill-in the missing words; enough copies of practice sheets with modified cloze sentences for every child in the group; a transparency of the cloze sentences children are to complete.

Directions:

1. Make an overhead with several cloze sentences like the ones below. Model how to use context and suffixes (or prefixes) to decide which word belongs in each blank. Make another overhead transparency for the practice cloze sentences individuals or pairs will complete after you have introduced the activity.

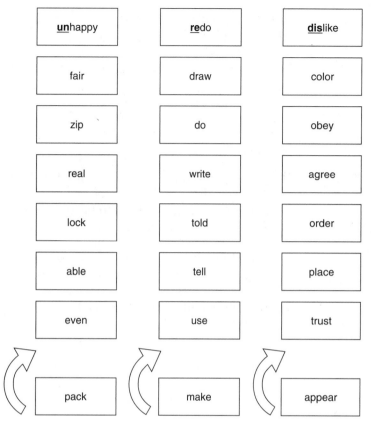

Figure 6-7   In this sorting activity, readers pay attention to prefixes and base words, talk about how prefixes affect word meaning, and cross-check for accuracy and meaning.

1. The man _____ his house bright red.
   (painted, painting, painter)
   After John threw a ball through the window, Mrs. Jones had to _____ the broken glass.
   (replace, displace, placed)
   Tom _____ the door and peeked into the room.
   (opening, opens, opened)
2. Give children a copy of the cloze sentences. Ask them to decide which word best fits the context.
3. After the children have completed the cloze sentences, show them the transparency of the sentences they just read. Invite individuals to circle the proper words on the transparency. Discuss children's choices. Talk about how prefixes and suffixes affect word meaning.

6.7 *How Many Words Can You Make?*
(Use with Prefixes and Suffixes)

Skill: Read and write words with prefixes and suffixes.

This game-like activity gives children valuable practice thinking of affixed words and remembering how to spell them.

Things You'll Need: Nothing special.

Directions:

1. Have children line up in two teams. Write a base word on the board. The teams talk among themselves and write the base word with different prefix and suffix combinations on scratch paper.
2. Alternating teams, ask a child from a team to go to the board and add a prefix or suffix to the base word. Have a child from each team add different prefixes and suffixes to the base word. For example, for the base word *limit*, a child from team A might write *limited;* team B, *limitless;* team A, *unlimited;* and so forth. Remember to start with a different team each time you write a base word on the board.
3. Depending on children's needs, you may want to ask them to add only prefixes or only suffixes. Every correct answer earns one point. Writing must be legible for the team to earn a point. The team with the most points wins.

6.8 *Word Hunts (Use with Prefixes and Suffixes)*

Skill: Read words with prefixes and suffixes.

Hunting for words with prefixes and suffixes is a good small group or learning center activity that is appropriate for children from late second through sixth grade.

Things You'll Need: Print that is appropriate for children's reading level, including a variety of magazines, coupons, and newspapers; a highlighter for each child.

Directions:

1. Give children a variety of age-appropriate print, such as old magazines, coupons, and newspapers.
2. Children use a highlighter to flag words with the prefixes or suffixes you specify.
3. Write the words on the board; use them when making affix wall charts.

6.9 *Complimenting Classmates (Use for Suffixes)*

Skill: Read and write words with suffixes.

Children in fourth, fifth and sixth grade use their knowledge of suffixes to write compliments for their classmates.

Things You'll Need: One piece of oak tag cut in the shape of a shield for every child in your class; several thesauruses.

Directions:

1. Review adjectives like the compliments *cheerful* and *artistic*. Discuss also how suffixes can change a noun (*friend*) or a verb (*imagine*) into an adjective (*friendly* or *imaginative*), and how -*er* and -*est* show comparative relationships, such as *kind, kinder,* and *kindest.*
2. Give each child an oak tag shield. Have each child write his or her name in *pencil* at the top of the paper, above the shield. Have each child write one compliment in *pencil*—a positive character trait—on the shield of every classmate. When writing, children cannot (a) use worn-out adjectives or (b) use the same compliment twice. For example, if Tom uses *imaginative* to describe a classmate, then no one else can write *imaginative* on that child's shield.
3. Make sure that each child has written one compliment on each shield. Return the shields to their owners.
4. Have the shield's owner trace over the penciled compliments in ink. Any mistakes children accidentally make when writing the original compliments are easily erased, making the finished shields smudge-free and error-free. Laminate shields and put them on the bulletin board. Fourth graders made the shield in Figure 6-8.

6.10 *Suffix Chart*

Skill: Read and write words with suffixes.

Children working together in groups combine base words with suffixes to create a chart that shows the same base words with many different suffixes.

Things You'll Need: Each cooperative group needs the following: a large piece of oak tag; a ruler; a dictionary; a pencil; a set of directions; a large piece of plain paper; colorful markers.

Directions:

1. Make a base word-suffix chart ahead of time. Show it to the children and leave it on display as a model.
2. Distribute to each group a set of directions, a large piece of oak tag, a ruler, a colored marker, and a dictionary. Directions consist of two

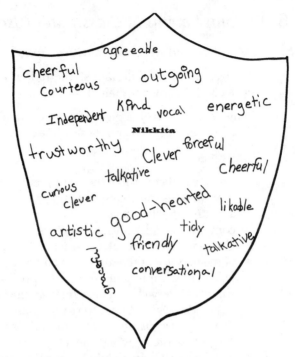

Figure 6-8 Making shields to compliment classmates gives readers opportunities to better understand adjectives and to consider how suffixes affect word meaning.

TABLE 6–3 *Sample Base Words and Suffixes for the Base Word-Suffix Chart*

Base Words				Suffixes	
act	calm	drive	last	-ed	-ing
blame	cheer	elect	like	-er	-ive
bold	color	happy	play	-est	-ly
bubble	cool	help	pass	-ful	-s/es
burn	create	jump	sick		

pages: One page is a list of 20 words and 8 suffixes, as shown in Table 6–3. The second page explains the following steps for developing a chart showing the same base words with many different suffixes:

1. Use a ruler to make a chart with 21 rows and 9 columns.
2. Color in the first box in the top row. Begin next to the colored box. Write one suffix in each box at the top of each column. When finished, you should have written: *-ed, -er, -est, -ful, -ing, -ive, -ly,* and *-s/es.*
3. Write one of the words in the first box in every row. Begin writing words in the row under the colored box. Write the 20 words in alphabetical order.
4. Write base word-suffix combinations in the rows. BEFORE writing the base word-suffix combinations, check in the *dictionary* to be sure that you are writing REAL words.
5. Leave spaces empty when you cannot make a real word with the base word-suffix combination. Use a colored marker to color in each empty space.
6. Sign the names of everyone in your group on the back of the chart when it is finished.
7. Share your chart with the class.

Table 6–4. shows a base word-suffix chart grid completed by a group of fourth graders.

6.11 *Cartoons (Use with Prefixes and Suffixes)*

Skill: Read and write words with suffixes.

Children create their own cartoons using dramatic illustrations, dialogue balloons, and words with the prefixes and suffixes they are learning in your classroom.

Things You'll Need: Large pieces of construction paper or oak tag; colored markers.

Directions:

1. Have children divide a large piece of oak tag into boxes. Each box will be used for one scene in the cartoons children are to write.
2. After deciding on a story line, children divide the story into four scenes, create fictional characters, write dialogue that uses a smattering of designated prefixes and suffixes, and illustrate their work, as shown in the cartoon in Figure 6-9.
3. Give writers opportunities to share their cartoons with their classmates. When children share their cartoons, have them point out base words with affixes. Talk about how the affixes affect word meaning and, if your classroom reading program is currently focusing on derivational suffixes, discuss how these suffixes sometimes change a word's grammatical function.

TABLE 6–4   Completed Base Word Suffix Chart

	-ed	-er	-est	-ful	-ing	-ive	-ly	-s/es
act	acted				acting	active		acts
blame	blamed				blaming			blames
bold	bolded	bolder	boldest				boldly	
bubble	bubbled	bubbler			bubbling		bubbly	bubbles
burn	burned	burner			burning			burns
calm	calmed	calmer	calmest		calming		calmly	calms
cheer	cheered			cheerful	cheering			cheers
color	colored			colorful	coloring			colors
cool	cooled	cooler	coolest		cooling			cools
create	created				creating	creative		creates
drive		driver			driving			drives
elect	elected				electing	elective		elects
happy		happier	happiest				happily	
help	helped	helper		helpful	helping			helps
jump	jumped	jumper			jumping			jumps
last	lasted				lasting			lasts
like	liked				liking			likes
pass	passed				passing	passive		passes
play	played	player		playful	playing			plays
sick		sicker	sickest				sickly	

Figure 6-9 Writing cartoons is a natural opportunity to use suffixes and to explore the contribution that suffixes make to word and passage meaning.

6.12 *Suffix Shoeboxes*

Skill: Read and write words with suffixes.

In this game-like activity, two teams draw suffix cards out of a shoebox, select a base word from a chalkboard list, and then write the base word-suffix combination. In so doing, children get practice reading and writing words with suffixes and you, the teacher, have an opportunity to target nettlesome base word-suffix combinations, such as correctly spelling *CVC* (*mopped*) and *VCe* (*moped*) words when adding suffixes.

Things You'll Need: A shoebox; cards with base words.

Directions:

1. Put several suffix cards in a shoebox, such as *-ed, -ing, -ly, -s/es, -er, -est,* and *-ly.* Write several base words on the board, like *talk, hop, slow, hope, try, jump, please, short, fast, large, drive, simple, happy,* and so forth.
2. Divide the class (or group) into two teams. Alternating from team to team, a child draws a suffix card from the shoebox, goes to the board, selects one of the base words (*hop,* for example), writes the word, and adds the suffix (*hopping*). If the base word-suffix combination is a meaningful, correctly spelled word, the team gets a point, and that base word is erased.
3. Continue playing until all the words are erased. Take the opportunity to discuss examples of nettlesome base word-suffix combinations, such as when and when not to double the final consonant or change the *y* to *i* before adding a suffix to a base word.

6.13 *Pin-Up Suffixes*

Skill: Read words with suffixes.

This activity can be used for practice with the suffixes the children are learning. It is appropriate for large and small groups of first graders and third graders.

Things You'll Need: One lightweight rope several yards long; construction paper cut into either rectangles or objects that are consistent with the theme of a book children are reading; clothespins; a shoebox; 3-inch-by-5-inch cards with base words. Put the 3-inch-by-5-inch word cards in the shoebox.

Directions:

1. Write a suffix on the board, such as *-ed,* and a few base words, perhaps *jump, hop, help,* and *hope.*
2. Demonstrate how to add *-ed* to the base words to make *jumped, hopped, helped,* and *hoped.* Explain that there are lots of words in the sack (or the shoebox), but that *-ed* (or any other suffix the children are learning) cannot be added to every one of them.
3. Children pick a word from the shoebox or sack and then decide if *-ed* can be added to it. If so, children write the word with the *-ed* suffix on a piece of construction paper (or a shape consistent with a theme in a book children are reading), and use a clothespin to put the word on the line, as shown in Figure 6-10. Children put words that cannot have an *-ed* added to the side of the shoebox or sack.
4. After all the words with *-ed* are pinned up, read them in chorus and have children practice writing them on the board. Reinforce the concept of adding suffixes to base words. In this example, you would want to

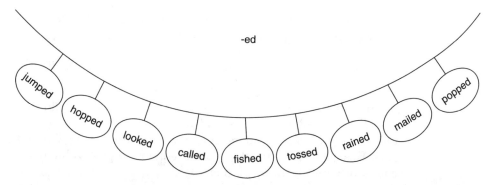

Figure 6-10 In this example, children pin up words to which the suffix *-ed* can be added. Later, words are taken down and children write them on the board with the suffix.

reinforce the idea of doubling the final consonant when adding *-ed* to CVC words by asking children to write words like *hopped* and *hoped* on the board. And then you would want to talk about why the consonant (*p*) in *hop* is doubled when adding *-ed* and why the *p* is not doubled when adding *-ed* to *hope*.

5. End by asking children to find words with doubled consonants on the pin-up line.

6.14 *Memory Game (Use with Prefixes or Suffixes)*

Skill: Read words with prefixes or suffixes.

This is another version of the memory game in which players remember which two facedown cards of 20 (or fewer) match. Children remember which pairs of base words and prefixes or suffixes make a match, such as *tall-taller* or *happy-unhappy*.

Things You'll Need: Cards with pairs of base word and base word prefix or suffix combinations, such as *joy-joyous, happy-happier, happy-unhappy,* and *like-dislike.*

Directions:

1. Put cards face down in rows. Players flip up two cards, one at a time.
2. If the base word card and the base word affix card match (*joy-joyous*), the player keeps the two cards. If not, the cards are flipped face down again, and the next player takes a turn flipping cards face up.
3. The player with the most cards wins.

6.15 *Words and Branches (Use with Prefixes, Suffixes, or Greek and Latin Roots)*

Skill: Read and write words with prefixes, suffixes, or Greek and Latin roots.

This activity uses a tree to illustrate how many different words are built by adding prefixes and suffixes or contain Greek and Latin roots. It is appropriate for third graders and above who are learning prefixes and suffixes and for fourth graders and above who are learning Greek and Latin roots. This activity is suitable for children working individually, in learning centers, or with a learning partner.

Things You'll Need: Pencils; dictionaries; copies of base words and branches; paper with several drawings of different trees, as shown in Figure 6-11.

Directions:

1. Review base words, prefixes, and suffixes, or Greek and Latin roots. Give children the base words and branches paper (see Figure 6-11).
2. Explain that each tree shows the many different "branches" that may be created by adding prefixes and suffixes to a single base word, or contain Greek and Latin roots.

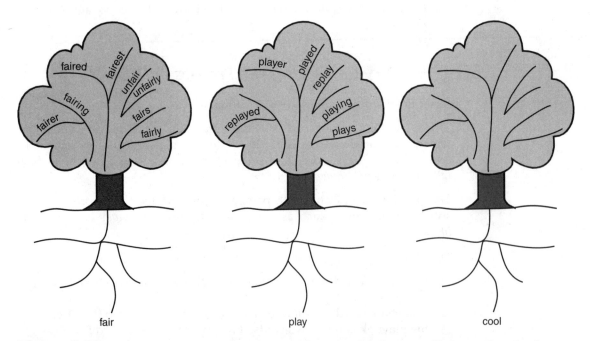

Figure 6-11   Writing words on branches that grow from the same base word helps readers develop more in-depth knowledge of the relationship among prefixes, suffixes, and base words.

3. Children think about the word at the base of each tree, decide which prefixes and suffixes can be added to that base word, and then write those words on the branches. Or children look for words that belong to the same meaning family—share the same Greek or Latin root. Children may consult dictionaries.

4. Children share the base words with affixes that grew from the base word tree or words in a meaning family with a shared Greek or Latin root.

6.16   *Syllable Word Building*

Skill: Identify syllables and combine syllables to spell words.

Children combine syllables into words and cross-check to make sure that the combined syllables make real words. This activity is appropriate for children working individually, with a learning partner, or in a center.

Things You'll Need: Cards with syllables on them.

Directions:

1. After discussing syllable patterns, give each child or set of learning partners a few syllable cards. Children put the syllable cards together to build words, cross-check for meaning, and then write the words they build.

2. When finished, discuss the words the children built. Talk about how syllables help us read new words. Discuss, too, the importance of cross-checking to be sure that the words are real, not nonsense. Table 6–5 shows an example of separate syllables and words that might be built from the syllables.

6.17   *Roundup (Use with Prefixes, Suffixes, or Greek and Latin Roots)*

Skill: Read and write words with prefixes, suffixes, and Greek and Latin roots.

Teams compete for three days to find words with the prefixes, suffixes, or Greek and Latin roots they are learning in your classroom.

Things You'll Need: Nothing special.

Directions:

1. Create groups of four to six readers. Ask the groups to find as many words as possible in three days that include the prefixes, suffixes, or Greek and Latin roots they are learning in your classroom.

2. Teams write the words on a sheet of paper and indicate where the words were found. Teams earn one point for each word they find. At the end of the third day, teams share the words and, if appropriate,

TABLE 6–5	*Syllable Word Building*

Syllables	
car	par
ty	pet
son	per
ter	bat

Words
party
carpet
person
petty
carpenter
Carter
batty
batter
car
pet
son
Bart

teams get a prize for finding different types of words, such as (a) the most words, (b) the most unusual word, (c) the longest word, or (d) the word with the most syllables.

6.18 *Coin-a-Word (Use with Common Greek or Latin Roots)*

Skill: Read words with Greek and Latin roots.

Children use common Greek or Latin roots to coin their own words. (*Astroport*, the word at the beginning of this chapter, is the invention of a fifth grader.)

Things You'll Need: Nothing special.

Directions:

1. Children work individually or in pairs to coin words by combining Greek and Latin roots, write a definition for the coined words, and illustrate their new words.

2. Put the coined words and illustrations on bulletin boards, along the chalk tray, or anywhere they are in plain view. Discuss the coined words. Children then decide in which meaning family the coined words belong. For instance, the coined word *bioforce* belongs in the *bio-* meaning family with words like *biology* and *biography.*

6.19 *Chalkboard Meaning Families (Use with Greek or Latin Roots)*

Skill: Read and write words with the same Greek or Latin roots.

This activity illustrates how common Greek and Latin roots are found in many English words. It is suitable for end-of-year fifth and sixth graders who are reading words with Greek and Latin roots in content area textbooks.

Things You'll Need: Oak tag sentence strips cut in half; markers; masking-tape loops; dictionaries.

Directions:

1. Select two or three common Greek or Latin roots that usually come at the beginning of words. Write on the board several long words that begin with the Greek or Latin roots, such a *geography, biology,* and *microscope.*
2. Talk about how common Greek and Latin roots contribute to word meaning. Discuss how *bio* means *life, geo* means *earth,* and *micro* means *small.*
3. Write the Greek or Latin roots on sentence strips. Tape the strips fairly far apart on the board. Distribute dictionaries, blank oak tag strips, markers, and tape to small groups. Assign (or ask groups to choose) one of the Greek or Latin roots on the oak tag strips.
4. Each group then finds words in dictionaries and context area textbooks that include the roots. Groups write the words they find on oak tag strips and tape the strips under the designated roots on the board, as shown in Figure 6-12.
5. Conclude by inviting a volunteer from each group to explain how their Greek or Latin root contributes to word meaning.

6.20 *Word Webs (Use with Prefixes, Suffixes, or Common Greek and Latin Roots)*

Skill: Read words with prefixes, suffixes, or Greek and Latin roots.

Word webs begin with a single, often-used prefix, suffix, or Green or Latin root and then spin off into many different miniwebs, as shown in Figure 6-13. Webs with prefixes and suffixes are appropriate for third through fifth

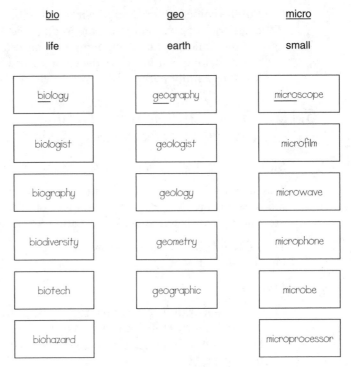

Figure 6-12   Creating words. In writing words with often-used Greek and Latin roots, children learn how these roots contribute to the meaning of many different words. Words found in *Merriam-Webster's Elementary Dictionary: The Student's Source for Discovering Language*, (2000), Springfield, MA: Merriam-Webster, Inc.

graders, while webs with common Greek and Latin roots are best suited for fifth and sixth graders. This activity is most successful when readers work cooperatively in groups.

Things You'll Need: Dictionaries; a large piece of chart paper for each cooperative group; colored construction paper; colorful markers.

Directions:

1. Write an often-used prefix, suffix, or Greek or Latin root in the center of the board and draw a bubble around it.
2. Write a word with the prefix, suffix, or Greek or Latin root to the upper right of the first bubble; draw a bubble around it; and draw a straight line from this word to the prefix, suffix, or Greek or Latin root, as shown in Figure 6-13.
3. Challenge readers to think of another word that includes the same prefix, suffix, or Greek or Latin root. Add suggested words to the web, drawing bubbles around them, and drawing a line from each word (called a web strand) to the prefix, suffix, or Greek or Latin root in the center.

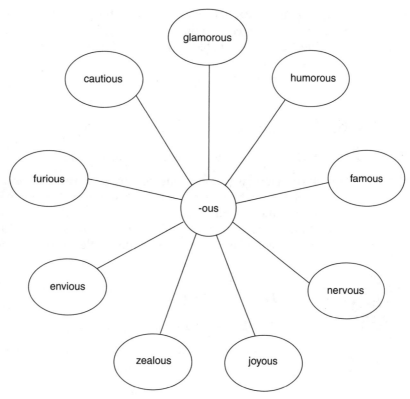

Figure 6-13 Word web for the suffix *-ous*. Creating word webs helps readers draw the conclusion that many words share the same prefix, suffix, or Greek or Latin root.

4. Children now are ready to work together in small groups to make their own word webs, using words found in materials they study throughout the day, as well as words they find in dictionaries, wall charts, signs, and posters.
5. After webs are perfected to the satisfaction of group members, invite the groups to share their webs with the entire class, and to explain the connections among words, telling why and how each word is a member of the meaning family. Figure 6-13 shows a word web for the suffix *-ous*.

SPARE-MINUTE ACTIVITIES FOR TEACHING SYLLABLES

6.21 *Tactile Syllables*

Skill: Identify the syllables in long words.

Children can actually feel syllables as they pronounce words. Have children lightly touch their chins with the back of their hands. You say a word and the children repeat it. In saying a word, children will notice that their chins drop as they pronounce the vowel sounds. Each chin movement represents one syllable. Count the syllables in a word. Write the word on the board and repeat the process, noting how many syllables the children feel. Divide the written word into syllables; discuss how syllable cues help us read new long words.

6.22   *Syllable-by-Syllable Decoding*

Skill: Read long words with several syllables.

Write a long word on a sentence strip, such as *retirement*. Gently fold the strip so that only the first syllable, *re*, shows. Ask children to read the first syllable. Reveal the second syllable, *tire*, and ask children to read it. Then ask the children to read the two syllables together. Unfold the strip to reveal the last syllable, *ment*. Have children read the whole word, *retirement*.

6.23   *Slashed Syllables*

Skill: Identify the syllables in long words.

Write several long words on the board. Have volunteers come to the board, put slashes between syllables, and read the words.

6.24   *One-, Two-, and Three-Syllable Word Sort*

Skill: Identify the syllables in long words.

Put masking tape loops on cards with one-, two-, and three-syllable words. Children take turns sticking the cards to the board. One-syllable words go under the numeral 1; two-syllable words, under 2; three-syllable words, under 3. Use this activity with children in third through fourth grade.

SPARE-MINUTE ACTIVITIES FOR TEACHING PREFIXES, SUFFIXES, OR GREEK AND LATIN ROOTS

6.25   *Wall Charts (Use for Prefixes, Suffixes, and Words with Greek and Latin Roots)*

Skill: Read words with prefixes and suffixes or Greek and Latin roots.

Make large wall chart lists of words with prefixes, suffixes, or Greek and Latin roots. In making large wall charts, readers think about words that include the multiletter chunks they are learning in your classroom, read the words, and then refer to them when participating in many different classroom reading and writing activities.

6.26 *Prefix-Suffix Circle*

Skill: Read words with prefixes and suffixes.

This is another variation of the peel-off strategy. Here, children (1) circle prefixes and suffixes, (2) underline the base word, (3) pronounce each part, and (4) blend the parts together (Archer, Gleason, & Vachon, 2003).

6.27 *Prefix-Suffix Definitions*

Skill: Read words with prefixes and suffixes.

Tape cards with prefixes and suffixes to the board. Move over a few feet and tape cards with prefix-suffix definitions to the board. Children match the definitions to the prefixes and suffixes by moving the cards to line up definitions with the correct prefix or suffix.

6.28 *Prefix-Suffix Peel Off*

Skill: Read and write words with prefixes and suffixes.

This is a quick version of a paper and pencil exercise. You can have children write on the board or write on a blank piece of paper. Children draw three columns. Have them label the first column *Prefix*, the second *Base Word*, and the third *Suffix*. You pronounce words and children write the base words, the prefixes, and the suffixes.

6.29 *Add the Right Suffix*

Skill: Read and write words with suffixes.

Working in pairs or individually, children read base words, two- or three-suffix choices, and then write the base words with the appropriate suffix.

Base Word	Suffix	Base Word + Suffix
long	er/ ment/ ly	longer
joy	ment/ ing/ ful	joyful
hand	er/ tion/ y	handy
move	ly/ able/ tion	moveable
happy	ness/ ed/ able	happiness

INSIGHT INTO WORD MEANING AND PRONUNCIATION

Many English words have affixes attached to them; others are built from borrowed Greek and Latin roots; still others are shortcuts—contractions—for writing words separately. The multiletter chunks in word structure give readers insight into word meaning, which explains why these multiletter groups are so important for word recognition (Nagy, Anderson, Schommer, Scott, & Stallman, 1989). On the other hand, syllables, while seldom providing readers with insight into meaning, do help readers figure out the pronunciation of long words.

Insight into the meaning and pronunciation of long words becomes increasingly important as children move up in the elementary grades. As children move from third to fourth, fourth to fifth, and fifth to sixth grade, they come into contact with more and more long words in content subject and leisure reading material. Many of these words are not in readers' speaking and listening vocabularies. When readers combine their understanding of the multiletter chunks in word structure with sentence structure and meaning context cues, they are able to learn these new words. Now, at last, vocabulary learning by reading surpasses learning by speaking and listening.

By the time children leave the elementary school and move on to middle school, they are learning more new words through reading and writing than through talking and listening. The power of literacy transforms children; it opens them to new ideas, new information, new intellectual horizons, and new English words. It also gives them tools for lifelong learning and lifelong reading pleasure.

Children who have had a great many reading and writing opportunities and still cannot use word identification strategies to read new words need extra help. These children have limited reading vocabularies. Consequently, they are often frustrated when reading and writing. Younger children who lack reading fluency cannot read age-appropriate library books on their own. Ideas and concepts in content area textbooks vex older children because the technical vocabulary is out of their reach. As a teacher, you are responsible for ferreting out children's stumbling blocks and providing the additional support and instruction that they require to succeed. This is the topic of the next chapter.

REFERENCES

Archer, A. L., Gleason, M. M., & Vachon, F. L. (2003). Decoding and fluency: Foundations of skills for struggling older readers. *Learning Disabilities Quarterly, 26,* 89–101.

Ayers, D. M. (1980). *English words from Greek and Latin elements.* Tucson: University of Arizona Press.

Bhattacharya, A., & Ehri, L. C. (2004). Graphosyllabic analysis helps adolescent struggling readers read and spell words. *Journal of Learning Disabilities, 37,* 331–348.

Carlisle, J. F. (2000). Awareness of the structure and meaning of morphologically complex words: Impact on reading. *Reading and Writing: An Interdisciplinary Journal, 12,* 169–190.

Carlisle, J. F., & Stone, C. A. (2005). Exploring the role of morphemes in word reading. *Reading Research Quarterly, 40,* 428–449.

Deacon, S. H., & Kirby, J. R. (2004). Morphological awareness: Just "more phonological?" The roles of morphological and phonological awareness in reading development. *Applied Psycholinguistics, 25,* 223–238.

Duncan, L. G., & Seymour, P. H. K. (2003). How do children read multisyllabic words? Some preliminary observations. *Journal of Research in Reading, 26,* 101–120.

Ehri, L. C. (2005). Learning to read words: Theory, findings, and issues. *Scientific Studies of Reading, 9,* 167–188.

Gentry, J. R. (2006). *The New Science of Beginning Reading and Writing.* Portsmouth, NH: Heinemann.

Gibson, E. J., & Guinet, L. (1971). Perception of inflections in brief visual presentations of words. *Journal of Verbal Learning and Verbal Behavior, 10,* 182–189.

Hackett, J. K., Moyer, R. H., & Adams, D. K. (1989). *Merrill Science.* Upper Saddle River, NJ: Merrill/Prentice Hall.

Henderson, E. H. (1990). *Teaching spelling* (2nd ed.). Boston: Houghton Mifflin.

Invernizzi, M. A. (1992). The vowel and what follows: A phonological frame of orthographic analysis. In S. Templeton & D. R. Bear (Eds.), *Development of orthographic knowledge and the foundations of literacy* (pp. 105–136). Hillsdale, NJ: Erlbaum.

Ives, J. P., Bursuk, L. Z., & Ives, S. A. (1979). *Word identification techniques.* Chicago: Rand McNally.

Mahoney, D., Singson, M., & Mann, V. (2000). Reading ability and sensitivity to morphological relations. *Reading and Writing: An Interdisciplinary Journal, 12,* 191–218.

Merriam-Webster. (2000). *Merriam-Webster's elementary dictionary: The student's source for discovering language.* Springfield, MA: Author.

Miller, G. A. (1956). The magical number seven, plus or minus two: Some limits on our capacity for processing information. *Psychological Review, 63,* 81–97.

Nagy, W. E., Anderson, R. C., Schommer, M., Scott, J. A., & Stallman, A. C. (1989). Morphological families and word recognition. *Reading Research Quarterly, 24,* 262–282.

Nagy, W., Berninger, V. W., & Abbot, R. D. (2006). Contributions of morphology beyond phonology to literacy outcomes of upper elementary and middle-school students. *Journal of Educational Psychology, 98,* 134–147.

Nagy, W. E., Diakidoy, I. N., & Anderson, R. C. (1993). The acquisition of morphology: Learning the contribution of suffixes to the meaning of derivatives. *Journal of Reading Behavior, 25,* 155–170.

Neuhaus, G. F., Roldan, L. W., Boulware-Gooden, R., & Swank, P. R. (2006). Parsimonious reading models: Identifying teachable subskills. *Reading Psychology, 27,* 37–58.

Nunes, T., Bryant, P., & Bindman, M. (1997). Morphological spelling strategies: Developmental stages and processes. *Developmental Psychology, 33,* 637–649.

Santa, C. M. (1976–1977). Spelling patterns and the development of flexible word recognition strategies. *Reading Research Quarterly, 12,* 125–144.

Singson, M., Mahony, D., & Mann, V. (2000). The relation between reading ability and morphological skills: Evidence from derivational suffixes. *Reading and Writing: An Interdisciplinary Journal, 12,* 219–252.

Stuart, M., & Coltheart, M. (1988). Does reading develop in a sequence of stages? *Cognition, 30,* 139–181.

Templeton, S. (1991). *Teaching the integrated language arts.* Boston: Houghton Mifflin.

White, T. G., Power, M. A., & White, S. (1989). Morphological analysis: Implications for teaching and understanding vocabulary growth. *Reading Research Quarterly, 24,* 283–304.

White, T. G., Sowell, J., & Yanagihara, A. (1989). Teaching elementary students to use word-part clues. *The Reading Teacher, 42,* 302–308.

Wysocki, K., & Jenkins, J. R. (1987). Deriving word meanings through morphological generalization. *Reading Research Quarterly, 22,* 66–81.

CHAPTER 7

Teaching English Language Learners and Children at Risk

This chapter explains how to help English language learners and children at risk develop effective word identification strategies. You will learn about the best practices for teaching English learners and how children's home language may affect learning to read English. This chapter also explains why some children struggle with word identification and what you can do to help them. You will learn how to give extra help to at-risk learners who over-rely on picture cues or do not effectively use the analogy-based strategy and letter-sound phonics to read and learn new words.

KEY IDEAS

- Some English language learners need extra help because the language spoken at home is different from the language of instruction at school.

- English language learners and children who speak English as their first language develop phonemic awareness and phonics in a similar way and in a similar sequence.

- Phonemic awareness activities help English learners pay attention to English sounds.

- Some children are at risk because they do not effectively use phonics to read and learn new words.

- At-risk learners become better readers when their teachers pair phonics instruction with reading connected text.

- It is important to strike a balance between (a) the knowledge and abilities children bring to reading and writing, and (b) the challenges of reading interesting and age-appropriate literature and of writing for a variety of purposes.

Perhaps you are wondering why the first illustration in this chapter—Figure 7-1—is a seesaw. As it turns out, a simple playground seesaw demonstrates a fundamental principle of physics that has a great deal of relevance to teaching and learning. Seesaws are simple levers. The purpose of levers is to make it easier to lift heavy loads, in this case the weight of playmates at either end of the seesaw. The seesaw board is the lever and the support on which the board is balanced is called the fulcrum.

The weight of the playmates in Rich's drawing in Figure 7-1 is about equal, so the effort needed to push each playmate into the air is exactly the same. Should a heavier playmate get on one end, the lighter playmate will be stuck in the air and the lighter playmate must push harder. If the heavier playmate weighs quite a bit more, the lighter playmate will not have the strength, or force, to lift the load of the

Figure 7-1   A simple seesaw demonstrates a fundamental principle of physics that is relevant to supporting literacy in today's classrooms.

heavier playmate. Moving the fulcrum changes the balance point. With a new balance point, the lighter playmate can exert the force necessary to lift the heavier playmate (load).

Just as seesaw playmates differ in weight, so do the children we teach differ in the knowledge, abilities, and strategies they bring to reading. While some children develop a full complement of word identification strategies through the normal reading and writing experiences in your classroom, others do not. Just as the success of a seesaw hinges on finding the right balance point between the force and the load, so does the success of learning and using word identification strategies hinge on finding the right balance point between children's abilities and reading and writing activities they engage in.

Sometimes regular classroom activities are too complex for the knowledge and strategies children bring to activities. Under this condition, children are in a similar position to that of a lightweight seesaw playmate who lacks the strength to lift a heavier child. When this happens, children need extra support and help from their teachers. Children succeed when classroom activities are roughly in balance with their ability to use word identification strategies. In practical terms, this means finding activities with which children are successful and then using those activities to improve achievement.

ENGLISH LANGUAGE LEARNERS

English language learners bring to your classroom rich ethnic, cultural, and language backgrounds. They also bring to reading a different complement of sentence (syntactic) structures and vocabulary. Your classroom reading program must build on children's ability to speak and understand English. Neither you nor I would consider attempting to learn to read a second language, say French, without any knowledge of French words and French sentence structure. We would first learn something about the words, sounds, and structure of the French language. Then we would begin to learn to read French. Likewise, children who do not speak English as their first language need to learn something about English words, sounds, and structure before we teach them to read.

There is a mutually supportive relationship among learning to speak, read, and write English, provided that children enter into reading instruction with some understanding of spoken English. When children understand how the English alphabet represents sounds, they become more aware of English words. Similarly, instruction in reading vocabulary not only increases children's reading comprehension, but also extends their use of spoken English. This, in turn, enhances children's abilities to form thoughts in English when they write.

Native language literacy is important for balancing the load and the force. It is easier for children to learn to read and write English when children are literate in their first language (Royer & Carlo, 1991). If children can read their home language and if that language uses an alphabet, children may bring to your classroom some, if not all, of the word identification strategies described in this book, albeit applied to reading new words in their home languages.

Children whose families speak languages other than English and who are not literate in their native language are most successful when they have opportunities to observe, infer, and grasp connections between spoken and written language, and when they have opportunities to develop phonemic awareness and learn letter names and phonics letter-sound patterns. After children have some understanding of spoken English, one way to strike a balance is to explore English words and sounds along with reading easy English stories.

Phonemic Awareness

Phonemic awareness in English is just as important for English learners as for children who speak only English (Chiappe, Siegel, & Wade-Woolley, 2002). English learners may generalize phonemic awareness in their first language to the English language (Manis, Lindsey, & Bailey, 2004). From a practical perspective, this means that English learners with better phonemic awareness in their home language are also likely to have better phonemic awareness in English. These children are likely to develop phonemic awareness at a faster pace and with less instruction than children who are not aware of the individual sounds in their home languages. Therefore, you will want to carefully observe children as they develop phonemic awareness and be ready to provide extra instruction and support, especially to children who do not have phonemic awareness in their home language.

English learners and English-only children develop phonemic awareness in a similar way (Chiappe et al., 2002). Therefore, you can use the same phonemic awareness activities for the English learners and the English-only children whom you teach. You do not need to prepare special phonemic awareness lessons for English learners, and it is not necessary to modify instruction for them. The ongoing phonemic awareness instruction in your classroom will benefit English learners and English-only children alike. However, in spite of following a common developmental pathway, English learners often perform less well on phonemic awareness and phonics tasks than their English-only classmates (Rupley, Rodriquez, Mergen, Willson, & Nichols, 2000). The challenge is to accelerate learning so that English learners progress at the same pace as English-only children. The English learners who do not have phonemic awareness in their home language may require the most intense instruction sustained over a longer period of time.

Differences between students' first language and English also affect learning to read. All the sounds in English may not be present in children's home languages. For instance, Spanish does not have the short /a/ heard in /bad/, the short /e/ in /bed/, the short /i/ in /bid/, or the short /u/ in /bud/ (Helman, 2004). This makes it more difficult for Spanish-speaking children to hear these sounds and, by extension, more difficult to develop phonemic awareness and learn phonics.

In order to develop an awareness of the sounds in English words, children must differentiate one English sound from another. Learning to read English depends more on children's ability to discriminate and identify English sounds than on children's ability to correctly pronounce sounds (Birch, 2002). In developing the ability to differentiate one English sound from another, children create mental representations of sounds that they then associate with letters when learning letter-sound phonics. The implication for your classroom reading program is that correct or near correct pronunciation is not critical if your students are able to discriminate one English sound from another.

Generally speaking, English learners with better English pronunciation find it easier to develop phonemic awareness than children whose English pronunciation is less well developed (Roberts, 2005). This said, you do not need to delay teaching phonemic awareness until English learners accurately pronounce English sounds. Phonemic awareness activities actually help English learners pay attention to English sounds. For instance, when you ask "What sound do you hear at the beginning of *mouse*?" you help children notice /m/ and give children practice pronouncing /m/. When you ask "Which doesn't belong? *Man-top-mouse*?" you draw children's attention to English sounds at the beginning of words and, additionally, help children learn the sounds of English.

You will notice that the proper pronunciation of English sounds has the greatest effect on children's ability to read aloud. Therefore, along with phonemic awareness instruction, you will want to offer children many and varied opportunities to sound out words and to read connected text instead of focusing on correct pronunciation.

Phonics

The English learners and English-only children in your classroom will learn phonics letter-sound patterns in a similar sequence (Chiappe et al., 2002; Rupley et al., 2000). Although English learners and English-only children follow a similar learning sequence, many English learners tend to learn phonics at a slower pace (Denton, Anthony, Parker, & Hasbrouck, 2004). Try grouping English learners and English-only children according to their ability to learn and use phonics. You can expect English learners to benefit from phonics instruction that lasts somewhat longer than is customary for English-only children. It is also important to supplement the ongoing phonics instruction in your classroom. English learners who learn phonics at a slower pace will benefit from extra, intense, and highly focused phonics instruction (Lesaux & Siegel, 2003).

Teach phonics instruction early, in kindergarten and first grade when the classroom reading program focuses on teaching word identification. When you provide early, supplemental phonics instruction over an extended period, English learners improve in decoding, word reading, comprehension, and fluency (Gunn, Smolkowski, Biglan, & Black, 2002). Early phonics instruction that is well-planned, sustained, and supplemental increases the possibility that English learners will read as well as the average readers in your classroom by the end of second grade (Lesaux & Siegel, 2003). And as you develop and implement early, intense, and supplementary instruction, model how to use phonics, give children practice using phonics to spell, and support children as they apply phonics while reading.

Structural Analysis

Children who speak a Romance language at home, such as Spanish or French, may have some familiarity with some of the prefixes, suffixes, and root words of English (Manzo, Manzo, & Thomas, 2006). Begin by teaching prefixes, suffixes, and Greek and Latin roots that are common to English and to children's home language (Pérez Cañado, 2005). Teaching common word parts makes it possible for children to generalize what they know about their home language to English.

Keep structural analysis meaning-based. Identifying and inferring the meaning of long words not only helps children read new words, but also helps them learn what the words mean in the reading context. Discuss how meaningful word parts—the free and bound morphemes found in prefixes, suffixes, and root words—affect the meaning of English words, as explained in Chapter 6. Demonstrate how the structure of long words consists of smaller, meaningful chunks; show children how to find these chunks; demonstrate how to use word structure to infer word meaning. And when teaching English learners about syllables, emphasize how syllables help us pronounce long words.

Teach word meaning along with structural analysis. When you teach English learners about the structure of English words, emphasize word meaning. For example, in teaching compound words, you might enrich speaking, listening, and reading ability by discussing the meaning of the words individually and then the meaning of the compound. Talk about how complex words are made of smaller word parts. Show children how to find these parts, discuss the meaning of the parts and, if focusing on syllables, how the sound helps us identify complex words.

Word Meaning

Vocabulary consists of (a) all the English words English language learners know and (b) how much children know about those words. Words label concepts. For example, *cat* refers to a furry, four-legged animal that purrs; *catty,* to spiteful behavior; *catty-corner,* to diagonal objects; *cat walk,* to a narrow elevated walkway. Each variation on the word *cat* conveys remarkably different information and invokes vastly different visual images. What children understand while reading and how they use words while writing depends, at least in part, on how much they know about the English language and the myriad of English words that label a multitude of concepts.

Cognates are words with similar sounds and meanings in two languages, such as *exit* and *éixto* (Spanish). This makes cognates a convenient bridge between children's home languages and English. English learners who know a cognate in their home language have some insight into the meaning of the same words in English. The more overlap there is between languages, the greater the number of cognates that we may use to develop students' understanding of English words. English and Spanish share many cognates. Therefore, developing the ability to recognize cognates in these two languages is particularly important for Spanish-speaking English-language learners. The possibility of misidentifying meaning not withstanding, teaching cognates increases children's English vocabulary (Carlo, August, & Snow, 2005).

Therefore, you will want to take advantage of cognates when the English word and the word in children's home language share a common meaning.

Children are bound to bring different life experiences, native language vocabulary, and concepts to our classrooms. It is important to find out whether children understand the concepts that English words label before teaching English vocabulary. There are three possible relationships among children's word knowledge and concepts:

- Children may already know the concepts and have the words for these concepts in their home languages but may not know the English labels for the familiar concepts. These children will have little or no trouble learning English words through conversation, classroom discussions, and reading. For example, Spanish-speaking children may know the spoken word /gato/ (*tomcat*) in their home language and recognize tomcats when they see them. These children need to learn the English word (/cat/) for a familiar concept and native language word they already know. Once children recognize the English word /cat/ and understand that in English the word *cat* may refer to either a male or a female cat, they are then ready to learn the written word for *cat*.
- A second possibility is that children already have a concept of cat but have not learned the native language word (/gato/) for that concept. When words are common, as we see in the example of *gato*, it may be wise to enlist the assistance of a native language speaker to develop the native language word. In teaching the English word *cat*, we want to link that word (/cat/) with the previously learned concept (*tomcat*). In this example, we also would want to slightly adjust children's concept so as to understand that in English /cat/ may refer to both male and female cats, while in Spanish *gato* refers only to tomcats.
- A third possibility is that children do not have the concept or know the word in their home language. Should an English word represent a concept that children do not understand, we will need to help them develop both the concept and the English word for that concept. Simply teaching the English word is not helpful because children do not understand the meaning of the English word they are learning. If children do not yet understand the concepts that English words label, then you will want to create learning opportunities to develop both the concepts and the vocabulary through using Internet activities, viewing films, interacting with CD-ROMs, taking field trips, demonstrating word meaning, discussing pictures that represent concepts, and listening to stories that offer some explanation of the concepts.

English language learners develop competence using English language in social settings before they develop the competence needed for reading, writings, and learning from text (Drucker, 2003). Greater language proficiency is needed for reading and writing than for interacting socially. English learners who effortlessly converse with their classmates in your classroom and on the playground may not have sufficient English language competence to support high achievement in reading and writing.

Some of the English learners in your classroom may know significantly fewer words than English-only children, and the vocabulary gap may not close even after two years of schooling (Hutchinson, Whitely, Smith, & Connors, 2003). English learners need to see, hear, read, and write words many times and in many different contexts. Children benefit when your classroom environment encourages speaking, hearing, reading, and writing in many different contexts. Use pictures and demonstrations to teach word meaning (Presta, 2004). Preteach key words, use exaggerated gestures to dramatize words, teach words and the concepts they represent, develop vocabulary before you ask children to read, and ask children to sound out with phonics only when children already know word meaning.

Children's home language influences learning to read and write English. Sometimes you will observe the influence of children's home language as they read and write, as shown in Juana's story in Figure 7-2. When Juana writes, she combines her knowledge of English with a rich knowledge of Spanish, her home language. Notice that Juana replaces *of* with *de*, the Spanish word that would ordinarily be used in this syntactic structure. Notice, too, that Juana writes *ticher* for *teacher*. The letter *i* in Spanish represents the sound heard in *routine*, not *line*, so Juana's spelling is consistent with her first language heritage. Juana also is aware of the way that the English alphabet represents sound, as you can see in her spelling of *tois* for *toys*. You can expect Juana to learn the rimes, phonics letter-sound patterns, and the

Figure 7-2   The written messages of children who speak languages other than English at home, such as Juana, whose family speaks Spanish, may reflect a combination of children's home language and English.

multiletter chunks in word structure in basically the same order as children who speak English as their first language, although, depending on the child, at a somewhat slower pace.

Chan, whose story is shown in Figure 7-3, has attended English-speaking schools longer than Juana. Chan brings greater knowledge of spoken and written English to reading and is therefore capable of lifting greater loads—he reads and understands more challenging materials than Juana. Even so, Chan's home language, Vietnamese, sometimes crosses over into written and spoken English. For instance, when Chan writes, he does not always include all function words such as prepositions and conjunctions. And when Chan reads aloud, he pronounces *mother* as /muder/ and leaves out most plurals, possessives, and many other word endings, thus reading *wanted* as /want/. This is so even though Chan's story is a retelling of a familiar book, *The Great Kapok Tree* (Cherry, 1990), which his teacher read several times in class, and the class discussed a good deal in relation to science.

Chan and Juana, like all readers of English, must automatically recognize the pronunciation and meaning of words, as explained in Chapter 1. Languages may overlap with English up to 20% (Graves, Juel, & Graves, 1998). The greater the

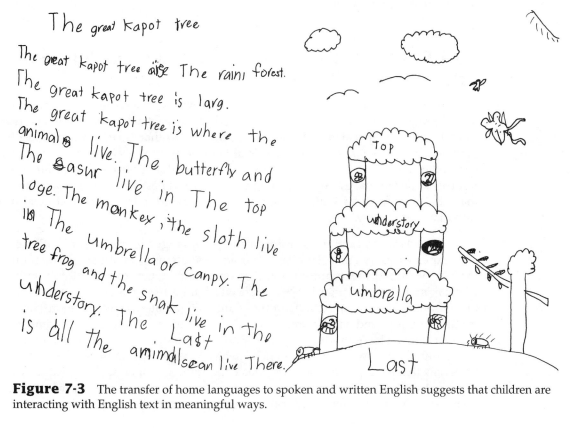

Figure 7-3   The transfer of home languages to spoken and written English suggests that children are interacting with English text in meaningful ways.

overlap in languages, the more information children bring to learning to speak, read, and write English. Juana's home language, Spanish, has a good deal of overlap with English, while Chan's home language, Vietnamese, has relatively little overlap. This means that, for children like Chan, you may need to concentrate more time and attention on building the background needed to understand English vocabulary and sentence structure.

When children are gaining an understanding of English words, they need lots of support, including support from the reading context. Interestingly, you may find that English learners are better at reading words in context than in lists (Wong & Underwood, 1996). Consequently, you may observe that English learners benefit from the cues to words found in the reading context, whereas the native English speakers in your classroom may show no difference in their ability to read words in lists or in context.

The crossover, or transfer, of home languages to spoken and written English (substituting *de* for *of*, spelling *teacher* as *ticher*, omitting word endings and conjunctions, and using verbs inappropriately) suggests that children are interacting with English text in meaningful ways. Transfer is an important sign of progress toward English literacy. Though the home languages Juana and Chan speak result in different types of transfer, you can expect children like these to learn to speak and read English equally well.

BEST PRACTICES FOR TEACHING READING AND SHARING LITERACY WITH ENGLISH LANGUAGE LEARNERS

Both Juana and Chan are moving toward accomplished use of written English, each at a different point on a continuum. You must determine what types of materials are most likely to help balance the load and the force—that is, to simultaneously support children's strategic use of our alphabetic writing system and enhance comprehension. One thing you can do is to support children as they become literate in their home languages. Another thing you can use is best practice to balance the load and the force to support developing the word identification strategies important for literacy.

1.   Adapt instruction to children's English language proficiency, culture, and experiences. English language learners will remember more information (Malik, 1990) and make more elaborate connections when they read culturally familiar materials (Pritchard, 1990) than when they read materials that are far afield from their home cultures. Culturally unfamiliar materials require more background building and call for more explicit explanations than culturally familiar materials. If you have children in your classroom who come from different cultural backgrounds, you will want to match materials with each culture, if possible. Materials that are a good fit for Hispanic children may not be such a good fit for Arabic, Asian, or Native American children. This underscores the importance of being sensitive to children's cultural heritage and personal life experiences.

2. **Use culturally familiar text to assess reading ability.** Culturally unfamiliar text is not a good measure of reading ability and, in fact, is likely to underestimate English learners' actual reading achievement (Garcia, 1991). Children are better readers of the materials in your classroom—better at comprehending storybooks, novels, articles, and poems, and better at remembering information and concepts in content subject textbooks—when text is culturally relevant, but worse readers when text is culturally unfamiliar. So, if you wish to get an informal assessment of children's reading abilities, use materials that correspond to children's prior knowledge and experience and avoid materials that are detached from children's lives.

3. **Connect children's life experiences and home language with your classroom reading program.** It is important to connect children's everyday life experiences, concepts, and cultural values with your classroom reading program. Welcome parents and other adults who speak children's home languages into your classroom as resources for sharing language and culture (in this case, Spanish for Juana and Vietnamese for Chan). Ask resource persons to talk about their home culture and to volunteer in your class when possible. And when you do this, invite adults to help your class celebrate some of the holidays in children's home cultures. Ask adults to bring traditional dress and foods to your classroom and to demonstrate art and dance.

Encourage children to talk about their life experiences and incorporate those experiences into your everyday classroom routine. Cook children's traditional foods; write signs in children's home languages; and make bulletin boards, wall charts, and labels in both English and the children's home languages. Use pictures and real objects (an orange, a fork, a toy car) to support classroom discussions whenever possible. Find books and magazines written in children's home languages or use books and magazines that include words from children's home languages. Read books and traditional tales that embrace children's cultures; role-play, retell, and illustrate stories, folktales, and poems. Such activities build a strong context for learning and provide ways to honor the cultures of children as well.

4. **Develop children's ability to speak their home language and English (Miller, et al., 2006).** Language competence facilitates reading text written in English and in children's home language. On the one hand, children with better competence speaking English have better comprehension of text written in English and their home language. In the other direction, children with better competence in their home language have better comprehension of text written in the home language and in English. Consequently, when children's ability to speak English and their home language improves, it is likely that children's comprehension of text will also improve.

5. **Use predictable books to practice and reinforce English language patterns and vocabulary.** Predictable books—books with repeated phrases or sentences— hold a special promise because they bring English syntax and English words within easy reach of young children who are beginning to read a language different from the one spoken at home. Because the same English language patterns recur over and over, predictable books encourage young, beginning readers to anticipate sentence structure. Since the same words are read many times, children have many chances

to remember them, thereby building their reading vocabularies. The same characteristics that make predictable books useful for younger children also make these books beneficial for older children who are novice readers of English (Arthur, 1991). Do not hesitate to share predictable books with older children who are crossing the threshold of English literacy, provided, of course, that books are culturally and developmentally appropriate.

6.   Read aloud to children. When you read aloud, children have opportunities to develop a sense of the structure of stories, enjoy literature, and have experiences with English print that may not be available in their homes. Select from a wide variety of books, including books that are set in children's home countries and reflect children's cultural heritage. If you teach emergent and beginning readers, reread familiar books to give children multiple opportunities to hear the same English sentences and words. Older children enjoy listening to you read books one chapter at a time. Read to children often and make reading aloud a normal part of your school day and an integral component in your classroom reading program.

7.   Have children write often and for a variety of purposes. Children whose families speak languages other than English at home express their thoughts in writing long before they speak English proficiently (Hudelson, 1984). Writing helps children reflect on meaningful messages in print, creates opportunities to use English sentence structure and vocabulary in meaningful ways, and supports insight into our English alphabetic writing system. Look for ways to combine read-aloud stories with writing activities, such as asking children to write about a memorable event or a fascinating character. If you teach young children, cut out the stories children write, fasten the stories to construction paper, and staple construction paper sheets together to make a giant accordion-style book. Accordion books link reading and writing directly and are wonderful resources to share with younger children. Then you might read aloud the accordion books and ask children to read the books in chorus. Older children enjoy creating and publishing their own versions of favorite books and poems, not to mention rewriting the lyrics of songs, raps, and chants.

Use the language experience approach with the less accomplished readers in your classroom and dialogue journals with more accomplished readers. Language experience is an approach whereby children read stories they write or dictate. These stories are based on their own life experiences and reflect their own spoken language. Reading their own stories directly links the text with the children's cultural background and daily experiences. Added to this, the words in language experience stories are a rich source of onsets, rimes, and letter-sound patterns to include in activities described in earlier chapters.

Dialogue journals are two-way communications between children and their teachers. These journals are particularly beneficial for children who read and write English with enough independence to put their thoughts on paper. When children like Chan write dialogue journals, they share their thoughts with their teachers. Their teachers, in turn, write reactions to children's messages, including personal comments and descriptions of relevant life experiences. This gives children opportunities to extend and refine their ability to use the alphabet to write, as well as opportunities to learn how to form their thoughts in such a way as to communicate with English-speaking readers. Should you choose to use dialogue journals with the children whom you teach, you can expect children's confidence with written language to improve and their command of spoken English to increase as well (Nurss & Hough, 1992).

All things considered, the greater the connection among everyday reading and writing activities and children's home language and culture, the more opportunities children have to use word identification strategies and to learn to speak, read, and write English words. Your challenge is to balance the load and the force to foster the development of word identification strategies, nurture literacy, and ensure that all children become competent, meaning-driven readers. Balancing the load and the force creates a supportive learning environment; honors children's individual differences, needs, and preferences; and provides the basis on which children successfully read a variety of material for information and for pleasure.

CHILDREN AT RISK

When your classroom reading program includes strong phonics-based instruction along with practice reading for meaning, children at risk because of poor decoding become better readers. You learned how phonemic awareness (Chapter 2) and phonics (Chapter 5) contribute to developing reading fluency. At-risk children succeed when classroom activities (the load) are roughly in balance with their ability to use word identification strategies (the force). In practical terms, this means finding activities with which children are successful and then using those activities to improve achievement. This brings us to the children in your classroom who are at risk of reading difficulty because they do not have good word identification skills and thus have not developed a large reading vocabulary.

CHILDREN WHO OVER-RELY ON PICTURE CUES

When children over-rely on picture cues, they take advantage of some, but not nearly enough, of the information available in written language. These children do not use analogy or letter-sound-based phonics. They overlook words, focusing instead on pictures and on creating their own stories that coincide with the picture content, and not necessarily with the meaning of the words on the page.

Shandra

First-grader Shandra, whose story is shown in Figure 7-4, over-relies on picture cues. If you were to listen to Shandra read easy books with which she is familiar, you would hear something akin to fluent reading. Shandra's fluency is misleading, however, because she memorizes the text. She thinks about print, but she does not pay attention to the rimes and phonics letter-sound patterns in words. For this

Figure 7-4 Children who are glued to pictures by the end of first grade may be trying to figure out exactly which written symbols—letters, numbers, or shapes—make up words.

reason, Shandra recognizes a mere handful of words. What's more, the words she reads with ease in familiar, memorized stories are seldom recognized when she meets them in other reading materials.

Shandra is developing insight into rhyme. However, she has not developed enough phonemic awareness to segment or blend sounds. From Shandra's writing, we might infer that she understands that written language is made up of letters and that writing goes from top to bottom and from left to right on the page. Shandra also seems to be developing awareness of punctuation and is working out exactly which written symbols make up words and which do not. Even with these understandings, toward the end of the year, Shandra has fallen far behind her classmates.

After a year of kindergarten and most of first grade, Shandra is still a prealphabetic word learner and a precommunicative speller. She knows how to read and write her name; can name some, but not all, of the letters; and recognizes a few words. In these respects, because she has developed some understandings from spending nearly two years in school, Shandra's print knowledge does not resemble that of a typical prealphabetic child entering kindergarten. However, Shandra does not know letter names and does not understand the alphabetic principle, which is a hallmark of prealphabetic word learners. To make up for this lack of insight, Shandra has become very good at interpreting pictures. When she reads short books that she has not memorized, she combines picture cues with her background knowledge to construct plausible stories.

What Shandra Needs to Learn   For starters, Shandra needs to become more print-focused. She needs to learn letter names and a sound for each letter. She needs to learn how the onsets, rimes, and phonics letter-sound patterns represent sound. She must also increase phonemic awareness and learn to spell by matching letters with the sounds in words she wishes to write. Additionally, Shandra needs to learn to cross-check, self-monitor, and self-correct to keep word identification meaning centered. The most immediate aim is to help her strategically use onsets and context cues and then to use onsets and rimes in word family words to decode unfamiliar words. Although the ultimate goal is for Shandra to develop the ability to use all the strategies described in this book, the letter-sound and structural analysis strategies will demand (load) more than Shandra is able to successfully handle (force) at this time in her literacy development. In studying beginning sounds and word family rimes, however, Shandra will begin to gain insight into the sounds in words and move toward developing sound awareness and blending.

Teaching Phonemic Awareness   Children like Shandra benefit from phonemic awareness activities that first target beginning sounds and rhyme and then *quickly* move on to ending sounds and middle sounds. As we learned in Chapter 2, this is the typical sequence in which phonemic awareness develops. Since spoken rhymes are easier to detect than individual sounds, the load is lighter when activities help children develop sensitivity to the rhyming sounds in words and heavier when activities focus on the middle and ending sounds in words. Beginning sounds are relatively easy to identify from a phonemic awareness standpoint. Beginning letter-sounds plus the reading context give children considerable insight into the identity of unfamiliar words. Use activities like those described in Chapter 2. As you use these activities, share books with rhyming words, engage children in language play that offers them opportunities to enjoy, use and repeat rhyming language, and teach children the sounds represented by the letters and rimes in words.

Teaching Shandra to Pay Attention to Print   Because of the mutually supportive relationship between phonemic awareness and letter-sound knowledge, you can expect Shandra's awareness of the beginning sounds in words to improve as she learns how to use onsets and context cues together to read new words. Show children like Shandra how to read to the end of the sentence and then to think of a word that makes sense and begins with the sound that the first letter represents. In this way, children stay focused on meaning and at the same time have opportunities to become aware of the beginning letters and sounds in words.

Read aloud to children like Shandra. And when you read aloud, draw children's attention to print—that is, to the words, letters, and letter-sound patterns in the text. Focusing on the print results in significantly better phonemic awareness and more knowledge of words and letters than focusing only on the storybook pictures (Justice & Ezell, 2002). Also call attention to print by pointing out words in your classroom that begin with the same sounds and letters, make lists of words that begin with the same sound, and ask children to find examples of words with the same beginning letter-sounds in familiar storybooks. Use tongue twisters, celebrate onsets and alliterative shopping lists (Chapter 4) to teach beginning letter-sound associations. Activities in Chapter 4 that can be modified to emphasize onsets are word family hunts, binders, train tickets, rime pickup, chains, and sticky note books. Also look in Chapter 5 for activities that can be adapted to focus on beginning letter-sounds.

To reinforce the concept that specific written words represent specific spoken words and encourage children to pay more attention to print, ask children like Shandra to point to each word as it is read. If you are not already sweeping your hand under words as you read them aloud, now is the time to do so. Talk about print; point out individual words in big books, poems, and familiar storybooks; make wall charts of often-used words; and ask children to arrange word cards into sentences. When asking children like Shandra to arrange words into sentences, bear in mind that (a) arranging words into sentences is easier when children match the individual words on cards with the words in a sentence you have written on an oak tag strip, (b) it is more difficult to arrange individual words into sentences that children have already dictated to you, and (c) the most difficult form of this easy activity is to give children word cards and to ask children to arrange the cards into the sentences you dictate.

Predictable books offer immediate success, in part because children easily memorize the repeated text and in part because the pictures typically tell the story. Predictable books are best used when children are just entering into reading and, therefore, are appropriate for Shandra and children like her. Predictable books will help children develop many critical and preliminary concepts, such as (a) reading is meaningful, (b) print is important, (c) writing goes from left to right and from top to bottom on pages, (d) white spaces separate words, and (e) there is a one-to-one match between spoken words and written words.

Children like Shandra frequently memorize predictable books, so make sure that children actually look at the words when reading. And as soon as Shandra has mastered basic book-handling skills and understands that reading is meaningful and that spoken words match written words, it is time to move beyond predictable books. Children with book-handling skills and who can match spoken words with written words benefit from lots of opportunities to combine context and beginning letter-sounds to identify and learn new words. Of course, children like Shandra also need opportunities to read and write word family words.

Activities that highlight written rime are important for children like Shandra because rime knowledge paves the way for development of the analogy strategy. To help Shandra and children like her expand their knowledge of rimes, invite them to work collaboratively with other children to write word family words on large pieces of chart paper. This activity is appropriate for many children, so include children like Shandra who are glued to picture cues, as well as better readers who bring more in-depth letter-sound knowledge to reading. When the charts are complete, tape them to the chalkboard and challenge children to explain in their own words why words are included in lists and to think of other words that might be added. In so doing, children have opportunities to think critically about spelling and everyone has a chance to participate.

As Shandra tunes into the rhyme in spoken language and the rime in written words, the lessons in Chapter 4 that become helpful include word family word building, rewriting familiar poems, paper plate word families, word family fishing, eggs, chains, train tickets, and towers. Since Shandra already may have made sticky note books for beginning letter-sounds, making sticky note books for word family words requires less explanation. This allows for more time spent on talking about word family words, writing word family words, and reading word family sticky note books. In addition, give children like Shandra ample opportunities to find rimes in the words they read in storybooks and poems, and to learn the sounds that the individual letters in rimes represent.

CHILDREN WHO DO NOT EFFECTIVELY USE ANALOGY-BASED PHONICS AND LETTER-SOUND PHONICS

Children who do not effectively use the analogy or the letter-sound strategy tend to misidentify words, get bogged down in the middle of words, blend sounds into the wrong words, and associate the wrong sounds with rimes or letter-sound patterns. These difficulties impair word identification and, of course, interfere with comprehension. You will notice that, while the fluent reading vocabulary of these children does increase over time, the pace of vocabulary growth is much slower than that of average readers. Because children's fluent reading vocabulary is limited and because children cannot effectively use the analogy and letter-sound strategies to read new words, they may bypass many of the words authors write, opting instead to reconstruct the meaning of stories from their own prior knowledge, picture cues, and perhaps a few letter and sound cues.

When children read stories about familiar events, relying predominantly on background knowledge, picture cues, and a few letter and sound cues, they may seem literate. In fact, material that closely parallels children's life experiences is understood remarkably well, given the fact that children do not read many of the words authors write. These are the children about whom you hear teachers say, "He doesn't know many words in the story, but his comprehension is good." Or "Even though she doesn't know many of the words, her comprehension is okay." Bypassing a large number of words does not work at all well when pictures do not tell the story and the reading materials do not closely parallel children's own lives. This approach fails altogether when the reading material introduces new ideas, concepts, and information. To take a closer look at children who have difficulty using analogous rimes and phonics letter-sound patterns when reading new words, consider the following descriptions of three children who do not effectively use the analogy or the letter-sound strategies. The first child, Raymond, brings less knowledge of letter-sound patterns and less phonemic awareness to reading and writing than Melissa, the second child, and Mike, the third child.

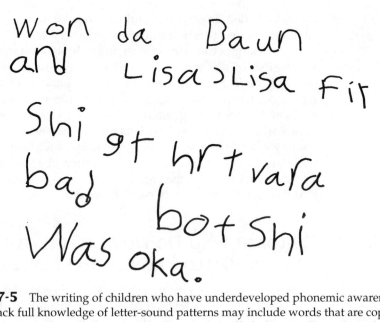

Figure 7-5 The writing of children who have underdeveloped phonemic awareness and who lack full knowledge of letter-sound patterns may include words that are copied, high-frequency words spelled conventionally, words spelled phonetically, and words in which the sounds do not match the letters.

Raymond

By the end of the second grade, Raymond's reading progress has come to a near standstill, as can be seen in Figure 7-5. His reading vocabulary is growing very slowly, which has a negative effect on comprehension. When he meets an unfamiliar word while reading, Raymond looks for picture cues and/or letter-sound cues from the beginning (and sometimes ending) letters in words. We can infer from his story in Figure 7-5 that Raymond uses some knowledge of onsets and ending letters when he writes and that he is working out how vowel letter patterns represent sounds in words. He copies words from the print in his classroom, such as *was, Lisa,* and *bad,* and he conventionally spells a few high-frequency words in his fluent vocabulary, such as *and* and *go.* Although letters and sounds are not always completely on target, some of the letters Raymond chooses are similar to the sounds in words.

Raymond's spelling includes a few words that are spelled semiphonetically (spelling that includes some, but not all, of the important sounds in words), as we see in his use of *gt* for *got* and *hrt* for *hurt.* Sometimes Raymond spells phonetically by writing letters that he thinks represent the sounds he hears in words, as in *bot* for *but, won* for *one,* and *vara* for *very.* The way he pronounces the /ot/ in /bot/ is not far from the sounds heard in /but/. This is also true for the word *very,* spelled *vara.*

Although Raymond strategically uses some letter-sound patterns when he spells, he is a long way from spelling conventionally and a long way from reading the kinds of books his second-grade classmates enjoy. Raymond is moving from partial alphabetic word learning into alphabetic word reading, as evidenced by his use of the *VC* short vowel pattern and his attempts to represent other vowel patterns. From his writing we can infer that Raymond has not made a full transition into the use of letter-sound patterns, as is expected of an end-of-year second grader. To develop the foundation on which the efficient and effective use of word identification strategies rests, the load and the force must be brought into balance to nurture Raymond's use of word identification strategies and, through effective use of word identification strategies, the expansion of his fluent reading vocabulary.

What Raymond Needs to Learn   The most immediate aspects of phonemic awareness that children like Raymond need to develop are the abilities to identify and blend individual phonemes. You will want to develop phonemic awareness through direct instruction (Chapter 2) combined with teaching onsets and word family rimes (Chapter 4) and the letter-sound patterns of phonics (Chapter 5). If children have difficulty with both the analogy and letter-sound phonics, as is the situation with Raymond, then rimes are the place to begin. Teaching children like Raymond to use rimes helps them become aware of relationships among written and spoken language and helps them overcome their over-reliance on the sounds represented by the first and last letters in words (Greaney, Tunmer, & Chapman, 1997). Hence, the most immediate things that children like Raymond need to learn about our writing system are (a) how rimes represent sounds, (b) how to strategically use analogous rimes to identify unfamiliar word family words, and (c) how the letters in phonetically regular rimes in word family words (rimes that sound like they are spelled) represent sound. As children begin to gain insight into the way that rimes represent sound, call attention to the individual letter-sound associations within the rimes and call attention to the vowel letter-sound patterns in rimes.

Teaching Phonemic Awareness   Children like Raymond may have difficulty detecting individual sounds in spoken words. Assuming that children already are aware of beginning sounds and rhyme, you will want to focus their attention on ending sounds and, when children are able to identify ending sounds, turn children's attention to sounds in the middle of words.

Look in Chapter 2 for activities to develop the ability to detect rhyme and the individual sounds in words. And when you share these activities with children like Raymond, be sure to include arm blending, which is also described in Chapter 2. Children like Raymond may find blending quite difficult, and arm blending is a highly successful technique. Arm blending is easy, gives children a visual and kinesthetic platform from which to blend, and transfers to many different reading situations. The description in Chapter 2 says to divide words into individual sounds, which places high demands on children who are not completely aware of the middle sounds in words. To lighten the load, divide words into beginning sounds (onsets) and rimes. Hence, the word /bat/ would be separated into /b/ and /at/, which is well within Raymond's capability. Modify the directions for arm blending in Chapter 2 by placing your hand in the crook of your elbow when you say /b/ and then on your wrist when you say /at/. Then, when Raymond has blended /b/ + /at/, ask him to repeat the whole process, only this time to blend /b/ + /a/ + /t/. Learning to blend individual phonemes into words increases the force children like Raymond bring to reading, which means they are then capable of reading materials in which authors use more challenging words. Combine phonemic awareness activities with teaching onset-rimes and letter-sound patterns with reading, and with plenty of opportunities to write.

Teaching Phonics   If children like Raymond are to develop greater force, they must bring greater knowledge of the rimes in word family words and a better understanding of letter-sound patterns to reading. Additionally, children must use word identification strategies to support comprehension. Once children know a handful of frequently occurring rimes in word family words, challenge them to look inside the rimes to discover the manner in which the letters in phonics patterns represent sounds. The idea is to use what children know, in this case a few high-frequency rimes, as a basis for teaching something they do not know—the letter-sound patterns of phonics. Teach children to look inside rimes to analyze the vowel patterns. When children do this, help them understand that one vowel in a short word most likely represents a short sound (*VC* pattern). For example, you would teach Raymond how *VC* rimes in word family words in the *an* (*man, tan, fan*), *ad* (*mad, had, glad*) and *at* (*mat, fat, hat*) all represent the short *a* sound. As children look for letter-sound patterns in rimes, children's knowledge of letter-sound relationships increases. Their ability to use this knowledge while reading also improves. In this way, children use their knowledge of common rimes to learn how a phonics letter-sound pattern—in this example, the *VC* short vowel pattern—represents the sounds of a whole host of different vowel and consonant combinations.

Next, compare and contrast the *VC* short vowel pattern in common rimes with the *VCe* long vowel pattern. An effective way to do this is to challenge children to think of words that include a *VC* or a *VCe* pattern in their spelling. Analyze the spelling of *VC* words—*mad, tap, dim*, and *fin*—and *VCe* words—*made, tape, dime*, and *fine*. Discuss the sounds that vowel letters represent in these two patterns; talk about how and when children might use this information as they read. Then invite children to work with a partner or in small groups to make charts of words that are spelled with *VC* (short vowel) and *VCe* (long vowel) patterns. Ask children who have less knowledge of letter-sound patterns to work with those who have more knowledge. Encourage children to find words that include the *VC* and *VCe* letter-sound patterns on the word wall, bulletin boards, and wall charts in your classroom. Support children as they work with one another to make charts, share finished charts with the whole class, display charts in your classroom, and use them as references. (Consult the letter-sound patterns in Chapter 5 that are less, more, and most challenging and look in Appendix B for an explanation of letter-sound patterns.)

The effect of beginning with large segments of spoken and written language (rimes) and then moving to smaller segments (letter-sound patterns) is that activities progress from less demanding to more demanding. Hence, the load (the demands of reading new words) is first brought into line with the force (children's abilities). Then the load can gradually increase as the force children bring to reading grows—that is, as children learn the sounds that the letters in patterns represent and use this knowledge to read new words.

Melissa

At the end of second grade, Melissa is far behind her classmates. When she meets an unfamiliar word, Melissa sometimes, but not always, considers the beginning letter. When the pictures are highly supportive of the text, Melissa's comprehension is good. When pictures do not help tell the story, Melissa creates in her mind a plausible story, filling in details from her background knowledge. Because Melissa's reading development lags far behind her peers, the load (the type of reading expected of end-of-year second graders) and the force (Melissa's underdeveloped phonemic awareness, rudimentary knowledge of letter-sound patterns, and weak fluent reading vocabulary) are significantly out of balance. It is the load imposed by the reading difficulty of second-grade books, not the ideas in the books, that creates the mismatch.

When someone else reads to her, Melissa easily understands stories written on or above her second-grade level. Melissa dictated her experience of a snake in the rabbit hutch to her teacher, reprinted in Figures 7-6 and 7-7. From her story, we

One day I was on my mommy's bed watching T.V. Then my mom said, "I am going to go check on the baby rabbits." When she got to the rabbit cage, she opened the back and saw a black snake eating the baby bunnies. The mother rabbit was in the back corner. My mom saw her shivering and she thought she was scared. Then she ran to the house as fast as she could. She called my grandma and grandpa and they sent Matt and my grandma over to kill the snake. Then Matt got a shovel and opened the back door and mommy held the door. Then he tried to hit the snake with the shovel, but he missed the snake. Then the snake crawled out of the back of the pen and went under the barn. They put something on the ground that snakes don't like the smell of to keep the snake from ever coming back. Matt and grandma went home and mommy and I went back in the house.
The End

Figure 7-6   Melissa dictated this story about a snake in the rabbit hutch to her second-grade teacher. Melissa's story shows us that she effectively uses spoken language when telling about the events in her life.

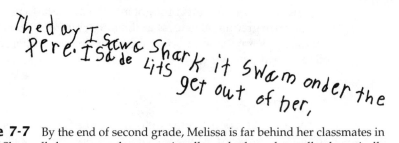

Figure 7-7   By the end of second grade, Melissa is far behind her classmates in reading. She spells known words conventionally, and others she spells phonetically. Sometimes she looks on the word wall for words she wishes to write but does not know how to spell.

can infer that Melissa is not at a loss for words when talking and that she has a sense of the sequencing of events and of cause and effect. She has a rich family background and has been read to since she was a very young child. As you might expect, Melissa also uses language effectively when communicating with her friends and adults. Melissa's difficulty, then, is not a lack of prior knowledge, early print experiences, or spoken language.

At this point in her development as a reader, Melissa is hampered by her underdeveloped reading vocabulary, low phonemic awareness, poor knowledge of letter-sound patterns, and ineffective use of the letter-sound strategy. Melissa spells the words in her reading vocabulary conventionally; other words she spells phonetically, as we see in Figure 7-7. She knows enough about letter-sound patterns to be beyond the partial alphabetic stage. She has made the transition into alphabetic word learning and the phonetic stage of spelling, yet her progress moving through alphabetic word learning is very slow. While many of her second-grade classmates are entering the consolidated word learning stage, Melissa lingers in the alphabetic stage.

Melissa's reading vocabulary is growing very slowly, her reading progress is minimal, and she does not like to write. If Melissa is to succeed, there must be a better balance between the load (reading demands) and the force (Melissa's abilities and knowledge). Melissa frequently confuses words, cannot remember words, and ignores letters in words—most often the vowel letters. If her sight word reading vocabulary and her ability to comprehend grade-level chapter books are to develop, Melissa must consider all the letters in words, including the trick vowels (Chapter 5). She must forgo overdependence on picture cues and guessing without enough letter-sound information, and she must learn to efficiently and effectively use the analogy and the letter-sound strategies in combination with sentence structure and meaning cues, as well as learn to cross-check, self-monitor, and self-correct to keep decoding meaning-based.

What Melissa Needs to Learn   Melissa readily identifies rhyming words, so you will want to focus instruction on developing her ability to segment and blend the sounds in words. Melissa needs to improve her ability to separate words into sounds, substitute sounds in words (exchange the /p/ in /pig/ for a /d/), thereby making /dig/), add sounds, delete sounds, and blend sounds (see Chapter 2). Melissa already has learned to read word family words, she uses high-frequency rimes when spelling, she knows how to find words on the word wall, and she knows the *VC* short vowel pattern. At this point in her development as a reader, Melissa needs to learn more about the letter-sound patterns of phonics and how to use these patterns when reading new words.

Teaching Phonemic Awareness   Melissa easily separates short words (words of two phonemes, such as *me* and *so*) into individual sounds. However, Melissa has to carefully think about sounds before separating three- and four-sound words into phonemes. Whereas Melissa's second-grade classmates effortlessly divide a word like /mad/ into sounds, Melissa ponders her answer. As word length increases, Melissa has more and more trouble identifying and manipulating the individual sounds in words. When blending, Melissa omits, adds, and rearranges sounds, which interferes with use of the letter-sound strategy. Melissa and children like her are very weak blenders.

To further develop Melissa's phonemic awareness, combine the sound awareness and blending activities in Chapter 2 with the lessons and activities in Chapter 5 that teach letter-sound patterns. As mentioned in Chapter 2, there is a mutually supportive relationship between phonemic awareness and letter-sound knowledge. Children like Melissa are in just the right position to take advantage of this two-way (phonemic awareness and letter-sound knowledge) relationship. Of the activities in Chapter 2, we find colored sound squares, interactive spelling, and sound boxes with letters to be especially helpful. In using colored sound squares, write the letters on the squares after Melissa has used them to identify the sounds in words. Writing letters in sound squares and sound boxes reinforces and extends Melissa's letter-sound knowledge, while at the same time developing phonemic awareness. As for blending sounds, Melissa needs lots of direct instruction and practice blending three- and four-sound words. Arm blending is remarkably beneficial for Melissa and children like her. Combine arm blending with sliding sounds together (both explained in Chapter 2). When using blending activities, encourage children like Melissa to pay attention to the *middle* sounds in words, to pay special attention to correct blending when using the letter-sound strategy, and to always cross-check for meaning.

Teaching Phonics   Melissa already knows the sounds represented by the single consonant, consonant cluster (blend), and consonant digraph patterns. Generally speaking, it is the vowel letter-sound patterns that are the most troublesome for children like Melissa. Use the lesson letter-sound pattern word building (described in Chapter 5) to develop vowel letter-sound knowledge. When building words, ask children like Melissa to make changes that affect the vowel patterns, such as changing *VC* into *VCe* long vowel words (changing *mad* into *made* or *plan* into *plane*), changing *VC* words into *VV* long vowel words (changing *me* into *meet* or *set* into *seat*), changing *VC* or *VCe* words into *r-controlled* words (change *cat* into *car; cage* into *care; date* into *dare*). Consult Chapter 5 and Appendix B for other vowel patterns to highlight when building words. Of course, you will want to always have children begin building words with patterns they know and then use this knowledge to help them learn new phonics patterns.

The puzzles activity in Chapter 5 combines phonemic awareness with letter-sound patterns and thus reinforces and extends the foundations on which the letter-sound strategy rests. The children we teach succeed when they first solve puzzles as a whole group activity. Then, when children are confident of their own ability, we ask them to solve puzzles individually. We also find the small group chalkboard sort, compare-contrast charts, and letter-sound cloze (described in Chapter 5) to be very beneficial in calling special attention to vowel patterns. After children apply basic vowel patterns when reading and spelling, teach other letter-sound patterns and how to use them (these patterns are described in Chapter 5 and Appendix B).

Children like Melissa benefit from reading decodable books—books with words that are spelled like they sound and therefore can be pronounced using the letter-sound strategy. Decodable books give children practice using letter-sound patterns while reading (Mesmer, 2001). Using letter-sound patterns in turn reinforces children's knowledge of the sounds the letters represent (Juel & Roper-Schneider, 1985). Because so many words can be successfully identified with knowledge of letter-sound patterns, decodable books help children like Melissa appreciate the benefits of applying the letter-sound strategy when reading. Melissa and children like her need many and varied opportunities to use phonemic awareness, particularly blending, along with letter-sound knowledge when reading and spelling new words. The more opportunities children have to apply knowledge of phonemic awareness and letter-sound patterns, the more likely they are to succeed.

Melissa's reading ability will improve as she develops more phonemic awareness, knowledge of letter-sound patterns, and the ability to strategically use this information to identify and learn new words. As Melissa's reading vocabulary expands, she will be able to read more difficult chapter books and content area books, and hence the load (the requirements of grade-level reading materials) and the force (what Melissa knows and can do) will come into balance.

Mike

Mike, whose story is shown in Figure 7-8, has learned to read and spell onsets and common rimes, and he is able to read and spell some letter-sound patterns. Even so, Mike has not learned enough about letter-sound patterns to support reading the material his fourth-grade classmates enjoy. Hence, the force that Mike brings to reading and writing is far less than the load imposed by everyday fourth-grade reading and writing activities.

When Mike writes, he conventionally spells highly frequent words, such as *it, all, you, bad, day*, and *have*. He also spells phonetically, as we see in the word *weight*, written as *wate*. In so doing, Mike uses the *VCe* long vowel pattern (*ate*), which suggests that he has some knowledge of this more challenging vowel letter

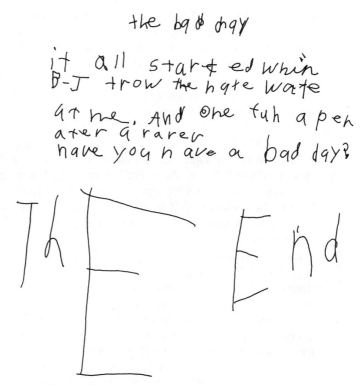

Figure 7-8 The reading and writing ability of children like Mike, who is midway through the fourth grade, will improve when they increase sound awareness and knowledge of letter-sound patterns.

pattern (Chapter 5). Mike still has a good deal to learn about letter-sound patterns in words, because even with the support of story context, we cannot figure out words such as *fuh* (intended to be the word *thing*), *ararer* (meant to be *another*), and *hate* (supposed to be *heavy*). Like Melissa, Mike has moved beyond the semiphonetic stage of word learning. Also like Melissa, Mike's development as a reader is encumbered by his inability to effectively use the letter-sound strategy to read and learn new words. While Mike struggles with the letter-sound patterns in words, his classmates are using multiletter chunks to add words to their reading vocabularies. Other fourth graders in his class are at the consolidated word learning stage (explained in Chapter 6) and are transitional spellers. Nevertheless, the beginning sentence in Mike's story introduces readers to action and his thoughts flow logically. What's more, Mike is an enthusiastic learner when the load and the force are in balance.

What Mike Needs to Learn   Mike needs to learn more about the letter-sound patterns in words, and he needs to be able to strategically use this knowledge when he reads and writes. As a fourth grader, Mike also needs to develop the knowledge of, and ability to use, the multiletter chunks in word structure to read and learn new words. Mike has to increase his awareness of the individual sounds in words and improve his ability to blend sounds together. Mike must continue to be meaning focused; to use context cues along with letter-sound patterns and the multiletter chunks in word structure; and to self-monitor, self-correct, and cross-check for meaning when reading new words.

Teaching Blending   It is critical that Mike's blending ability improve, because at present Mike typically adds, deletes, and rearranges sounds when he blends. Asked to blend /l/ + /a/ + /m/ + /p/, Mike may say something like /slamp/, /lap/, or /plam/. Arm blending, discussed in Chapter 2, does not appeal to Mike because he does not want to use something so obvious in front of his fourth-grade friends. As an alternative, have Mike tap the side of a table (or desk) with his pencil for each sound to be blended. Many of the older children we teach find that this is an effective and acceptable technique to use while reading in school.

Finger blending, explained in Chapter 2, is another beneficial way for children like Mike to blend short words. The slide sounds together activity is helpful, provided that it is modified to be appropriate for older children. Instead of drawing a slide on the board, as described in Chapter 2, give Mike and other children sheets of paper with slides on them. Mike then writes letters on the slide himself (beginning at the top and ending near the bottom), blends the sounds represented by letters, and writes the whole word at the bottom of the slide. Writing letter-sound patterns or the multiletter chunks in word structure (the *-ing* in *jumping*) down the slide and the whole word at the bottom helps children like Mike develop phonemic awareness as well as knowledge of letter-sound and word structure cues. When writing the prefixes and suffixes—as well as other multiletter chunks in word structure—on the slide, have children write the entire group at once (*-ing, -ed,* or *re-,* for example). In so doing, children develop sensitivity to and an understanding of multiletter chunks that make up the structure of long words.

Teaching Letter-Sound Phonics and Structural Analysis   If you have children like Mike in your classroom, they are likely to develop greater ability to segment words into sounds as a consequence of learning more about letter-sound patterns. Teach Mike to recognize and use the letter-sound patterns that he has not yet learned and model for him how to apply this knowledge when reading new words. Additionally, teach fourth graders like Mike the high-frequency prefixes and suffixes and show children how to divide long words into affixes and base words (Chapter 6).

You can expect the word building activities (Chapter 5) to be effective and to shorten the time readers like Mike spend catching up with their classmates (Tunmer & Hoover, 1993). The use of letter-sound pattern cloze sentences (also described in Chapter 5) focuses attention on letter-sound patterns while keeping words in context. Venn diagrams are a good way to demonstrate the way that a single letter-sound pattern represents more than one sound, and sorting will give Mike beneficial practice thinking about letter-sound patterns in words (Chapter 5). Compare-contrast charts, puzzles, letter-sound bingo, picking what works for me, and blocks also give children like Mike useful practice thinking about and using letter-sound patterns (Chapter 5).

We like to use small white boards (or mini-chalkboards) to help children like Mike learn and use letter-sound patterns. Ask children working in small groups to spell words that contain the letter-sound patterns you are teaching. For example, if you are helping children learn and use the *Vr* pattern, then you might ask them to spell words like *car, sir, mother,* and *store.* Ask children to explain why they put the *r* in words when spelling and to listen for the /r/ in the words as they say them aloud. And when you have an opportunity to observe how children spell words, you see right away who uses letter-sound patterns correctly and who does not. Misspelled words are not penalized in any way. Children simply erase misspellings and fix words with minimal disruption to learning. As children spell, talk about letter-sound patterns, compare and contrast words, and discuss word meaning.

We know it is important for children like Mike to develop greater phonemic awareness and letter-sound knowledge. Yet we also know that the average fourth grader has moved well beyond alphabetic word learning. It is important to include Mike in the ongoing, grade-appropriate aspects of learning the multiletter chunks in word structure. Introduce Mike to fourth-grade prefixes and suffixes, as well as prefixes and suffixes from earlier grades that Mike has not yet learned. The graffiti activity, explained in Chapter 6, is beneficial because the word finding and word writing focus is well within the competence of a child like Mike. So, too, is the complimenting classmates activity (described in detail in Chapter 6). Children like Mike are quite capable of making the honor shield. An added benefit is that the honor shield may very well boost Mike's self-esteem when he reads the compliments of his friends. By having Mike participate in a small group, you can effectively balance the load and the force in using activities like webs and suffix chart, both explained in Chapter 6.

All things taken together, children benefit most when they have a great many experiences in reading and writing, and many opportunities to use the analogy, letter-sound, and multiletter chunk strategies when reading and spelling. As children use the letter-sound strategy, their awareness of the sound in words and knowledge of letter-sound relationships simultaneously increase. With greater phonemic awareness and greater knowledge of letter-sound patterns, children's ability to use the letter-sound strategy also improves. Children will notice and use the multiletter groups in word structure. As a consequence, the force that children like Shandra, Raymond, Melissa, and Mike bring to reading is greater and, by extension, the load these children are capable of lifting is heavier. By carefully and systematically adjusting the balance between schoolwork and ability, we help children succeed, gain self-confidence, develop greater capacity to express themselves in writing, enjoy reading increasingly more difficult books, and eventually become independent readers who have a large fluent reading vocabulary.

REFERENCES

Arthur, B. (1991). Working with new ESL students in a junior high school reading class. *The Journal of Reading, 34,* 628–631.

Birch, B. M. (2002). *English L2 reading.* Mahwah, NJ: Lawrence Erlbaum Associates.

Carlo, M. S., August, D., & Snow, C. E. (2005). Sustained vocabulary-learning strategy instruction for English-language learners. In E. H. Hiebert & M. L. Kamil (Eds.), *Teaching and learning vocabulary: Bringing research to practice* (pp. 137–153). Mahwah, NJ: Lawrence Erlbaum Associates.

Cherry, L. (1990). *The great kapok tree.* New York: Harcourt Brace.

Chiappe, P., Siegel, L. S., & Wade-Woolley, L. (2002). Linguistic diversity and the development of reading skills: A longitudinal study. *Scientific Studies of Reading, 6,* 369–400.

Denton, C. A., Anthony, J. L., Parker, R., & Hasbrouck, J. E. (2004). Effects of two tutoring programs on the English reading development of Spanish-English bilingual students. *The Elementary School Journal, 104,* 289–305.

Drucker, M. J. (2003). What reading teachers should know about ESL learners. *The Reading Teacher, 57,* 22–37.

Garcia, G. E. (1991). Factors influencing the English reading test performance of Spanish-speaking Hispanic children. *Reading Research Quarterly, 26,* 371–392.

Graves, M. F., Juel, C., & Graves, B. (1998). *Teaching reading in the 21st century.* Boston: Allyn & Bacon.

Greaney, K. T., Tunmer, W. E., & Chapman, J. W. (1997). Effects of rime-based orthographic analogy training on the word recognition of children with reading disability. *Journal of Educational Psychology, 89,* 645–651.

Gunn, B., Smolkowski, K., Biglan, A., & Black, C. (2002). Supplemental instruction in decoding skill for Hispanic and non-Hispanic students in early elementary school: A follow-up. *Journal of Special Education, 36,* 69–79.

Helman, L. A. (2004). Building on the sound system of Spanish: Insights from the alphabetic spellings of English-language learners. *The Reading Teacher, 57,* 452–460.

Hudelson, S. (1984). Kan yu ret an rayt en ingles: Children become literate in English as a second language. *TESOL Quarterly, 18,* 221–238.

Hutchinson, J. M., Whiteley, H. E., Smith, C. D., & Connors, L. (2003). The developmental progression of comprehension-related skills in children learning EAL. *Journal for Research in Reading, 26,* 19–32.

Juel, C., & Roper-Schneider, D. (1985). The influence of basal readers on first grade reading. *Reading Research Quarterly, 20,* 134–152.

Justice, L. M., & Ezell, H. K. (2002). Use of storybook reading to increase print awareness in at-risk children. *American Journal of Speech-Language Pathology, 11,* 17–29.

Lesaux, N. K., & Siegel, L. S. (2003). The development of reading in children who speak English as a second language. *Developmental Psychology, 39,* 1005–1019.

Malik, A. A. (1990). A psycholinguistic analysis of the reading behavior of ESL-proficient readers using culturally familiar and unfamiliar expository text. *American Educational Research Journal, 27,* 205–223.

Manis, F., Lindsey, K., & Bailey, C. (2004). Development of reading in grades K–2 in Spanish-speaking English-language learners. *Learning Disabilities Research & Practice, 19,* 214–224.

Manzo, A. V., Manzo U. C., & Thomas, M. T. (2006). Rationale for systematic vocabulary development: Antidote for state mandates. *Journal of Adolescent & Adult Literacy, 49,* 610–619.

Mesmer, H. A. E. (2001). Decodable text: A review of what we know. *Reading Research and Instruction, 40,* 121–142.

Miller, J. E., Heilmann, J., Nockerts, A., Iglesias, A., Fabiano, L., & Francis, D. J. (2006). Oral language and reading in bilingual children. *Learning Disabilities Research and Practice,* 30–43.

Nurss, J. R., & Hough, R. A. (1992). Reading and the ESL student. In S. J. Samuels & A. E. Farstrup (Eds.), *What research has to say about reading instruction* (2nd ed.), (pp. 277–313). Newark, DE: International Reading Association.

Pérez Cañado, M. L. (2005). English and Spanish spelling: Are they really different? *The Reading Teacher, 58,* 522–530.

Presta, K. (2004). Incorporate sensory activities and choices into the classroom. *Intervention in School and Clinic, 39,* 172–175.

Pritchard, R. (1990). The effects of cultural schemata on reading processing strategies. *Reading Research Quarterly, 25,* 273–295.

Roberts, T. A. (2005). Articulation accuracy and vocabulary size contributions to phonemic awareness and word reading in English language learners. *Journal of Educational Psychology, 97,* 601–616.

Royer, J. M., & Carlo, M. S. (1991). Transfer of comprehension skills from native to second language. *Journal of Reading, 34,* 450–455.

Rupley, W. H., Rodriquez, M., Mergen, S. L., Willson, V. L., & Nichols, W. D. (2000). Effects of structural features on word recognition of Hispanic and non-Hispanic second graders. *Reading and Writing: An Interdisciplinary Journal, 13,* 337–347.

Tunmer, W. E., & Hoover, W. A. (1993). Phonemic recoding skill and beginning reading. *Reading and Writing: An Interdisciplinary Journal, 5,* 161–179.

Wong, M. Y., & Underwood, G. (1996). Do bilingual children read words better in lists or in context? *Journal of Research in Reading, 19,* 61–76.

APPENDIX A

Rimes for Word Reading and Spelling

Rime	Words
ab*	blab, crab, dab, drab, flab, gab, grab, jab, lab, nab, slab, stab, tab
ace	brace, face, grace, lace, pace, place, race, space, trace
ack*	back, black, clack, crack, hack, jack, knack, lack, pack, quack, rack, sack, shack, slack, smack, snack, stack, tack, track, whack, wrack
ad	bad, cad, dad, fad, gad, glad, had, lad, mad, pad, sad, tad
ade	blade, fade, glade, grade, jade, made, shade, spade, trade, wade
ag*	bag, brag, crag, drag, flag, gag, hag, jag, lag, nag, rag, sag, shag, slag, snag, stag, swag, tag, wag
ail*	bail, fail, frail, hail, jail, mail, nail, pail, quail, rail, sail, snail, tail, trail
ain*	brain, chain, drain, gain, main, pain, plain, rain, slain, Spain, sprain, stain, train
ake*	bake, Blake, brake, cake, fake, flake, Jake, lake, make, quake, rake, sake, shake, take, wake
ale*	bale, dale, gale, hale, kale, male, pale, sale, scale, shale, stale, tale, vale, wale, whale
all*	ball, call, fall, gall, hall, mall, pall, small, squall, stall, tall, wall
am*	clam, cram, dam, ham, jam, Pam, ram, Sam, slam, scram, swam, tam, tram, yam
ame*	blame, came, fame, flame, frame, game, lame, name, same, shame, tame
amp	champ, clamp, cramp, damp, lamp, ramp, stamp, tramp

an*	ban, bran, can, Dan, fan, Jan, man, Nan, pan, plan, ran, span, Stan, tan, than, van
and	band, bland, brand, grand, hand, land, sand, stand, strand
ane	bane, cane, crane, Jane, lane, mane, pane, plane, sane, vane, wane
ang	bang, clang, fang, gang, hang, pang, rang, sang, slang, sprang, twang
ank*	bank, blank, clank, crank, dank, drank, flank, frank, hank, lank, plank, prank, rank, sank, shrank, spank, stank, tank, thank, yank
ap*	cap, clap, flap, gap, lap, map, nap, rap, sap, scrap, slap, snap, strap, tap, trap, wrap, yap, zap
ash*	bash, cash, clash, crash, dash, flash, gash, hash, lash, mash, rash, sash, slash, smash, stash, trash
at*	at, brat, cat, chat, fat, flat, hat, mat, pat, rat, sat, scat, slat, spat, tat, that, vat
ate*	crate, date, fate, gate, hate, Kate, late, mate, plate, rate, skate, slate, state
aw*	claw, draw, flaw, haw, jaw, law, maw, paw, raw, saw, slaw, thaw
ay*	bay, clay, day, gay, gray, hay, jay, Kay, lay, may, nay, pay, play, ray, say, stay, stray, sway, tray, way
eam	beam, cream, dream, gleam, ream, scream, seam, steam, team
ear	clear, dear, fear, gear, hear, near, rear, shear, smear, spear, tear, year
eat*	beat, cheat, feat, heat, meat, neat, peat, pleat, seat, treat, wheat
eck	check, deck, fleck, heck, neck, peck, speck, wreck
ed*	bed, bled, bred, fed, fled, led, Ned, red, shed, sled, sped, Ted, wed
eed*	bleed, breed, deed, feed, freed, greed, heed, need, reed, seed, speed, steed, tweed, weed
eep	beep, bleep, cheep, creep, deep, jeep, keep, peep, seep, sheep, sleep, steep, sweep
eer	cheer, deer, jeer, leer, peer, queer, sheer, sneer, steer
ell*	bell, cell, dell, dwell, fell, jell, sell, shell, smell, spell, swell, tell, well, yell
en	Ben, den, glen, Gwen, hen, men, pen, ten, then, when, wren
end	bend, blend, fend, lend, mend, rend, send, spend, tend, trend

est*	best, chest, crest, jest, lest, nest, pest, rest, test, vest, west, zest
et	bet, get, jet, let, met, net, pet, set, vet, wet, yet
ew*	blew, brew, crew, dew, drew, few, flew, hew, knew, mew, new, pew, slew, stew
ice*	dice, lice, mice, nice, price, rice, slice, spice, twice
ick*	Dick, brick, chick, click, flick, kick, lick, nick, pick, prick, quick, Rick, sick, slick, stick, tick, thick, trick, wick
ide*	bide, bride, glide, guide, hide, pride, ride, side, slide, snide, stride, tide, wide
ig	big, dig, fig, gig, jig, pig, rig, swig, twig
ight*	bright, fight, flight, fright, knight, light, might, night, right, sight, slight, tight
ill*	bill, chill, dill, drill, fill, frill, gill, grill, hill, Jill, kill, mill, pill, sill, shrill, spill, still, thrill, will
im*	brim, dim, grim, him, Jim, Kim, rim, skim, slim, swim, Tim, trim
in*	bin, chin, din, fin, gin, grin, kin, pin, sin, skin, spin, tin, thin, twin, win
ind	bind, blind, find, grind, hind, kind, mind, rind
ine*	dine, fine, line, mine, nine, pine, shine, spine, swine, vine, wine, twine
ing*	bring, cling, ding, fling, king, ping, ring, sing, sling, sting, string, swing, thing, wing, zing
ink*	blink, clink, drink, fink, kink, link, mink, pink, rink, sink, shrink, slink, stink, think, wink
ip*	blip, chip, dip, drip, flip, grip, hip, lip, nip, pip, rip, sip, ship, skip, slip, snip, strip, tip, trip, whip
it*	fit, hit, kit, knit, lit, pit, quit, skit, sit, wit
ob*	blob, Bob, cob, fob, glob, gob, knob, job, lob, mob, rob, slob, snob, sob, throb
ock*	block, clock, cock, crock, dock, flock, hock, jock, knock, lock, mock, pock, rock, sock, shock, smock, stock
og	bog, clog, cog, dog, fog, frog, hog, jog, log, smog
oil	boil, broil, coil, foil, soil, spoil, toil
oke*	broke, choke, coke, joke, poke, smoke, spoke, stoke, stroke, woke, yoke
old	bold, cold, fold, gold, hold, mold, scold, sold, told
ong	gong, long, prong, song, strong, thong, tong, wrong

op*	bop, chop, crop, drop, flop, hop, lop, mop, plop, pop, prop, shop, slop, stop, top
ore*	chore, core, fore, lore, more, pore, score, shore, snore, sore, spore, store, swore, tore
orn	born, corn, horn, morn, scorn, sworn, thorn, torn, worn
ot*	blot, clot, cot, dot, got, hot, jot, knot, lot, not, plot, pot, rot, Scot, shot, slot, spot, tot, trot
ought	bought, brought, fought, sought, thought
out*	bout, lout, scout, shout, snout, spout, sprout, pout, trout
ow*	(long o) blow, bow, crow, flow, glow, grow, know, low, mow, row, show, slow, snow, stow, throw, tow
ub	club, cub, dub, flub, grub, hub, nub, pub, rub, scrub, shrub, snub, sub, tub
uck*	buck, chuck, cluck, duck, luck, muck, pluck, puck, shuck, snuck, struck, stuck, suck, truck
ug*	bug, chug, drug, dug, hug, jug, lug, mug, plug, rug, shrug, slug, smug, snug, tug
um*	bum, chum, drum, glum, gum, hum, mum, plum, rum, scum, slum, sum
ump*	bump, chump, clump, dump, grump, hump, jump, lump, plump, pump, rump, slump, stump, thump, trump
un	bun, fun, gun, nun, pun, run, shun, spun, stun, sun
ung	clung, dung, flung, hung, lung, rung, slung, sprung, strung, stung, sung, swung, wrung
unk*	bunk, chunk, clunk, drunk, dunk, flunk, gunk, hunk, junk, punk, shrunk, skunk, slunk, spunk, stunk, sunk, trunk
ust	bust, crust, dust, gust, just, must, rust, thrust, trust
ut	but, cut, glut, gut, hut, jut, nut, rut, shut, strut
y*	by, cry, dry, fly, fry, my, ply, pry, shy, sky, sly, spy, spry, sty, try, why, wry

---

Note: Pronunciation of /og/ may vary for children in different regions.

*Rimes with an asterisk are part of many different words, according to Cheek, Flippo, and Lindsey (1997) and/or Fry (1998).

**ow is pronounced with a long /o/ as in /know/.

Cheek, E. H., Flippo, R. F., & Lindsey, J. D. (1997). *Reading for success in elementary schools*. Dubuque, IA: Brown & Benchmark.

Fry, E. (1998). The most common phonograms. *The Reading Teacher, 52*, 620–622.

APPENDIX B

Letter-Sound Patterns

CONSONANT PATTERNS

Single Consonants

Single consonant letters represent the sounds heard in the following words:

B,b	boat	buffalo	P,p	pig	popcorn
C,c	cat	city	Q,q	queen	quack
D,d	dog	donkey	R,r	ring	rabbit
F,f	fish	fox	S,s	sun	daisy
G,g	goat	gem	T,t	turtle	table
H,h	hat	hippopotamus	V,v	van	valentine
J,j	jet	jam	W,w	wagon	wave
K,k	kite	kangaroo	X,x	fox	exit
L,l	lion	lamp	Y,y	yo-yo	yellow
M,m	moon	monkey	Z,z	zipper	zoo
N,n	nut	nest			

- *W,w* and *Y,y* act as consonants when they are onsets, as in *wagon, wait, yellow,* and *barnyard*.
- Though *Y,y* represents the consonant sound heard in *yellow* when it is an onset, *Y,y* also acts as a vowel in many letter-sound patterns.
- *X,x* seldom represents the sound heard in *x-ray*, a favorite example in ABC books. Though *X,x* represents several sounds, the /ks/ in *fox* (particularly at the end of words) and the /gz/ in *exit* are most common.
- Consonants that represent more than one sound, such as *c, g,* and *s,* are explained later.

Qu

When *Q,q* is present in spelling, it almost always precedes *U,u*.

Beginning qu /kw/ Sound		*Middle qu /kw/ Sound*		*Final que /k/ Sound*	
quack	quick	acquit	inquire	antique	physique
quaint	quiet	banquet	liquid	boutique	plaque
quarter	quit	conquest	request	critique	statuesque
queen	quote	eloquent	require	oblique	technique
question	quiz	frequent	sequin	opaque	unique

- Words spelled with *que* are borrowed from French and reflect the influence of French on our spelling system.
- Occasionally the *u* in *qu* is silent and represents the /k/ heard in *mosquito, quay, croquette,* and *quiche*. This occurs so seldom in English words that it does not merit specific attention.
- *Q,q* occurs without *u* in a few words, as in *Iraq*, but this is so rare in English that it does not warrant special consideration, either.

Double Consonants

Formed whenever the same consonants are side by side, the sound represented is usually that of a single consonant, as in *rabbit* and *cotton*.

- When there is a double consonant in a word, the consonant sound most often goes with the preceding vowel to form a pattern, as in *rabbit* (/rab/) and *mitten* (/mit/). The exception occurs when words are joined together to make compounds, in which case both sounds may be heard, as in *headdress* and *bookkeeper*. For the purpose of dividing words into syllables, the syllable division is between the double consonants (*rab - bit, mit - ten*), and the first syllable is most often the syllable that is accented.
- In some words spelled with a double *c*, the first *c* represents the sound of /k/ in *kite* and the second the /s/ in *save*, as in *accent, accept,* and *accident*.
- When suffixes are added to some words, such as *slam* and *wrap*, consonants are doubled, as in *slamming* and *wrapped*. Whereas it is relatively easy to infer the pronunciation of double consonants, it is much more challenging for children to learn when (and when not) to double consonants in writing suffixes.

Consonant Clusters (or Blends)

The sounds represented by letters in a consonant cluster are joined together during pronunciation. Some teachers' manuals refer to this pattern as a consonant blend.

Two-Letter Clusters

bl Cluster

black	blank	blanket	blew	blink	block	blood	blouse	blue	blur
blade	blast	bleach	blind	blip	blond	bloom	blow	bluff	blush
blame	blaze	blend							

cl Cluster

claim	clasp	clean	climb	clog	clown
clam	class	cliff	cloak	close	club
clap	claw	clear	clock	cloth	clue
clash	clay	clip	clod	cloud	clump

fl Cluster

flag	flash	flesh	flip	floor	flu
flake	flat	flew	float	flop	fluff
flame	flea	flight	flock	flour	flute
flare	fleet	fling	flood	flow	fly

gl Cluster

glad	gleam	glory
glade	glen	gloss
gland	glide	glove
glance	gloat	glow
glare	glob	glue
glass	globe	glum
glaze	gloom	glut

pl Cluster

place	play	plug
plain	please	plum
plan	plod	plume
plane	plop	plump
plank	plot	plunge
plant	plow	plus
plate	pluck	plush

sl Cluster

slam	slid	slob
slant	slice	slop
slap	slick	slope
slave	slide	slot
sled	slim	slow
sleep	slip	slouch
sleet	slit	slump

br Cluster

brag	break	broil
brain	breeze	broke
brake	brick	brook
branch	bride	broom
brass	brim	brow
brave	bring	brown
bread	broad	brush

cr Cluster

crab	creek	cross
crack	creep	crow
craft	crew	crown
crash	crib	crumb
crate	crime	crush
crawl	crisp	crust
cream	crop	cry

dr Cluster

drag	drew	drool
drain	drift	droop
drank	drill	drove
drape	drink	drown
draw	drip	drug
dream	drive	drum
dress	drop	dry

fr Cluster

frame	friend	from
frank	Friday	front
freak	fright	frost
free	frill	frown
freeze	frisky	frozen
French	frock	fruit
fresh	frog	fry

gr Cluster

grab	graph	grin
grade	grasp	grind
grain	graze	groom
grand	great	ground
grape	green	group
grass	greet	grow
grave	grew	growl

pr Cluster

prank	prim	proof
press	prime	prose
pretty	print	proud
prey	prize	prove
price	prod	prowl
prick	prom	prune
pride	prong	pry

tr Cluster

track	tray	troop
trade	treat	truck
trail	tree	true
train	trial	trunk
tramp	tribe	trust
trap	trick	truth
trash	trip	try

sc Cluster

scab	scarf	scorn
scald	scoff	scotch
scale	scold	scour
scalp	scone	scout
scan	scoop	scowl
scar	scope	scuff
scare	score	scum

sk Cluster

skate	skid	skipper
skeet	skiff	skirt
skein	skill	skit
skeleton	skim	skulk
sketch	skimp	skull
skew	skin	skunk
ski	skip	sky

sm Cluster

smack	smelter	smolder
small	smile	smooch
smart	smirk	smooth
smash	smite	smother
smear	smock	smudge
smell	smog	smug
smelt	smoke	smut

sn Cluster

snack	snatch	snob
snag	sneak	snoop
snail	sneer	snore
snake	sneeze	snort
snap	sniff	snout
snare	snip	snow
snarl	snipe	snug

sp Cluster

space	speed	spin
spade	spear	spit
span	spell	spoon
spank	spend	sport
spare	spice	spot
spark	spider	spun
speak	spill	spy

st Cluster

stack	star	stew
stag	start	stick
stage	state	still
stain	stay	stir
stair	steal	stone
stamp	stem	stop
stand	step	store

sw Cluster

swam	sweat	swing
swamp	sweep	swipe
swan	sweet	swirl
swap	swell	swish
swarm	swept	Swiss
swat	swift	switch
sway	swim	swoop

tw Cluster

twain	twelve	twine
twang	twenty	twinge
tweak	twice	twinkle
tweed	twig	twirl
tweet	twilight	twist
tweeze	twill	twitch
twelfth	twin	twitter

- The two-letter clusters *sk, sm, sp*, and *st* occur at the beginning and the end of words, as in *mask, prism, clasp*, and *last*. All the other two-letter clusters occur at the beginning of words, not the end.
- The letters *wr* do not form a cluster. The *w* is silent, as in *wrap, write*, and *wreck*.
- Some letter combinations, such as *nd, mp, ld, nt, lk*, and *nk*, form a cluster at the end of words, as in *stand, jump, held, sent, talk*, and *sink*. Try teaching consonant clusters at the end of words as rimes (see Appendix A).

Three-Letter Clusters

scr Cluster

scram	screech	scrod
scramble	screen	scroll
scrap	screw	scrooge
scrape	scribble	scrub
scratch	scribe	scruffy
scrawny	scrimp	scrunch
scream	script	scruple

spl Cluster

splash	splice
splat	splint
splatter	splinter
splay	split
spleen	splotch
splendid	splurge
splendor	

spr Cluster

sprain	sprightly	spruce
sprang	spring	sprung
sprawl	sprinkle	spry
spray	sprint	
spread	sprite	
spree	sprocket	
sprig	sprout	

squ Cluster

squab	squall	squash	squeal	squeeze	squish	squirrel
squabble	squander	squawk	square	squid	squire	squirt
squad	square	squeak	squash	squint	squirm	

str Cluster

straight	strap	stream	strict	stripe	stroke	struck
strain	straw	street	strike	strive	stroll	strum
strand	stray	strength	string	strode	strong	strung
strange	streak	stretch	strip			

The following letters in these three-letter clusters represent only two sounds:

chr Cluster

christen	chronicle
Christmas	chrysalis
chrome	chrysanthemum
chromosome	
chronic	

sch Cluster

schedule	scholastic
schema	school
schematic	schooner
scheme	
scholar	

thr Cluster

thrash	thrift	throne
thread	thrill	throng
threat	thrive	throttle
three	throat	through
thresh	throb	throw

- Except for *Christmas, school,* and *schedule, chr* and *sch* are not often present in the words younger children are likely to read and spell.
- This is not the case for *thr*, which is part of many words.
- Teach the three-letter clusters after readers know common two-letter clusters.

Consonant Digraphs

The letters in a consonant digraph represent one sound that is different from the sounds the letters represent individually.

ch Digraph

chain	chart	chew
chair	chat	chicken
chalk	chase	child
chance	cheat	chin
change	check	chip
chapter	cheer	choose
charge	cheese	

ph Digraph

phantom	philosopher	phosphorus
pharaoh	philosophy	photo
pharmacy	phobia	photograph
phase	phone	photosynthesis
pheasant	phoneme	phrase
phenomenon	phonics	physical
philodendron	phonograph	physics

sh Digraph

shack	she	short
shade	sheep	shot
shake	shell	should
shape	ship	shovel
shark	shirt	show
sharp	shoe	shut
shave	shop	shy

th Digraph (Voiceless)

thank	thief	thirteen
thatch	thigh	thirty
thaw	thin	thorn
theater	thing	thought
theft	think	thousand
theme	third	thumb
thick	thirst	thunder

th Digraph (Voiced)

than	then	those
that	there	though
the	these	thus
their	they	thy
them	this	

	wh Digraph			*tch Digraph*	
whale	whether	whir	batch	glitch	patch
what	which	whirl	blotch	hatch	pitch
wheat	whiff	whisper	catch	hitch	scotch
wheel	while	whistle	clutch	hutch	sketch
wheeze	whim	white	ditch	itch	switch
when	whine	whopper	Dutch	latch	watch
where	whip	why	etch	match	witch

- Other sounds that the *ch* digraph represent are the /sh/ heard in *chivalry* and the /k/ heard in *choir*. The sound in *chirp* is the most frequent sound. Advise readers to try this sound first.
- The digraph *ph* commonly represents the /f/ heard in *phone*. Every now and then *ph* represents the sound of /p/, and sometimes *ph* is silent.
- The digraphs *ch, ph, sh,* and *th* occur at the beginning of words, in the middle of words—such as *franchise, dolphin, bishop,* and *heathen*—and at the end of words, such as *perch, graph, fish,* and *teeth*.
- The letters *th* represent two sounds—the sound heard in *thank* (called voiceless) and that heard in *than* (called voiced). Advise readers to first try the voiceless /th/ in *thank*.
- When *wh* precedes *o*, it represents the /h/ in *who*. The /hw/ sound in *white* is much more common. Encourage readers to try this sound first. In some Americans' speech, the /h/ is not pronounced in a word such as *white*; just the /w/ is pronounced. This reflects readers' normal pronunciation and hence should not interfere with word identification.
- When the letter *e* follows the digraph *th* at the end of a word, such as in *bathe*, the *th* represents the voiced sound heard in *that*. This explains the difference in pronunciation between *cloth* and *clothe*, and *teeth* and *teethe*.
- The digraph *tch* occurs at the end of words, as in *catch, itch, match,* and *stretch*. Whereas readers should have no trouble inferring that the *t* in *tch* is silent, they must remember to include the *t* in spelling.
- The *ck* (which represents the /k/ at the end of words such as *back*) and the *ng* are not included here because they are quicker to learn as part of the rimes *ack, eck, ick, ock,* and *uck,* or the rimes *ang, ing, ong,* and *ung,* as shown in Appendix A.
- As an onset, the digraph *gh* represents /g/, though few English words begin with *gh*. When *gh* is not an onset, there are two options: the *gh* is silent, as in *thigh*, or it represents /f/ as in *laugh*. When words include the sequence *ght*, the *gh* is silent, as in *bought* and *night*. Look in appendix A for examples.

S,s

As an onset *S,s* represents the /s/ in *sack*, never /z/. Only two alternatives, /s/ or /z/, are possible when *s* is a middle or the last letter in a syllable.

	/s/ Onset			*/s/ Final Sound*			*/z/ Sound*	
sack	seed	sight	bass	grass	moose	amuse	ease	music
salt	self	sign	boss	goose	plus	arise	fuse	nose

save	sell	six	bus	horse	this	as	has	please
saw	send	soap	chase	house	toss	cause	his	rose
sea	set	sock	dress	kiss	us	closet	hose	those
seal	sick	soft	fuss	lease	verse	cousin	is	was
see	side	sun	gas	loss	yes	daisy	lose	wise

- The words *sure* and *sugar* are exceptions; the *s* in the beginning of these words represents the sound of /sh/.
- If *i* or *u* follow *s* in the middle of a word, the *s* may represent the sound heard in *mansion* or in *pleasure*.
- When *-es* is a suffix as in *dishes* or *washes*, the *-es* represents /z/.

Ca, co, cu

When *c* precedes *a*, *o*, and *u* (*ca, co, cu*), the *c* usually represents the /k/ heard in *kite* (called a hard sound).

ca Pattern			co Pattern			cu Pattern		
cab	camel	card	coal	comb	core	cub	cup	curl
cage	camp	cart	coat	come	cork	cube	cupid	curse
cake	can	case	coach	cone	corn	cuddle	cusp	curve
calf	cane	cast	cob	cook	cost	cue	cur	cusp
call	cap	cat	code	coop	cot	cuff	curb	custom
calm	cape	catch	cold	cop	cove	cull	curd	cut
came	car	cause	colt	cord	cow	cult	cure	cute

Ce, ci, cy

In the *ce*, *ci*, and *cy* patterns, the *c* usually represents the sound associated with the /s/ in *soap* (called a soft sound).

ce Pattern		ci Pattern		cy Pattern
cease	cent	cider	circumstance	cycle
cedar	center	cigar	circus	cyclone
ceiling	century	cinch	cirrus	cylinder
celery	ceramic	cinder	citizen	cymbal
cell	cereal	cinnamon	citrus	Cynthia
cellar	ceremony	circle	city	cypress
cement	certain	circuit	civil	cyst

- As an onset, the *c* in *ci* represents /s/, but in the middle of words, *ci* represents the /sh/ sound, as in *social*.

Ga, go, gu

When *g* precedes *a*, *o*, and *u* (*ga*, *go*, *gu*), the *g* usually represents the sound associated with the /g/ in *gate* (called the hard sound).

ga Pattern			*go* Pattern			*gu* Pattern		
gable	game	gate	go	gone	gore	guard	gulch	guppy
gag	gang	gather	gob	gong	gorilla	guess	gulf	gurgle
gage	gap	gauze	goal	good	gossip	guest	gull	gush
gain	gape	gave	goad	goof	got	guide	gulp	gust
gait	gas	gawk	goat	goon	gourd	guild	gum	gutter
gal	gash	gay	gold	goose	govern	guilt	gun	guy
gale	gasp	gaze	golf	gopher	gown	guitar	gunk	guzzle

Ge, gi, gy

In the *ge*, *gi*, and *gy* patterns, the *g* usually represents the sound associated with the /j/ in *jelly* (called the soft sound).

ge Pattern		*gi* Pattern		*gy* Pattern	
gelatin	genius	giant	digit	gym	clergy
gem	gentle	gibe	engine	gypsy	ecology
gender	genuine	gigantic	fragile	gyroscope	energy
gene	geography	gin	legion	allergy	geology
general	gerbil	ginger	logic	analogy	lethargy
generic	germ	giraffe	magic	apology	strategy
generous	gesture	gist	margin	biology	zoology

- The combinations *ge* and *gi* are not as dependable as the others. Support readers as they learn to first try the sound of /j/ in *jelly* for ge and gi and, if that fails, try the sound of /g/ in goat.

VOWEL PATTERNS

Short Vowel Sounds and Short Vowel Patterns

a	in *apple*
e	in *edge*
i	in *igloo*
o	in *octopus*
u	in *umbrella*

VC Short Vowel Pattern

The *VC* pattern usually represents a short sound. This pattern consists of one vowel in a one-syllable word or in a single syllable. Short vowel sounds are often indicated by a breve (căt), a single vowel preceding one or more consonants, as in *VC-at; CVC-cat; CCVC-chat* or *slat; CCVCC-black; CCVCCC-thatch; CCCVC-scrap; CCCVCCC-splotch*. The number of consonants following the vowel in this pattern does not affect the short vowel sound, although, of course, there are exceptions.

VC Short Aa					*VC Short Ee*			
bad	cat	mad	sat		bed	hem	men	red
bag	dad	man	tab		beg	hen	met	set
ban	fan	map	tag		bet	jet	net	shed
bat	fat	nap	tan		den	led	peg	sled
cab	gas	pan	wag		fed	leg	pen	ten
can	had	rag	van		fled	less	pep	vet
cap	ham	sad	yam		gem	let	pet	web

VC Short Ii					*VC Short Oo*			
bib	dim	him	lit		box	drop	jot	nod
bid	din	hip	mix		cob	fox	lob	not
big	dip	his	pig		cod	gob	lop	pod
bin	fin	hit	pin		cop	got	lot	pond
bit	fit	kid	rib		cot	hop	mob	pop
did	fix	kit	rim		crop	hot	mom	pot
dig	hid	lid	sit		dot	job	mop	top

VC Short Uu			
bud	cup	hum	pup
bug	cut	hut	rug
bum	dug	jug	run
bun	fun	lug	sub
bus	gum	mud	sun
but	gun	mug	tub
cub	hug	nut	tug

- Sometimes the vowel in a *CVC* pattern represents a long sound, as in *cold* (old), *colt* (olt), *find* (ind), *night* (ight), and *child* (ild). Considered within the context of rimes, combinations like these are quite predictable and, hence, best learned as rimes in word family words (see Appendix A). Advise readers to try the short vowel first and, if that does not produce a meaningful word, to try a long sound.

VCCe Short Vowel Pattern

In the *VCCe* pattern, the vowel generally represents a short sound and the *e* is silent. A consonant pattern before the vowel forms a *CVCCe* (*dance*) or *CCVCCe* (*chance*) sequence; it does not affect the sound the vowel in the *VCCe* pattern represents.

CVCCe		CCVCCe	
badge	rinse	blonde	prance
dance	since	bridge	prince
dense	dodge	bronze	sconce
fence	fudge	chance	smudge
ledge	judge	fringe	trance
sense	lunge	glance	twinge
hinge	nudge	pledge	

- *dge* usually represents /j/ and the final *e* is silent. Never an onset, *dge* is included in the spelling of many different words, and hence readers have ample opportunities to learn this pattern through reading and writing.
- Many, though not all, of the words in the preceding list end with *ge* or *ce*. In spellings, the final *e* signals readers that the sound of the *c* is /s/ and the sound of *g* is /j/, consistent with the *ce* and *ge* patterns. Without the final *e*, readers might pronounce the final *c* as /k/ (*epic*) and the final *g* as /g/ (*chug*). In this way, the final *e* in these *VCCe* patterns makes our writing system a more predictable and dependable representation of sound.
- The *VCCe* short vowel pattern is challenging to spellers because the *e* may be dropped when suffixes are added, as in *lodging* and *dancing*.
- If the short vowel sound does not result in a meaningful word with a *VCCe* pattern, advise readers to try the long sound.

Long Vowel Sounds and Long Vowel Patterns

Long Vowel Sounds

a	in *apron*
e	in *eraser*
i	in *ice*
o	in *overalls*
u	in *unicorn*

VCe Long Vowel Pattern

In the *VCe* pattern, the *e* is silent and the preceding vowel usually has a long sound, which is often indicated by a macron (-). A consonant pattern before the vowel forms a *CVCe* (*save*) or a *CCVCE* (*shave*) sequence and does not affect the sound that the vowel in the *VCe* long vowel pattern represents.

aCe Pattern

bake	lace	safe
base	lane	sale
cake	made	same
came	make	shape
date	page	tape
face	pave	trade
game	rake	wade

eCe Pattern

cede
extreme
gene
scene
scheme
recede
theme

iCe Pattern

bike	hike	nice
dime	kite	nine
dine	life	price
drive	like	prize
file	line	side
fire	mile	smile
hide	mine	time

oCe Pattern

broke	nose	rope
close	note	rose
drove	phone	shone
froze	poke	smoke
globe	pole	stone
hole	robe	those
home	rode	throne

uCe Pattern

abuse	fuse
acute	huge
amuse	mule
cube	mute
cute	use
excuse	
fume	

- There are some marked exceptions to the *VCe* long vowel pattern, as we see in *have* and *love*.
- Words spelled with *r* usually conform to the *r-controlled (Vr)* pattern *(more)*.
- When the last syllable is *ate* or *ite*, and when the syllable is not stressed in pronunciation, the *a* and the *i* do not represent a long sound (*climate* and *granite*).
- Some borrowed words from French (*café*) are exceptions and are pronounced accordingly.

CV Long Vowel Pattern

In the *CV* pattern, the vowel usually represents a long sound.

Ca Pattern

basin	later
canine	major
crazy	nation
flavor	paper
haven	table
label	vapor
labor	volcano

Ce Pattern

be	media
feline	meter
female	regent
he	sequence
legal	we
me	zebra

Ci Pattern

China	rifle
digest	silent
giant	spider
lion	tiger
migrant	title
minus	tricycle
pilot	

Co Pattern

also	moment	polar	social
banjo	no	program	total
locate	nomad	rotate	vocal
molar	poem		

Cu Pattern

Ber*mu*da	*fu*qitive	*mu*seum	*pu*pil
*bu*gle	*fu*ture	*mu*sic	tri*bu*nal
*cu*cumber	*hu*man	*mu*tate	
*fu*el	*hu*mid	*pu*ny	

- There are many exceptions to the *CV* long vowel pattern, particularly if this pattern occurs in a syllable that is not accented—for example, the first syllable in *develop*.

The Letter Y,y as the Final Letter

The letter *y* at the end of a word acts as a vowel. When *y* forms a separate final syllable, it generally represents the sound associated with long *e*, as in *bunny* and *silly*. *Y,y* at the end of a word with *no other vowels* represents the sound associated with long *i*, as in *by* and *try*.

Final Syllable (long e)		*Only Vowel (long i)*	
any	funny	by	shy
army	lady	cry	sky
baby	melody	dry	spy
body	silly	fly	spry
bunny	study	fry	sty
candy	taffy	my	try
city	tiny	pry	why

- Tell readers to try the sound of long *i* in short words and the sound of long *e* in longer words. If one sound does not work, the other one has a good chance of being correct.
- When the *ly* is a suffix as in *deeply* and *cheaply*, it represents long *e*. Advise readers to try long *e* if they think the *ly* is a suffix and long *i* if they think it is part of the base word. If one sound does not work, the other probably will.

VV Long Vowel Pattern

In the *VV* patterns of *ai, oa, ay, ee, ey*, and *ea*, the first vowel usually represents a long sound and the second is silent.

ai Pattern		*oa Pattern*		*ay Pattern*	
bait	main	boat	oak	bay	may
claim	nail	coast	oat	clay	pay
drain	paint	coat	poach	day	ray
fail	sail	foam	road	gay	stay
jail	train	loaf	throat	jay	tray
maid	waist	loan	toad	lay	way

ea Pattern		*ee Pattern*		*ey Pattern*	
beach	meat	beef	green	alley	jockey
dream	peak	creek	keep	barley	key
heat	real	creep	meet	donkey	kidney
leaf	sea	deed	need	galley	money
leap	sneak	deep	peel	hockey	monkey
meal	treat	feel	queen	honey	turkey
mean	weak	feet	reef	jersey	valley

- Sometimes two adjacent vowels in the *VV* long vowel pattern are referred to as a vowel digraph because two letters represent one sound.
- Some teachers' manuals refer to the vowels in the *VV* long vowel pattern as a vowel team.
- *Y, y* is a vowel when it follows *a* and *e*, thereby creating the *VV* long vowel pattern of *ay* and *ey*.
- Most of the time, *ai* represents long *a*, but occasionally it represents the sound heard in *said* (seldom the sound in *plaid*). Tell readers to first try the long *a* sound and, should that fail to create a meaningful word, to try the sound heard in *said*.
- *ey* represents the sound in *key* and *they*. Advise readers to first try the sound of long *e* and, if that fails to produce a meaningful word, to try the sound of long *a*.
- *ea* sometimes represents the short *e* heard in *head*. Infrequently, *ea* represents a long *a* as in *great*. Advise readers to first try long *e* and, if that does not form a contextually meaningful word, to try short *e*.
- When two adjacent vowels are in different syllables, then both vowels represent a separate sound, as in *create*.

Other Vowel Patterns

Double oo

The double *oo* usually represents the sound heard in *school* or the sound heard in *book*.

oo in school		*oo in book*	
boot	room	brook	look
cool	scoop	cook	nook
food	smooth	crook	shook
hoot	soon	foot	soot
moon	spoon	good	stood
pool	tooth	hood	took
proof	zoo	hook	wood

- Advise readers to try one sound and, if that does not result in a sensible word, to try the other sound.

Vowel Diphthongs

Ow, ou, oi, and *oy* often represent the following sounds in pronunciation: *ow* in *cow; oi* in *oil; ou* in *out; oy* in *boy.*

ow Pattern		*ou Pattern*	
brow	growl	cloud	noun
brown	how	flour	ouch
clown	now	grouch	pound
cow	plow	ground	proud
crowd	scowl	hour	scout
down	town	loud	shout
gown	wow	mouth	trout

oi Pattern		*oy Pattern*	
boil	moist	annoy	ploy
broil	noise	boy	Roy
choice	point	coy	royal
coin	soil	decoy	soy
coil	spoil	enjoy	toy
foil	toil	joy	troy
join	voice	loyal	voyage

- *ow* also represents the long vowel sound /crow/, so readers have two sounds from which to choose: the /ow/ in /cow/ and the /o/ (long *o*) in /crow/. If one sound does not work, the other will.
- *oi* may be part of the multiletter groups *oise* (as in *noise*) and *oice* (as in *voice*). Encourage readers to draw these conclusions during the normal course of reading and writing.
- Though *ou* frequently represents the sounds heard in *out* and *cloud,* these two letters represent several other sounds in words; for example, *soul, tour, group, shoulder, encourage, could,* and *double. Your, pour,* and *four* are examples of other exceptions to the *ou* pattern. However, authors use words like *your, four, should, would,* and *could* so frequently that children learn to read them through normal reading and writing experiences.

Vr or r-Controlled Pattern

The r affects pronunciation so that vowels cannot be classified as short or long.

ar Pattern			
arm	dark	jar	tar
barn	far	mart	yard
car	farm	park	
chart	hard	star	

er Pattern		ir Pattern	
after	eager	bird	shirt
anger	enter	chirp	sir
butter	ever	dirt	skirt
cider	fever	fir	stir
clerk	her	firm	third
cover	over	flirt	twirl
verb	term	girl	whir

or Pattern		ur Pattern	
born	horn	blur	hurt
cord	porch	burn	nurse
corn	pork	burst	purr
for	port	church	spurt
force	sort	curb	surf
fork	store	curl	turf
form	torn	fur	turn

- The letters *ar* after *w* represent the sounds heard in *war* and *warm*, not the sound heard in *car*. This, however, is not overly difficult for observant readers to discover.

The au and aw Patterns

The *au* generally represents the sound in *fault*. The *aw* represents the sound in *straw*.

au Pattern		aw Pattern	
author	launch	awe	lawn
autumn	laundry	claw	raw
caught	maul	crawl	saw
cause	pause	draw	straw
caution	sauce	drawn	thaw
faun	sausage	fawn	yawn
haul	taught	jaw	

- The *au* and *aw* patterns are fairly reliable. The *au* does not occur at the end of words. The *aw* is used as an onset (*awe*), in the middle of words (*dawn*), and at the end of words (*draw*).

The ew and ue Patterns

The *ew* and *ue* patterns usually represent the sound in *blew* and *blue*.

ew Pattern		*ue Pattern*	
blew	grew	argue	pursue
brew	jewel	avenue	rescue
chew	knew	blue	statue
crew	new	clue	sue
dew	screw	due	tissue
drew	stew	flue	true
flew	threw	glue	value
		issue	

- The *ue* pattern cannot be counted on to represent the sound in *blue* when the *ue* follows a *q* or a *g* in spelling, as in *antique* and *guess*. When children have lots of experience reading and writing words spelled with these sequences, they learn the sounds these letters represent.

APPENDIX C

Generalizations for Adding Suffixes

-S, -ED, -ING, -LY, AND -ER TO WORDS

VC Short Vowel Words

Add -s and -ly to one-syllable words with the *CVC* short vowel pattern:

	-s		-ly
bat	bats	glad	gladly
clap	claps	sad	sadly
stop	stops	dim	dimly
dog	dogs	low	lowly
hat	hats	bad	badly
win	wins	mad	madly

-ed, -ing, -er

Double the last consonant before adding -ed, -ing, and -er to words ending with the *CVC* short vowel pattern:

	-ed	-ing	-er
jog	jogged	jogging	jogger
drop	dropped	dropping	dropper
plan	planned	planning	planner
slip	slipped	slipping	slipper
stun	stunned	stunning	stunner
trap	trapped	trapping	trapper

Doubling the last consonant keeps *VC* short vowel words with the *-ed, -ing,* and *-er* suffixes, such as *hop-hopping,* from being read as *VCe* long vowel words, like *hope-hoping.* Children need a lot of reading and spelling opportunities to successfully use this generalization when they write.

VCC Short Vowel Words

Simply add *-s, -ed, -ing, -ly,* and *-er* to words ending in a *CVCC* short vowel pattern:

	-s	*-ed*	*-ing*
rest	rests	rested	resting
talk	talks	talked	talking
jump	jumps	jumped	jumping
call	calls	called	calling
help	helps	helped	helping
land	lands	landed	landing

	-ly	*-er*
sick	sickly	sicker
hard	hardly	harder
cold	coldly	colder
calm	calmly	calmer
soft	softly	softer
warm	warmly	warmer

The reason we do not double the last consonant in the *VCC* short vowel pattern is that there is no chance of confusing these short vowel words with long vowel *VCe* words, as explained previously.

VCe Long Vowel Pattern

Drop the final *e* and then add the *-ed, -ing,* and *-er* to words ending with the *VCe* long vowel pattern:

	-ed	*-ing*	*-er*
race	raced	racing	racer
joke	joked	joking	joker
bake	baked	baking	baker
dine	dined	dining	diner
hike	hiked	hiking	hiker
shave	shaved	shaving	shaver

Add -s and -ly to VCe long vowel words.

	-s		-ly
bike	bikes	nice	nicely
face	faces	home	homely
hope	hopes	late	lately
home	homes	huge	hugely
game	games	love	lovely
rule	rules	live	lively

VV Long Vowel Pattern

When words end with a *VV* long vowel pattern followed by a consonant, add the -s, -ed, -ing, -ly, and -er without changing the base word:

	-s	-ed	-ing
need	needs	needed	needing
load	loads	loaded	loading
peel	peels	peeled	peeling
roam	roams	roamed	roaming
fail	fails	failed	failing
soak	soaks	soaked	soaking

	-ly	-er
cheap	cheaply	cheaper
deep	deeply	deeper
fair	fairly	fairer
broad	broadly	broader
plain	plainly	plainer
sweet	sweetly	sweeter

Words Ending in the VV Combinations of ay, oy, ey

Simply add -s, -ed, -ing, and -er to words ending in the *VV* combinations of *ay, oy,* and *ey*:

	-s	-ed	-ing
play	plays	played	playing
obey	obeys	obeyed	obeying
enjoy	enjoys	enjoyed	enjoying
spray	sprays	sprayed	spraying
stay	stays	stayed	staying
toy	toys	toyed	toying

	-er
play	player
gray	grayer
gay	gayer
spray	sprayer
employ	employer
buy	buyer

Words Ending in Y,y

When a word ends in a *y*, change the *y* to an *i* before adding *-es*, *-ed*, and *-er*:

	-es	-ed	er
carry	carries	carried	carrier
worry	worries	worried	worrier
dry	dries	dried	drier
busy	busies	busied	busier
fancy	fancies	fancied	fancier
copy	copies	copied	copier

Adding -es to Words Ending in s, ss, ch, sh, x, and z

Add *-es* to words that end in *s, ss, ch, sh, x,* and *z* as in:

	-es		-es		-es		-es
bus	buses	beach	beaches	leash	leashes	fox	foxes
toss	tosses	porch	porches	crash	crashes	fix	fixes
pass	passes	branch	branches	bush	bushes	mix	mixes
class	classes	bench	benches	rush	rushes	tax	taxes
dress	dresses	catch	catches	fish	fishes	buzz	buzzes
boss	bosses	bunch	bunches	wish	wishes	waltz	waltzes

White, T. G., Sowell, J., & Yanagihara, A. (1989). Teaching elementary students to use word-part clues. *The Reading Teacher, 42,* 302–308.

APPENDIX D

Greek and Latin Roots

Roots	Meaning	Examples
aer (o) (Greek)	air, atmosphere	aerial, aerospace
ann (Latin)	year	annual, anniversary
anthr (opo) (Greek)	human	anthropology, philanthropist
art (Latin)	skill	artist, artifact
aqua (Latin)	water	aquatic, aquarium
ast (er) (Greek)	star	astrology, astronaut
aud (Latin)	hear	audience, auditory
aut (o) (Greek)	self	autobiography, automobile
biblio (Greek)	book	bibliography, bibliotherapy
bio (Greek)	life	biology, biodegradable
cap (Latin)	head	cap, capital
cardi (Greek)	heart	cardiology, cardiogram
chrom (at) (Greek)	color	chromatic, chromosome
cycl (Greek)	circle, wheel	cycle, bicycle
dem (Greek)	people	democracy, democratic
dyna (Greek)	power	dynamite, dynamic
fid (Latin)	faith, trust	fidelity, confidential
fin (Latin)	end, limit	final, finite, finish
firm (Latin)	strong, firm	confirm, affirm
ge (o) (Greek)	earth	geography, geology
gon (Greek)	angle	polygon, hexagon
grat (Latin)	pleasing, grateful	gratitude, gracious
hydr (Greek)	water	hydrant, dehydrate
loc (Latin)	place, put	locate, allocate
magn (Latin)	great, large	magnitude, magnificent

mal (Latin)	poor, inadequate	malnourished, maladjusted
misc (Latin)	mix, mingle	miscellaneous
mit (Latin)	send, soften	transmit, mitigate
neg (Latin)	deny	negative, renegade
ne (o) (Greek)	new	neonate, neophyte
omni (Latin)	all	omnivorous, omnipotent
ortho (Greek)	straight	orthodontics, orthodox
phon (Greek)	sound	phonics, phonograph
phot (Greek)	light	photograph, photo
port (Latin)	carry	export, portable
press (Latin)	press, force	pressure, repress
psych (Greek)	mind	psychology, psychosis
quest (Latin)	seek, ask	question, quest
rupt (Latin)	break	disrupt, interrupt
sci (Latin)	know	science, conscience
scribe (Latin)	write	inscribe, subscribe
sen (Latin)	old	senile, senior
sens (Latin)	feel, think	sensation, sensory
serv (Latin)	serve, save	servant, preserve
son (Latin)	sound	sonic, resonance
spec (Latin)	look, see	spectator, inspect
strict (Latin)	draw tight	constrict, restrict
tact (Latin)	touch	tactile, contact
tele (Greek)	far away, distant	telescope, telephone
ver (Latin)	true	verdict, verify
vid (Latin)	see	video, evident
voc (Latin)	voice	vocal, invoke

Key Vocabulary

Accented Syllables   The stress given to syllables. Accent affects the way we pronounce the vowels in long words. The vowels in accented syllables, also called primary accents, tend to follow the pronunciation we would expect from their placement in letter-sound patterns.

Adding Sounds   Attaching a sound to a word, such as adding /p/ to /an/ to form /pan/ or /bee/ to /t/ to pronounce /beet/.

Affixes   The prefixes and suffixes attached to the beginning or end of words.

Alphabetic Principle   The principle that, in writing, letters represent sounds and, therefore, readers can pronounce any word that is spelled the way it is pronounced.

Alphabetic Word Learners   Children who are capable of reading new words by analyzing all the letter and sound patterns and then using this information to pronounce the new words they see in text.

Analogy-based Phonics   A phonics teaching approach in which children learn how vowels and consonants (*at, in, ap, up*) in words represent sounds (/at/ - /in/ - /ap/ - /up/) in familiar words and then use this information to read new words with the same patterns. Words that share the same pattern (*at*) belong to the same word family (*sat, hat, mat, pat, fat*).

Analytic Phonics   Whole-to-part-to-whole phonics instruction in which children first learn a group of basic sight words with certain phonics patterns and then learn how the letter patterns in known words represent sound.

Automatic Readers   Children who instantly recognize all the words in everyday text.

Base Words   The smallest real English words to which prefixes and suffixes are added (*play* or *elephant*, for example).

Blending   The ability to combine sounds into words. Children might combine onsets and rimes (/sh/ + /ip/ = /ship/) or individual phonemes (/p/ + /a/ + /n/ = /pan/).

Compound Words   Words that are formed when two words—for example, *finger* and *print*—are glued together to create a third word—in this case, *fingerprint*.

Configuration Cues   Configuration consists of a word's word shape, word length, or unique letters. Some beginning readers use configuration cues to identify new words.

Consolidated Word Learners   Children who read new words by identifying and pronouncing meaningful and nonmeaningful multiletter chunks in words.

Consonant Clusters   Two or more consonants that appear together and form a consonant blend (*bl, tr, sm, scr*) when pronounced.

Consonants   All the letters other than *a, e, i, o, u,* and *y* when *y* comes in the middle or at the end of a syllable.

Contractions   Words formed when one or more letters (and sounds) are deleted from other words, with the deleted letter(s) replaced by an apostrophe—a visual clue telling readers that a word is abbreviated, as in *hasn't, he's, she'll,* and *let's.*

Cross-checking Strategy   A strategy, used whenever readers identify new words, that involves making sure that identified words make sense in the reading context.

Decodable Books   Books that have an unusually high number of words that sound like they are spelled. Often these books consist of many words that represent a certain letter-sound pattern.

Deleting Sounds   Removing a sound or sounds from a word or syllable, such as taking the /b/ from /bit/ to pronounce /it/ or the /m/ from /seem/ to form /see/.

Derivational Suffixes   Word endings that change the part of speech, as in changing *read* (a verb) into *readable* (an adjective).

Digraphs   Two letters that represent a sound that is different from the sounds the letters represent individually, such as *sh* (ship), *th* (thud), and *ch* (child).

Diphthongs   The vowel-like sounds represented by *oy* and *oi* as heard in /boy/ and /oil/, and by *ou* and *ow* as heard in /out/ and /cow/.

Embedded Phonics   A strategy in which children learn only the phonics letter patterns they need to decode words in the books they are currently reading. Because embedded phonics uses a "teach as needed" stance, teachers and children do not follow a prescribed scope and sequence for learning phonics letter patterns.

Environmental Cues   Environmental cues consist of print in an everyday environment such as signs, logos and package labels. Beginning readers associate meaning with these cues.

Greek and Latin Roots   Word parts we borrowed from these two languages such at the port (from Latin meaning to carry) in portable.

Identifying Sounds   Recognizing the same sound or sounds in different words, such as indicating that /boy/ and /boat/ begin alike or that /book/ and /duck/ end alike.

Inflectional Suffixes   Word endings that clarify word meaning or make meaning more specific, as the -*s* added to *cats* or the -*ed* added to *played*.

Invented Spelling   A problem-solving stance in which words are spelled like they sound, such as *comin* for *common*.

Isolating Sounds   Pronouncing the beginning, ending, or middle sound in a word, such as saying that /man/ begins with /m/ or that /sun/ ends with /n/.

Letter and Sound Cues   In this book, the letter-sound and word structure cues that help readers identify words.

Letter-sound Patterns   Letters that routinely represent one or more sounds in words, such as the *ee* in *feet*, and *sh* and *or* in *short*.

Letter-sound Phonics   The systematic relationship among letters and sounds which is the principle that underpins all alphabetic languages and an approach for teaching these relationships. Children use the letter-sound phonics when they associate sounds with letters to pronounce words they do not recognize.

Manipulating Sounds   The act of deliberately changing the sounds in one word so as to pronounce a different word. Children might add a sound (/r/ + /at/ = /rat/), delete a sound (/rat/ − /r/ = /at/) or substitute one sound for another (change the /t/ in /rat/ to /n/ to pronounce /ran/).

Meaning Cues   Meaningful relationships among words in phrases, sentences, and paragraphs. Readers use these cues to determine whether an author's message is logical and represents real-world events and relationships.

Metacognitive Awareness   The self-awareness of what we know, how we know it, and how and when to use information. As it pertains to word identification, readers with metacognivitive awareness monitor their own reading, cross-check for meaning, and correct their own miscues.

Onset   The consonant(s) that comes before the vowel in a syllable or one-syllable word (the *s* in *sat* or the *ch* in *chat*).

Partial Alphabet Cues   A portion of the letter-sound relationships in a word's spelling, such as beginning or ending letter-sounds.

Partial Alphabetic Word Learners   These children use part of the alphabetic cues in spelling to identify words, such as associating the sound /m/ with monkey. As a consequence, children are apt to confuse mouse, mother and made for the word monkey.

Phonemes   The smallest sounds that differentiate one word from another. The /b/ in /bat/ is one phoneme, while the /h/ in /hat/ is another phoneme, as each sound differentiates one word (/bat/) from another (/hat/).

Phonemic Awareness   The ability to think analytically about the sounds in words, and the ability to act on the basis of this analysis to separate words into sounds and to blend sounds into words.

Phonetic Spellers   Children who correctly spell known words and spell new words the way they sound.

Phonetically Regular Words   Words that can be pronounced by associating sounds with letters.

Phonogram   The vowel and the consonants that come after it, such as the *an* in *man* and *can* or the *at* in *cat* and *mat.* Phonograms and rimes refer to the same letter groups inside short, one-syllable words or syllables.

Phonological Awareness   A broad term that refers to the awareness of and the ability to manipulate words, syllables, rhymes, and sounds.

Picture Cues   Suggestions about meaning that readers infer from the illustrations in storybooks.

Prealphabetic Word Learners   Children who use environmental print, pictures, and word configuration when reading. These children lack phonemic awareness, do not know letter-names (or know the names of only a few letters), and do not understand how letters represent sounds.

Precommunicative Spellers   Children whose writing shows no relationship between sounds and letters.

Prefix   A separate syllable attached to the beginning of words that either changes the meaning of the root word completely or makes meaning more specific.

Rhyme Awareness   The ability to identify words that rhyme (/bad/ and /mad/), do not rhyme (/bad/ and /dog/), and think of rhyming words (/bad/ - /sad/ - /had/).

Rime   The vowel and everything that follows it in a syllable or one-syllable word (the *at* in *sat* and *chat*).

Segmenting Sounds   Pronouncing each phoneme in the same order in which it occurs in a word, such as indicating that /mad/ consists of /m/ - /a/ - /d/.

Self-correcting   The process of rereading for accuracy so as to fix a previous miscue.

Self-monitoring   The ability to self-regulate one's own reading to be sure that it makes sense.

Semiphonetic Spellers   Children who spell known words conventionally and use letters to represent some, but not all, of the important sounds in words, such as writing a *p* for *park* or *fs* for *friends*.

Sentence Structure Cues   Cues readers use to decide whether an author's word order is consistent with English grammar. Readers use these grammar-based cues to predict words in phrases and sentences.

Sound Boxes   Connected boxes where each box represents a sound in a word.

Sound Stretching   Elongating sounds while pronouncing words, as in /fffiiinnn/. *Rubber banding* is another term for the same way of pronouncing words.

Structural Analysis   Analyzing the structure of words into large multi-letter chunks, including compound words, contractions, prefixes, suffixes, syllables, and Greek and Latin roots.

Substituting Sounds   Deleting a sound from a word and then adding another in its place to make a different word. Examples include substituting the /n/ in /man/ for a /t/ to pronounce /mat/ or substituting the /sh/ in /ship/ for a /ch/ to pronounce /chip/.

Suffix   Usually a separate syllable attached to the end of words that changes grammatical function, makes meaning clearer, or adds information.

Syllable   The basic unit of pronunciation. Each syllable has one vowel sound and, perhaps, one or more consonant sounds (/o/ + /pen/ = /open/). The number of syllables in a word equals the number of vowels heard.

Synthetic Phonics   Part-to-whole instruction in which children associate sounds with letters to read, or "sound out," new words.

Transitional Spellers   Children who conventionally spell known words and, when spelling is not already memorized, may represent sounds with incorrect letter-sound patterns or write letters in the wrong sequence.

Unaccented Syllables   Syllables that are not prominent in stress. Most vowels in unaccented syllables have a soft, or short, sound.

Vowels   The letters *a*, *e*, *i*, *o*, and *u*, and *y* when it comes in the middle (*cycle*) or at the end of a syllable or short word (*try*).

Word Family   A word group that shares the same rime or phonogram (*cat, rat, fat, sat, bat*).

Index